# CRACKING THE INTUITION CODE

# CRACKING THE INTUITION CODE

## Understanding and Mastering Your Intuitive Power

### GAIL FERGUSON

**CB**

CONTEMPORARY BOOKS

**Library of Congress Cataloging-in-Publication Data**

Ferguson, Gail.
    Cracking the intuition code : understanding and mastering your
intuitive power / by Gail Ferguson.
        p.    cm.
    Includes bibliographical references and index.
    ISBN 0-8092-2839-4
    1. Intuition (Psychology).    I. Title.
BF315.5.F47    1999
153.4'4—dc21                                                    98-33368
                                                                      CIP

Interior design by Scott Rattray

Published by Contemporary Books
A division of NTC/Contemporary Publishing Group, Inc.
4255 West Touhy Avenue, Lincolnwood (Chicago), Illinois 60646-1975 U.S.A.
Copyright © 1999 by Gail Ferguson
Printed in the United States of America
International Standard Book Number: 0-8092-2839-4
99  00  01  02  03  04  QP  18  17  16  15  14  13  12  11  10  9  8  7  6  5  4  3  2  1

To my children,

Jeffrey, Natalya, and David

*Dulcius Ex Asperis*

*Nature is unpredictable.*

WERNER HEISENBERG

*Where logic and evidence clash, it seems*

*prudent to stick with evidence, for this*

*holds the prospect of leading to a wider*

*logic, whereas the opposite approach*

*closes the door to discovery.*

HUSTON SMITH

# Contents

# Acknowledgments

I COULD NOT have written this book alone. From the beginning, I've drawn on speculations postulated by the world's greatest philosophers and conclusions that our finest scientists have tested tirelessly. Numbers of probing questions, astute observations, and, of course, doubts from analytical colleagues, enthusiastic students, fear-filled family members, puzzled friends, and legions of fascinated individuals worldwide have likewise contributed to my understanding of intuition.

I would like to acknowledge a few people in particular. In 1973, Dr. Hazel M. Denning, then a complete stranger, began plying me with questions and presenting opportunities for me to intuitively cross seemingly impassable mental boundaries. During the years, our lively discussions forced me to observe open-mindedly and think objectively about the facts I encountered there. Without her selfless generosity, patience, and friendship, I most certainly would have closed the doors on this subject long before I uncovered its riches.

In 1979, Dr. Douglas Bowman, then professor of religion and chaplain at the University of Redlands in California, opened my eyes to the great religions of the world. He taught wonderful lessons that laced together beautifully the inconsistencies in my five life spheres of family, academia, religion, my own intuitive behavior, and my rapidly expanding worldview. Week after fascinating week, he masterfully unrolled an impressive panorama of human values as they have evolved, endured, and died through religions and metaphysical teachings since the dawn of our search for meaning in life. Because of his keen insights into wise hearts and great minds, I began to understand that our tradition of beliefs has ever and always served as a conduit—one that continually channels our ideals into our behavior until we find real reasons to behave ideally.

I also thank my peerless champion and loving husband, Gayne Rescher, that man across the table ($\psi$-23), whose wry wit keeps me bent over double and whose astute observations stretch my thinking constantly.

Editor Matthew Carnicelli at NTC/Contemporary deserves both thanks and the prize of patience. He instantly captured the spirit of my work and calmly steered me—suggesting here, nudging there—until the dream and the book were one. Without him this volume would be much less. Thanks also to others at NTC/Contemporary, especially Nicole Adams, and to Regina Wells.

My profound thanks also to Jane Dystel, a literary agent *extraordinaire*. It is my good fortune that she holds an author to the same high standard of excellence as she demands of herself.

If this book opens new doors for anyone, it will be due in large part to all these thousands, yes, thousands, of people. I humbly thank every one.

# Introduction

THESE PAGES INTRODUCE my observations and conclusions on a puzzling subject debated by people around the world—our intuitiveness. I maintain that intuition is a sleeping giant of a capability within every one of us, a wonderful phenomenon of nature that we experience constantly, and a readily available tool for building a better future for humanity. My purpose in writing this book is to awaken the giant, because it is a powerful force behind our individual and collective ability to survive and flourish in an often hostile social and natural environment.

The book explains how intuition is irrevocably tied to our achievements. Interwoven in the text is the story of my twenty-five-year search to establish intuition's connection with evolution, biology, the great religions of the world, and everyday human behavior. The whole eye-opening investigation began with my simple desire to understand why I learned some things that society at large and people near and dear to me decreed I couldn't possibly know. The answers came slowly but surely, while I earned further academic degrees, mastered my own intuitiveness, and traveled the world as an itinerant teacher and consultant. This has so far been an endlessly astonishing adventure in discovery.

I am sticking my neck out here by proposing unequivocally that we as humans are born to succeed in life but cannot do so without the help of our innate intuition. The basis of my argument is that intuition continually provides well-timed accurate facts that guide us flawlessly in solving problems, making decisions, planning the future, and taking risks. To confirm this proposition, I introduce intuition's unbending natural laws, along with other of its basic elements, and illustrate its unique universal effects in ordinary situations. For example, when any one of us has a "sense" of imminent opportunity or danger, a "feeling" about the importance of an event, or a "certainty" that a seemingly unpredictable incident will occur, such a *feeling, sense,* or *certainty* is a fundamental intuitive experience so common to us all that we should know immediately what to do with its information. Knowing how to manage each intuitive effect will have a dramatic impact on our lives and accomplishments. Exciting possibilities await us all when intuition joins our repertoire of finely trained behaviors.

Part I discusses the nature of intuition, or perhaps more precisely stated, intuitiveness as part of nature and the human experience. The emphasis is on how it has evolved into our species as a sensory system, what seems to have forced it into existence, and why we should come to terms with it now. Part II is devoted to showing you how to master your own intuition and offers a universally applicable technique for triggering the intuitive process.

Throughout the book you will find dozens of accounts of intuitive experiences that illustrate the concepts discussed. Nearly all of these accounts are drawn from my family, close friends, and personal incidents. I use these as examples not because I consider us to be the only, or best, intuitive people around—we're not—but because I can be absolutely sure of the details, thus am able to explain intuition's normal process accurately for your greater understanding. Except in the cases of my family members, I have changed the names of the people involved.

Each account is prefixed with a number in parentheses that corresponds to the Index of Psi Effects on page 323. This should provide a point of departure for analyzing and experimenting with your own intuition. The reference numbers look like this: ($\psi$-1), ($\psi$-2), and so on. The symbol "$\psi$" represents the word "psi" and is pronounced "sigh." This is the twenty-third letter in the Greek alphabet and is used in the science community to represent specific human experiences called "psi effects." For generations these effects, often described as paranormal, have created great confusion and controversy in the general public, organized religion, and scientific sectors of society because no one has clearly understood what they do or where they belong in the scheme of natural events. I have concluded that these psi effects are the most visible elements of our intuitive capability. With the accounts as backdrop, I explain my reasons for this conclusion.

This is a complicated subject that has captured scientists' interest for more than a century. Yet, to date we have no convincing explanation for our intuitiveness. During my search I uncovered a vast array of evidence that yielded a new combination of facts previously unassociated with intuition—at least as far as I know. The newness notwithstanding, this amalgam offers a sound explanation for the consistent experiences and behavior that I classify as intuitive and which human beings have observed for thousands of years. From the first line of this book, my challenge has been to develop these findings intelligibly. As an explorer, I hope that I have managed to do so without detracting from either the fascination of the various accounts, the excitement of learning about this inborn human capability, or the thrill that rises with the realization that by training ourselves to use it our future existence might be much more wholesome, yet every bit as challenging as it is today. As a teacher, my hope is that I have said enough to give you the opportunity to think about the ideas, to test them personally, and to judge the conclusions for yourself.

# CRACKING THE INTUITION CODE

# Part I

# NATURAL INTUITION

Why do we:

▲ sense something's wrong when we're in danger?

▲ feel that an idea is right or wrong?

▲ just plain know that we should move forward on a plan?

How many of us:

▲ frequently know what another person is feeling?

▲ are convinced that we are guided in our big decisions and future plans?

▲ believe that anyone can correctly know others' feelings, the future, and the past?

Who among us:

▲ is intuitive?

▲ knows what it means to be intuitive?

▲ understands the importance of being intuitive?

In Part I we address these questions and their implications for each one of us. This section of the book is the story of human intuitiveness as I have observed it—its history, its purpose, its promise. Here we begin to move closer to understanding intuition at its core—what created it, the correct way to use it, and why it doesn't always work.

This is a look at intuition from a new perspective. I take a systematic approach. Beginning with a plain discussion of why we are all naturally intuitive, I introduce accounts that capture patterns in our daily behavior and expose intuition for what it is—an extremely exciting, healthy, everyday human ability. I focus on what makes it normal and demonstrate how it affects decisions and moves we make. I project how it could, and should, change *your* future as well as the future of humankind and the environment.

Part I gives you the facts necessary to take advantage of intuition—an option available to us all. Follow the arguments to learn why we should each develop and use this ability to set ourselves on courses of action that make it easier to be successful, to forge and sustain loving relationships, to develop our personal talents, and to succeed in our worldly work. After reading Part I, perhaps you will understand why I predict that by being a society that effectively uses intuition we will open a new chapter in the story of humankind. It will be the climactic chapter that reverses the projected dark ending of a self-indulgent species to one in which that species takes an evolutionary leap forward to new heights of achievement and cooperation.

# CHAPTER 1

# Why Are We Intuitive?

(ψ-1) THREE MONTHS after the Oklahoma City bombing on April 19, 1995, which killed 168 people and wounded scores of others, CNN aired an interview with one of the victims, a woman who was learning to walk on an artificial leg. In addition to a leg, she had lost two young children and her mother in the blast. The object of the report was for the audience to see real-life adjustments continuing, lest the nation's horror fade into memory. However, the interview took a surprising turn when the woman, speaking through tears of despair, remarked how often she wished she had followed her "instinct" that day. Leaving the reporter speechless, she continued, saying that while in the building, she had a distinct impulse to seize her family and leave immediately. She said she discarded the impulse at once as a silly notion, so she did not move. In the next minutes, her world exploded.

(ψ-2) On that same unforgettable April 19 morning, a college student in Pennsylvania was awakened from a sound sleep. He later wrote me this note:

*I remember waking up at 6:30 that morning, unusually early for me—you know how college students are who study half the night. And I just sat straight up in bed, because my head was filled with a very powerful thought:*

A lot of people are going to die in
Oklahoma City.

*I didn't do anything about it, only went back to sleep until about 9:30. Then I dressed and headed for the restaurant where I was working. For some reason, someone turned on the television. We discovered that regular programming on every channel had been preempted by a chaotic tragedy unfolding. The federal building in Oklahoma City had blown up just minutes before—at 9:04 central time. I looked up at the clock on the wall. It was 10:30, only twenty-six minutes after the blast, but four hours after I had intuited it.*

He closed his account by saying, "I asked myself why I got that message, because I was in no position to stop it, or warn anyone about it."

Accounts such as this repeat hundreds of times daily, in different contexts, throughout the world. People know! They learn. However, usually they understand neither what is happening at the time, nor how to use the information that they receive. The reason for this innocence is: They simply don't comprehend that this is their own intuition at work. Since intuition does follow particular patterns, even without our knowing, I can say absolutely that the woman in line and the student in bed were both being intuitive. I predict that, as human beings, we will all be able to use intuition naturally in the not-too-distant future to reach our full potential individually and to help every other living creature do the same. In these pages, you will learn why I am convinced that intuition is an ability working within every living human being.

Examine the marvel of these accounts: two people were aware of the same event—which had not yet happened! Neither is an expert on terrorism, nor had any acquaintance with the perpetrator or perpetrators, yet each one "knew" that a human tragedy was in the offing. Although they were 1,500 miles apart, each discovered it, in a different way. One, within the building, learned just in time to help her family and herself. Unbelievably, she was advised precisely what to do—"Run!" The other, who could not possibly be physically injured, was informed hours in advance. Who would disagree that their knowledge truly provided opportunity? This is the task of intuition. It empowers us to help one another and ourselves. Look at the evidence here. That morning the woman and the student had an opportunity to use their mysterious information and make constructive changes that would alter the future dramatically.

We can see that if the woman had understood that the impulse was as good as any boss's instruction, and had followed through, her personal life would not have taken such a radical turn. And, had the sleepy collegian been able to pick up a phone to report his premonition to, say, a national precognition center, his intuitive wake-up call could have been a wake-up call at least to alert local law enforcement agencies and at best to favorably alter the future of who knows how many people.

To even the most casual observer, it must seem as though each of these people had an opportunity to produce what might be considered a miracle—escaping unscathed from a calamity and foretelling a catastrophe. We all have to ask: Why did those two have that ability to be miracle workers? How could they have known? What is this thing called intuition? And, I ask you: How many people would like to think that this capacity is within our reach? How many doubt it? On the other extreme, how many have no doubt at all?

Let us begin to build a case for this phenomenon called intuition.

## What Do We Know?

A popular definition for intuition is: that human ability for attaining direct knowledge without evident rational thought. We have the most elementary example in these experiences just described, of two people who knew about a developing, cunningly planned, deadly event which, by rational standards, should have been unknown to all but the perpetrators. Now ask yourself the question that I ask myself repeatedly: If these two people intuited that information, how many others were also unaccountably notified *before* that bomb blew apart a solid building and hundreds of lives? How I would love to know that precise number!

## Redefining Intuition

Throughout my life I have had frequent cues like those the woman and man reported. I can remember several incidents when I was as young as five, but I actually began to pay attention to them around age eleven. ($\psi$-3) One of the first sharp memories is of the tragic day when I was "absolutely certain in my bones" that six-year-old Maynard would not be found alive. I had no doubt of that—despite the searchers' confidence when they set out on the first afternoon, into the woods around the village. ($\psi$-4) And, how could I ever forget the afternoon when my older sister and I were merrily playing piano duets? Despite her infectious giggling, I had what we called a "sure feeling" that she was desperately unhappy. ($\psi$-5) On another occasion, I wakened from a sound sleep, as if on cue, and "plainly knew" that my best friend was being crowned queen of her school prom at that very moment. I could "tell" she was bubbling with delight. ($\psi$-6) One youthful intuitive experience I recall made me unpopular in high school. I was assigned an "opportunity" to head a fund-raising venture, but I knew down to my "core" that I shouldn't take it. Although I was cautioned that this was not good citizenship, and could see by the faculty adviser's scorn that it was a bad choice, I had such a strong feeling "deep down" that something was wrong with the whole venture that I declined.

Passing time confirmed all these psi effects. The local boy's life *was* snuffed out. Those searchers found Maynard's body the next day in the frozen river; he'd fallen through the ice and drowned. I discovered that my sister *did* dread the future. Apparently some weeks before our duet-playing merriment, our family eye doctor had told her that she had an early symptom of multiple sclerosis, but she never breathed a word about it to me until twelve years later, when the fearful disease began taking over. My friend *was* crowned queen of her prom on that night I awakened; I heard the news with my own ears when she telephoned me to share her excitement directly the next morning. Six weeks after it began, the school fund-raising campaign failed miserably.

"Sudden inclinations." "Impressions." "Bone certainty." "Sure feeling." "Plain knowing." "Core" and "gut feelings." Those stray snippets of information, which burst to life everywhere, eventually landed in my head spontaneously. They came as reporters of facts, produced in uncomplicated ways that any youngster would certainly have caught. Many years later, I learned that they were what scientists had long since classified as "psi effects."

To my amazement, I had never stopped to wonder whether they were normal. Why? Innocence, probably. I began to notice them naturally, the way a newborn begins looking at objects and listening to sounds, and, before many days have passed, is able to respond to those phenomena as either threatening or gratifying. Nature decrees so much of our behavior—including receiving and learning quantities of information through sensory systems; it's part of being human.

Looking back, I can say that the intuitive information was invaluable. It helped me decide whether to remain or leave a place, which plan to change, how people truly felt, and, yes, how to predict future events. It was endlessly beneficial. Although no one ever taught me to use it, and although I made my share of mistakes with it through the years, I slowly gained insight into its obscure processes and purpose. In one test after another, results reflected back the vast range of readily available intuitive information and its ways to help me consistently with uncertainties. I gradually learned to work with it very effectively for solving immediate problems, testing my limits, and making plans. Now, dozens of years later, I have finally found the keys that make it possible for all of us to call on intuition whenever we need it, and to know what to do when it calls on us.

I am an educational psychologist. My history of exploring this phenomenon started in 1972, when I became interested in experiences such as those just described out of my past, which I now formally classify as "intuitive." Having a classical psychology background, I was also intrigued by the questions posed during the human potential movement, which began in the sixties; they were focused on the outer limits of human capabilities and how we learn. Of course, at the time, "intuition" was not the household word it is today. In the spring of 1973, I registered at the local college for an evening course intriguingly named "Your ESP* and How to Use It." Under the title in the catalog was the requisite explanatory subtitle "* Extra Sensory Perception." I drew only one solid conclusion from that class: We, as a species, had a lot to learn about our mental abilities.

Now fast-forward to 1999. How did I learn all that I am proposing to say here? It required two steps. Phase One was experimentation. Phase Two, graduate school. I began to search seriously because I had discovered that ESP was an umbrella phrase for "paranormal learning," "knowing the unknown," "gut feelings," "impulses," and dozens of other similar effects. To my surprise, they were all merely descriptors for that nameless method of learning information that I had used all my life. Amazingly, it had never once occurred to me that other people did not learn likewise. Imagine my puzzlement.

Probably I'd expected the instructor of that class to reveal something far more sensational and mysterious than she did, but I decided that if this *was* it, then I wanted to fully understand the big fuss about ESP. After extensive reading and debate, I decided to test myself and analyze this ability "to know" that people were calling extraordinary. I had no reason, yet, to think that it was anything but ordinary. Phase One began the search for ESP with its associated diverse, inexplicable paranormal phenomena— the psi effects. Six years later, I commenced Phase Two by entering graduate school, to study neurobiology and transpersonal psychology.

The first phase would be field testing. Hence I chose to test myself quietly, as a "psychic," doing what were acceptably called "readings" for inquisitive neighbors and friends. They came, listened, and went away, leaving startling words floating in the air behind them that emphatically described their view of the way I knew their information. Among other things, I heard "spooky," "strange," and "amazing," but I couldn't agree. This was *entirely* normal.

It was never my intention to gain a reputation as the person who could add insights to everyday concerns that people said they couldn't discover by themselves. But, of course, one person did tell another. Thus, I began making appointments! Owners of local businesses called on me for forecasts and information about trends. These usually were accurate. The heads of elite squads in two major metropolitan police departments asked me to work along with their teams to solve criminal cases; we were successful with one case after another. A psychologist called on me to pinpoint her clients' obscure mental problems; the information helped her work. As time went by, my consulting extended into the world. Law enforcement agencies asked for information—the

FBI, Scotland Yard, and the Israeli police, to name a few. Heads of large corporations, hospital staffs, governments, and the media called me in on sticky problems. Reports came back: the information helped! They'd made their decisions based on the "readings"; results were positive.

It was marvelous. My laboratory was vast: twenty thousand consultations and climbing. People were showing me the practical value of intuition in their lives and the world, *and* I was rapidly gaining insight into what I then called "the System," my pet name for the way I learned this knowledge that people so prized.

Then, 1979: time for Phase Two—graduate school, for more biology and psychology. Three private grants later allowed further research. In 1980, I hypothesized that the System is a sensory process. It would give us information that is different from all of our other senses. It had to be what for generations has been called "intuition," combined with those ancient, mystifying psi effects.

Teaching came next. I went from place to place—wherever people wanted to learn to intuit. It was during these classes that I found the crucial answer I needed. With my own eyes, I watched a small sample of humanity begin to discover its own intuition. In more than a dozen countries, women, men, and children living all styles of life, working in every imaginable profession, and crossing a staggering range of ages from five to eighty-five learned, one by one, to use intuition well and naturally. As they learned, I watched them help themselves come through untold numbers of threatening experiences and flourish to their full potential. To my delight, they were proving to me, at last, that intuition is completely normal among human beings. My hypothesis was confirmed.

## New Definition

Based on the evidence I've observed, I have redefined *intuition* to be: a sensory process in human beings triggered by particular kinds of interactions both inside and outside our bodies that influences our stability and optimal performance. It affects our behavior, feelings, and/or thoughts so that we either move involuntarily or receive factual information that provides direction for our decisions about what moves to make.

Now I can answer the question "Why are we intuitive?" I say with absolute certainty: We are intuitive because we are a species of animal evolved on earth by a natural process. We are born with capacities to cope with challenges and are charged with the responsibility to utilize the abilities to develop and reproduce. Living in an immense, ever-changing environment, we always need adequate information to (1) protect ourselves against predators that threaten our individual lives or other life forms, and (2) gain every personal advantage that provides us the opportunity to reach our full potential, and to do the same for other organic and mechanical systems.* Intuition is one of our innate abilities; it produces some of our required information. Evolutionary biologists would say that intuition's main purpose is physical growth and adaptation that will insure the perpetuation of our species. This, of course, is entirely correct.

## No Escape from the Factors "U"

Unhappily, a monstrous bombing with all the resulting misery is not an overly dramatic example of events occurring in our world today. More and more, we have become an impulse-driven society, pushed to the edge of despair and destructiveness by our own malcontentedness and mean-spiritedness. True, humankind has always walked a fine line of survival. From the beginning, circumstances decreed that we would have to roam about in environments that frequently would be hostile to us. Because we've taken multiple unanticipated blows from our own reverenced

---

*Regarding predators: Note that any terrorist is certainly to be counted as predatory, making us the prey.

Mother Nature's rampages—earthquakes, windstorms, fires, floods, attacks from wild beasts and, somewhere along the way, even from our own kind, which is as capable of vicious bestial raging as any other of nature's elemental forces—perhaps it isn't so astonishing that nature has gradually evolved helpful systems for getting ourselves safely through the ceaseless changes that impact our lives.

We came to life in a world full of unpredictable events and unknown conditions that we didn't understand, and yet we were equipped to adapt and survive. We've discovered the rules and the ropes slowly. For example, from the dawn of our existence we have been finding ways to provide adequately for our most constant physical needs—food, water, and thermal protection such as shelters and clothing for our warm-blooded bodies. However, we have more to discover. Every day, year, and epoch brings new challenges to recognize and survive.

Oddly, despite hundreds of millions of years of learning, the greatest predators on our well-being, both physical and mental, are evermore the same. Tragic experiences have taught that our vast bank of adaptive assets falls apart like quicksilver when we're faced with surprises cloaked in the Unknown indefinite present and the Unpredictable future. Call them the Factors "U."

As it was in the beginning, so it is now. They lurk where any phenomenon is concealed or secret. Too often we're caught defenseless, struggling in despair to help ourselves at the time we face an unknown—or worse, later, after the crisis, attempting to figure out rationally how to help ourselves the next time, if indeed there is a "next time." Generation after generation, we have wrung our hands, asking: What are we to do if we or our loved ones fall prey to wild things coming out of the jungles, both forested and asphalt? Our hunger to know about every event, both beneficial and malevolent, concealed in the present and cloaked as the future, is as old as the human race; to date, it remains unsatisfied.

We can't be faulted for not trying. From earliest times, we have attempted to regulate the quantity and quality of uncertainties that could, and would, swallow us up. Generally our methods involved straightening out the twisted interactions and rounding off the sharp turns in life's situations that would be blind corners. The result has been an ongoing creative evolution. Many times now, our species has taken control of the natural patterns of evolution by inventing new interactions of materials, mimicking those natural processes we figure out, and creating synthetic likenesses of elemental forms.

What has been our motive for adding our creative strains to natural structures? It appears to have been for our greater well-being and comfort. We've changed the order of nature at every turn, by introducing all manner of practical phenomena, from the stone ax, to fertilizer, to the greenhouse—to gain control of the agricultural climate and thus our food supply—to travel on water, rail, and wing, with the consequence of speeding up our pace of movement, which by now we've extended to global interaction, in the form of commerce, cultural exchange, and, regrettably, war.

Without ignoring our almost absurdly phenomenal success at fine-tuning one unknown after another, to meet the requirements we set as standard, we'd be foolish to think we'll ever be able to lock out the Factors "U" completely. Mother Nature's irrepressible elemental whims will always produce surprises, and the increasingly abusive forces rampant among our own species add intolerable tensions that create the ever-worsening uncertainties of destruction and death. In the final analysis, we obviously still roam in an extremely difficult environment.

Although our behavior has steadily become more complex and efficient since the evolutionary split that likely occurred to produce the hominid, or human, line between 1.5 and 2 million years ago, our development has neither solved nor eliminated one particularly sticky human problem. The phenomena might be different, and we might be able to anticipate many more hazards than we could in the first days of humankind, but a reality check says that the Factors "U" lurk all the same. Signs indicate that this is the way things are; we always will be prey to some looming forces of change. This being true, who wouldn't agree that we desperately need to find every possible way to know the unknown and unpredictable, before we destroy ourselves and the world with us? If you have even the slightest doubt, review one week's headline news in one small-town newspaper:

"LA NIÑA MAY BRING A FIERCE HURRICANE SEASON."

Emergency planners poring over projections worry about an exploding coastal population and wonder if all the new technology will be enough if evacuation is necessary. They fear that many new residents of the coast may not respond to warnings. Coastal communities could become death traps for stragglers.

"IN MEXICO CITY RANDOM CRIME IS OFTEN
JUST A TAXICAB RIDE AWAY."

Hailing a cab in Mexico's capital can be risky business. Crime and the fear of it have gripped Mexico City. Crimes are happening all over the place at all times of day in all parts of the city. The city's transportation secretary said that the overall crime problem is nearly unsolvable because of corruption and lack of respect for, or confidence in, authorities who should be preventing and punishing crime.

"SCHOOL SHOOTINGS LEAVE SURVIVORS CONFUSED."

Just as life starts to return to normal, to be filled with haircuts and soccer games and plans for summer, it happens again. Another angry youngster in another small town fires a gun.

"Patients question anti-malaria drug.
Sometimes severe side effects occur,
but doctors claim it's safe."

"The international scientific community is concerned about the safety of this drug," said the Berkeley, California, lawyer. "The bottom line is mefloquine is preventing a fatal disease," the researcher stated. "If 93 to 95 percent of the people who take the drug tolerate it with no problems, or minor problems, we have to keep this thing in perspective."

"The challenge of change."

Nearly half of the 3,000-plus acres in Ward 8 lie undeveloped and unspoiled—much as it was generations ago when residents farmed and fished. As the town considers how the area should be developed, the question arises: What are the environmental ramifications likely to be? Nobody can say.

Let's review this news of the week. The weather could surprise us. Authorities misguide us. Murderers might ambush us; medicine will, maybe, consume us; and the environment, perhaps, will be depleted. But we're not sure!

Could! Probably! Might! Maybe! Perhaps! We don't need to ask why we feel like victims on parade. The problem is as plain as the nose on your face. The Factors "U" are on the loose! We can't escape them. And this is unnerving. It sets us shivering, like brittle autumn leaves in the wind. Yet, we know, beyond question, that to yield to the enormous power that the unknowns and unpredictables seem to be wrenching from us influences how we function in all aspects of our daily life. The result of the present-day dilemma is that we're slowly building an impenetrable wall of fear and inflexible defenses. Why?

Because we feel helpless. Woven liberally among the plethora of hidden options for the good life are as many, or more, others that bring painful and destructive outcomes. Although they might be concealed under public officials' sugarcoated promises of well-being, or wrapped in optimistic parental plans and establishment programs, no one is exempt. We're prey when matters become unpredictable. It could be your home standing in the path of the hurricane, you climbing into that Mexico City taxicab, your son or daughter's school, you in that small percentage of allergic people, your own house and furnishings swallowed whole in the floodwaters of those "environmental ramifications." Multiply this by dozens of nations, hundred of states, millions of cities and towns, seven billion human beings, and think of the sheer weight on our psyches caused by our not knowing when personal safety and self-sufficiency will be smothered by destructive forces sewn from fibers of ignorance, greed for power, or even nature's furies; it can cause any wholesome adult to shake with indecision and any half-grown child to suffer miserably from chronic uncertainty.

Here is what has happened. For all of the promises, hopes, and dreams that should come true in a world so abundant with resources, too many of us feel threatened by the steady ratcheting up of impulses that lead to violence, whether it be in man, beast, or our most reverenced Mother Nature. To make decisions confidently in climates gone wild becomes overwhelming. Our traditional methods are inadequate: We've tried them all—learning from others, cool reason, trial and error, rational gambles, positive thinking, faith, second-guessing, even dumb luck—but the weight of our uncertainties only becomes more oppressive. It appears that the unknowns and unpredictables have become constant trappers, and we are their prey for life.

While we suffer stress fractures from head to toe about the gaping holes in our security, and wonder in frustration what to do to stabilize our worlds without unnecessary sacrifice, we are all thinking in the backs of our minds: There must be a law against all this. Surely we must possess the ability to regulate the uncertainties, and thus stabilize our existence and be free of these concerns. What must we do to be free?

We seem to have proven to ourselves that becoming "tougher" with our antagonistic authoritative laws and monstrous prodigious social and military defenses has not made life better. But be assured, there is a natural way. When we peer into nature's order, we discover that a solution exists. Grand changes over time clearly explain why any organism survives and evolves. It seems that nature's own gradual way of bringing change through the evolutionary process has not produced "tougher" living organisms; instead, it has increased their sensitivity, thereby helping to assure that an organism will survive and flourish. Improved sensitivity is our answer.

## A Law Does Exist

There is such a rule, and a far wiser course of action than building fear and more uncompromising defenses. An evolving sensory system has emerged at last, ready for us to activate it; it's natural and within our own physical bodies now. A new sense is ready and waiting to point out the route to personal safety, contentment, and optimal performance. It is, of course, our intuition, a tantalizing internal biotic control that will help us, one and all. It is the means by which we humans will return stability to our lives, to have the opportunities we need to take risks safely, to use our talents and reach our full potential. I propose that intuition is nature's evolutionary gift to us, a brand-new set of manageable controls to run our future.

The place to begin reconfiguring ourselves is in a candid view of what we are today. Let's establish that we, the human species, one by one, are indeed perennial victims—prey to be seized upon by countless grasping forces. Traditionally, we think of predators as wild consuming creatures and think of prey as physically smaller or more vulnerable ones. But, why limit the predatory power to only creatures? If prey is something capable of being seized and devoured, and the predator is the doer of the deed, then surely the Factors "U" are candidate predators, for is it not true that there inside them both is where our attackers await? Is it not true that in the unknown, a predator might be prowling?

Our keen awareness of our vulnerable position is starkly visible in the question we ask repeatedly: "Is it safe?" In this day and age, safeness is suspect across the land—in our schools, in the markets, in post offices, and in the dark clouds that might unleash a deadly freak tornado. Of all the people who are given a wonder drug prescription, we have to wonder ourselves who among us will fall into that unknown 7 percent and react "negatively," which in plain words means falling ill or even falling dead.

Why be so negative? For fair reasons: Terror and terrorists are real, and all around us. Yes, of course, where there is bad there is good. We have no question that all the possibilities for good and ill exist, but we have a valid problem. Ask anyone out there: Too many agree that the vital spirit is losing its spark. The glow of joy has faded. Without accurate facts that map out that road to personal success, we all seem to understand that we're traveling in the opposite direction. Despite our natural courage, innate talents, and desire to believe the best, nowadays we are forced to fear the worst.

No matter the confident assurances of perpetual protection from governing corners of our world. No matter the optimistic statistics that say the number of losers is definitely diminishing, that we can count on one hand those who won't make it. The real matter is toward another interest: What can we do? Our safety and accomplishments are personal rights. We want to know the rules that return them to us. We need individual direction for our actions.

## Managing Our Life on Earth

The problem we face is to get inside the systems of the "U" beasts and gain control *before* they turn disagreeable or deadly. I propose that intuition gives us a way to do this: It produces all the facts we ever need to manage unsafe situations successfully. This is the entire reason we are intuitive. All our natural advantages will flow from it. I am confident that nature's next evolutionary improvement is to establish intuitive sensitivity in our species, for intuitiveness is another facet to us—one that puts us at the helm on the sea of life.

The next big question is: How do we recognize our own intuition?

# Meet the Effects

($\psi$-7) IN THE early seventies, the American Mathematical Association held its international conference in Vancouver, British Columbia. Anticipating that two thousand or so preoccupied mathematicians and their guests might overtax the public transportation, the city fathers wisely provided an exclusive transit system. It ran a circuit from the campus of the host university to various lecture halls and places of local interest. When meetings finished on the last day, my husband and I decided to ride to the end of one line and stroll through the lively metropolis.

The bus filled to near bursting at the campus and emptied slowly until, at the last stop, we were the only passengers aboard. On my way to the exit, I noticed a scuffed attaché case on one seat and decided immediately to report it to the driver. However, other information silently overrode that decision:

*Pick it up.*

This terse instruction arose within my head. Since it made quite a strong impression, I deciphered the message easily. I knew by the mental feeling that I was receiving intuitive information about what to do with the abandoned briefcase. The instruction was accompanied by a "sense" that this was urgent; this too occurred within my head.

I had learned years before to recognize these intuitive instructions. Experience had taught me that the messages would be associated with an event in the real world and that I should treat them as important. Strange as it might seem I understood that there was a reason for that attaché case and the accompanying agitation catching my attention as plainly as any screaming fire siren would do.

In technical terms, I was intuiting. I was being informed about the location, movement, and mental state of the individual who owned that briefcase. I intuited, or learned, the information when I detected the instruction and urgency. The actual experience of detecting data, which I call a "mental experience" and psychologists classify as "perception," is one part of the intuitive process. Hereafter I shall use all three terms—detection, mental experience, and perception—to refer to the experience of learning via data supplied to us by our sensory systems. The human visual system, for instance, provides an extraordinary quantity of information. One quick glance allows a person with average vision to learn the location, size, shape, color, and texture of multiple objects; should those objects be in motion, the onlooker also detects, or perceives, their relative speed and direction.

For a familiar parallel think of noticing a car move along the street. How many visual details do you gather in that first glimpse? Take the thought further by asking what that moment of discovery "feels" like. Do you have any distinct internal sensations when you catch sight of the car's color, shape, or speed? In other words, what is your "mental experience" when you see that car? Most would answer that it is a "feeling of learning," or perhaps an experience of "simply knowing," all those facts about the car. And most are aware that those effects occur because they are seeing that car. These dynamic changes, which take place in our heads as we learn, are referred to technically as "perceptual effects"—visual effects, sound effects, tactile effects, and so forth.

We perceive the information that comes from many, but not all, of our sensory interactions with the world. For example, you don't normally detect gravity. Neither do you perceive the continual exchange of oxygen, carbon dioxide, and other gases in your lungs. On the other hand, you probably do perceive that you are "thinking" while adding or subtracting numbers in your head, and you certainly detect the discomfort of a sunburn.

When intuiting information, the mental experiences we detect and learn by are called *psi effects*. Through these psi effects, we learn facts about the objects we are intuiting in the same way that we experience "simply knowing" facts about a moving car. As part of gaining control over our intuition we are responsible for learning what these psi effects represent, just as we were required in early childhood to master the meaning of the perceptual effects—pain, pleasure, hot, cold, fear, thinking, and so on—associated with other experiences.

The psi effects I detected on the bus were strictly mental experiences, or perceptible effects, of a stimulus—in this case pure knowledge and a strong sense of pressure. Our days are filled with such occurrences. The real world surrounds us, but our perception of it takes place in the head through a wide variety of signaling effects that arrive in the brain. By learning the effects' patterns of information and what they mean, we discover what is happening to us and literally follow events in the environment, as they occur, the way we would a story. The more signals we can recognize, the more we learn. In all cases, that knowledge is the core of our security and success.

Each piece of information is coded in your brain, to tell you how things are. As an adult, you already know most of the

codes—that's a number, that's a color, there's a noise, this is how
I feel. You broke the codes long ago, starting the day you were
born and continuing on through your childhood. Now you use
their data automatically. On any given day, you perceive multitudes of visual effects, sound effects, and thermal effects of warm
or cold, for example. It's up to you to decide which of them are
useful enough to receive your undivided attention. Once you
have decided your focus, you gather the information, make a decision about what to do in response, and follow through with
action. The phone is ringing: Will you answer it or not? You are
getting colder: Will you go back indoors and put on a jacket? The
world comes into our heads this way for a natural reason. When
we know what is going on, we can decide what to do next.

On that day in the bus, I was learning about two specific
events in the environment: That briefcase had a destination, and
someone was upset. I knew this because without understanding
what I was doing, I had cracked the code of psi effects in my
early youth—at about the same time that I was learning to identify colors and count with numbers. By the time I was five, intuition's psi effects were as clear and informative to me as most
children's visual and sound effects are to them. No one ever spoke
to me about the intuitive way in which I learned. I understood
that psi effects were factual information and experienced them
personally—rather the same way that I experienced color: Red was
red, blue was blue, and so on. As I have already stated, I had no
idea whether or not other people had the same kind of information, because I never bothered to inquire. Intuition simply was a
splendid resource for accurate data, nothing more.

With this background, therefore, "Pick it up" meant just
that. I immediately understood that the instruction was somehow
directly connected to the lone briefcase, the way a jumbo jet is
connected with its trailing roar; in both there is a real, albeit invisible, physical connection. And the sense of urgency decoded into
a subtle impression in me of "straining" for time. The important

detail, which I understood, was that this strain was *imposed* on me; it could not possibly be my own. I was absolutely certain that it originated with someone else.

Today I can say that I was following my intuition, but on that particular afternoon in Vancouver, I had no such idea. Intuition always wove smoothly into the fabric of my experiences. As far as I was concerned, I was paying attention to some impressions in my head and decided to act on them, the same as anyone else in the world would do. Little did I know that within an hour, I would make a leap to understanding these effects that always came to me spontaneously. Little did I know, as well, that no one had ever drawn a map of the road to using our intuitive sensibilities intelligently; every inch of understanding it was up to me. This chapter traces my first steps of actual discovery, when I found the pattern of intuition in human experiences and the real-life reason we are intuitive. Here we're beginning to break the code of nature's psi effects. We will revisit and identify them in a wide range of accounts throughout the book.

Returning now to the bus: I knew it would be permissible, in fact advisable, to follow through on that succinct instruction. How did I know this? Because I'd experienced that kind of impression many times before. I understood what it meant; a predicament was evolving, even though it was impossible in that instant to pinpoint it geographically, explain it logically, or describe what my next move would be if I were to pick up the briefcase. Thus, I made my decision, reached over, grabbed it, tested the fasteners, and found they were locked. This done, I left the bus, without saying a word to the driver.

As soon as we alighted from the bus, I told my husband what had happened, took his arm, and asked him to stick with me. We were already half walking, half running. Between gasps, he posed some very sensible questions, such as, "Where are we going?" and "Wouldn't it be easier for the person to contact the transit company, rather than for us to chase blindly through a vast city we've never seen?" My terse answers told him I was concentrating, yet at the same time I was amused by a familiar, personal capricious notion that I was behaving rather like a bloodhound tracking a scent. I wondered: "Do *they* know where they're going?"

I certainly didn't. My moves now depended on my confidently following through on the instruction. This was easy; experience had taught me that intuition's movements are regulated in a natural way. As I had no doubts about being guided, I agreeably let the bloodhound loose, leaving it to my head to implement the instruction correctly.

By now we'd turned right from the bus onto a narrow sidewalk, then left, then right again, then had fairly flown along five city blocks, which to our surprise joined the main street. We turned again and went up a hill to the next corner. When we arrived, about twenty people were waiting for a signal to change. Although we were looking only at the backs of heads, I was "aware" that the owner of the briefcase was in this particular crowd. I studied that sea of strangers. Nothing visibly stood out about a medium-tall, dark-haired man toward the front, but I "knew," or intuited, instantly that the case belonged to him. We moved in his direction as quickly as the crowd would allow. Beside him at last, I caught his attention, held out the tattered briefcase for him to see, and inquired, "Is this yours?"

His eyes might have popped from his head, if such a thing were possible. As it was, they darted from the case to my face, to my mystified husband standing with me, and back to the case. Obviously bewildered, he stared at it vacantly until he regained his composure. Then he accepted it from me and told us his story, in a strong accent.

On the bus, he'd been so engrossed in his plans that he'd forgotten to pick up the case when he disembarked near the city center. As soon as he realized his mistake, he tried to track the bus, but that was futile. Now he was headed for campus, to find anyone who could help him. He'd felt so desperate. The most terrible part, he said, was that his plane was leaving in two hours for New York; it was the only flight that day that would take him to Paris and a tight connection. His home, he said cautiously, was Romania. He dared not arrive late.

My thoughts began to race. Romania! He lived behind the Iron Curtain! He *was* in a predicament—one that might be more dangerous for him than any of us in the free world could imagine. Foreign travel was rigidly controlled by the Communist Party, particularly for scientists. "Lateness" could mean trouble. No wonder he was frantic.

While speaking, he'd been fussing with a combination lock on the case. When it finally opened, he hurriedly rummaged through an unruly pile of papers, pulled out a thick booklet, and triumphantly whirled it around over his head.

"My tickets home!"

Smiling with delight, he shook my hand vigorously, as though he were pumping water from a well. And, quite unexpectedly, he heartily embraced my husband, who began gasping again, but this time in astonishment. Then, with a few light steps, this nameless man rejoined the crowd of strangers crossing the street, tickets waving over his head like branches in a wild wind. Slightly dazed, we turned back toward the heart of town, to continue our adventure of discovering the city. We smiled in amusement when my husband pulled out his map to guide us.

## Information Comes First

The mathematician's very serious problem was that he and his tickets had been separated. The damage done by the loss is clear: His plans were crumbling. To begin correcting the problem, he had to have the tickets in hand. But, how could he do this with no clue about their location? Common sense says that he would have to seek assistance quickly. It might have appeared in the form of someone at the university who would follow up with a mechanical call, by telephone, for example; his other option was less obvious: person-to-person contact, through the intuitive communication system. It would appear that everything depended on his getting the information to the right individual. Two matters governed which of these services would be most appropriate: his location, which was far away from any helpful person, and the short time until the plane departed. These severely restricted him and thus controlled the way in which he found his tickets.

This, I have learned, is the juxtaposition that intuition always makes first—it combines a phenomenon and intuitive people. We learn from it spontaneously. As we unravel the complexities of the intuitive process, this one fact never changes: The intuitor receives relevant information about the phenomenon. That information represents a contact between the intuitor and the phenomenon, which *must* occur to trigger the intuitive process. Contact between the phenomenon and the intuitor is always the first step in the intuitive process. Remarkably, I didn't figure out this very significant fact until I tripped over it—in a moment of pure insight.

## Aha!

The Vancouver attaché-case race with the clock took place four months after that class in ESP, so the intellectual concept of psi effects was no longer completely new to me. That introduction notwithstanding, I was doubtful that psi effects had anything to do with me. Maybe they did occur in other people's lives. Using them in isolation, as I obviously was, it probably comes as no surprise that I'd never thought about how they might influence events outside my little world—until that ecstatic man danced away with the crowd.

Perhaps it was seeing his great relief that precipitated what happened next, or maybe it was the class. I don't know. But, that day, the chase in Vancouver made me realize something new about the way things are in the natural order of life. The simple insight was that this was not the first time I had learned something from an inexplicable instruction in my head. In actual fact, I had had numbers of other such experiences, and when I followed them through exactly, the result was consistent. Someone or something always benefited! Then the clanging of truth: These experiences, I realized, all were psi effects. And finally, the frosting on the cake: I had the new idea. Those psi effects had an absolute purpose. They report useful information. Suddenly the facts fell together. The instruction experiences were repetitive, and when I did follow through, they invariably led to correcting a situation that was heading for trouble.

I almost felt the jolt of that realization. A lifetime of mental reports—hundreds, thousands of them, from high drama to pure comic—fit into a pattern. It meant that there had to be a basic function that was responsible for informing me mentally, in consistent patterned ways, about particular developing events (Factors "U") that needed my assistance if they were to come out right. I'd never thought of those thousands of mental effects as anything quite so structured.

To personally discover a great truth is to discover life itself. It's the lure, the "Ah," the "Look at that!" From the start, a mind soars. One previous experience after another begins to make sense by itself, and life, with the new truth in place, becomes less of an effort, more a connecting of the parts of a most wonderful whole. So it was for me. As details supporting my new find were liberated one after another that day, I wondered, for a fleet instant, why it had taken me thirty-five years to recognize this pattern as a consistent way of learning. But I couldn't stay long with reflection, because the story was evolving rapidly. My thoughts, transformed to racehorses, were coming into the stretch!

It had ever been thus: These experiences—the instructions and several others kinds of information I regularly perceived—all belonged in one group together. There could be no doubt.

And, they had to be what people were calling the "psi effects." I might have had hundreds, even millions or billions, of different commands during my lifetime—from parents, teachers, friends— but I was sure that a substantial number of them would fit into what I spontaneously decided to classify as the Instruction type of psi effect. And, with that, another certainty landed with a thud: It would be only one category of a larger collection.

The other psi effects would have their own distinct recognizable characteristics, just like the Instruction psi effect, which always commanded the very next move I should make. Though I'd never thought about it, this was true. The Instruction effect was always the same. Its information had never done anything more than provide details about the next move to make, and remarkably that was all. Now I understood that was *supposed* to be all. We should treat any Instruction psi effect the same way we would if it came from another source, such as a teacher or a ship's captain, because giving instructions would be all we could ever expect of it. People would have to understand this as a fact.

The discoveries poured down in a rush, bringing together new ideas, passing others by. First, a psi effect probably had the specific task of informing me so that I could make finer-tuned decisions than would be possible without it. Second, once I caught, or detected, the information, the psi effect would have accomplished its purpose. Third, I had better pay attention to it, because no other system within my mentality or body could produce the particular kinds of details that these psi effects provided. Finally, I drew my first solid conclusion: The Instruction is a viable source of reliable information; it is one psi effect.

This notion about the pattern of the Instruction was the element I needed, the intellectual starch, if you will, that stiffened my resolution to dig deeper into the world of psi effects. By the end of that day, I was certain of one more detail: There would indeed be other such effects, but not vast quantities of them. This would be an exclusive club. We'd probably uncover fewer than ten. As it was with Instruction, so it would be with the others: Each type would have its own particular kind of information to report; each would be purposeful. And, if experience held true, I would discover too that as the receiver, I would have a definite role in the process. Probably, if I used it correctly, it would improve life and remove a disadvantage, as the information from the Instruction effect had done for the dancing mathematician.

As the ideas grew and connected one to the other, a larger pattern jumped out from the basic concept of patterns. To my amazement, I'd landed on a solid rock of knowledge from the ages. Fact one was nothing new; teenage youngsters learn it in biology class: "Effects" are attached to our senses! Vision has visual effects. Hearing, sound effects. Body thermostat, heat and cold effects. Then, another leap: Could it be possible that the psi effects' diverse types of information were coming through a designated sensory system?

I remembered information-filled feelings from my childhood, especially in church. All kinds of facts flew through the air in that sparsely furnished Pilgrim sanctuary. Every Sunday morning between ten and eleven o'clock, while the pastor delivered his sermon, I would "learn" about the deepest concerns of the parishioners and events in the villagers' lives.

($\psi$-8) On one particular day, Dr. and Mrs. Stanstead—pillars of the church—had bright smiles on their faces, but I "felt" they were overflowing with distress. It was confirmed later in the week; they had learned on Saturday that their son was an alcoholic.

($\psi$-9) On another sunny Sunday morning, while the minister droned on with the seemingly endless Bible reading, a flitting bit of information skimmed along the edges of my concentration and effortlessly overrode his message. I suddenly "knew," without a doubt, that Beth Browning, seated three pews ahead of us, would be the only one admitted to the college that she—and everyone else—yearned to attend. Weeks later, one letter of acceptance from the school arrived. It was for Beth.

How had these facts arrived? I certainly understood the common sensory effects: They all reported as sensations in my brain, between my ears. Sound, for example, would have come from the outside world, along my auditory nerve, as part of the nervous system's function. Like the images that are known as visual effects and noises associated with sound effects, these psi effects also turned up and were perceptible within my head. Did that mean they were transmitted along my nervous system? I supposed so.

Next, I began to think more about vision. Would they work like that? Vision records information carried in light from the world around us through the pupils of our eyes. Inside on the retina, sensory receptors encode the light waves and convey the information along the optic nerves to multiple subdivisions of our brains. The visual system reports colors from the environment as one type of data; movement of objects, like cars, for another; and perspective, as in paintings, as yet another. Put them together as one function, and we have eyesight, or vision, with its range of visual effects—which we experience, or technically "perceive," in our heads as pictorial images.

I raced back to the Instruction in my head. What had happened when I was informed to "pick it up"? I was aware of receiving information. Different as it was from "seeing" a color, I understood that the psi effects might work on the same principle. I had perceived those words; certainly a system inside of me was responsible for that learning experience. I would draw my conclusions over the next few years, during which I had ample opportunity to observe that system at work.

It took longer to identify six other types of psi effects. By 1983, I had isolated a total of seven. Although many fine details have since fallen into place, adding one chapter of discovery after the next, when I think about the whole story, I always remember best that moment in Vancouver, when I made the leap that forced me through the most difficult challenge of all—coupling one three-word phrase with a real-life learning system that favorably influences the way we live our lives.

## Search for the Structure

The discovery just described happened after I'd delivered the briefcase. As the jubilant man turned back to the crowd, my husband punctuated his astonishment with a low whistle and soft-spoken "Impossible." Of course he meant that my little bloodhound act contradicted a few basic principles of cause and effect that we rationalists hold to be solidly true. By those sound laws, I had indeed just done the impossible. That whistle was the reason I began wondering: *Was* that an undoable feat?

While we walked, I began reflecting on the experience of the instruction, "Pick it up." It took no time to draw a parallel situation. What if the driver himself had given me that same instruction in a verbal command as I left the bus? Imagine his saying, "Ma'am, please pick up that case as you go by." I certainly would have understood immediately that this was a directive from someone who knew precisely what I should do with an object unfamiliar to me. What's more, I would have complied without hesitation.

My experience was only slightly different in that the information I perceived, also a clear directive, came from a remote source that somehow "knew" more than I did about the attaché case. True, it wasn't the bus driver, but having found the owner, we now had evidence that someone, who actually did know more than I, had needed me to take it.

And that was it, the leap to the next rung on the learning ladder: Clearly the words were a definite communication for me. The message had originated with another person, the Romanian mathematician. He was in contract with me. All that excitement of discovery followed from the simple realization of the effect's being a form of communication and ended with the idea of the Instruction's belonging to a small group of specific functions that most likely were generated from a sensory system.

The idea certainly seemed far-fetched, and I might have talked myself out of it had I not remembered a fairly recent similar situation when a completely different Instruction had succeeded in leading me to solve another urgent problem.

(ψ-10) It occurred one stormy morning. I was driving at the speed of traffic in the slow lane on a busy three-lane highway. A sharp impression caught my attention. It seemed urgent:

*Move to the left lane.*

Although I could see no danger around me, I began moving cautiously, across the second and into the outside lane. Glancing back where I'd been, I noticed the shiny new pickup truck that had just been ahead of me. What a shock it was to see it suddenly skid out of control, veer into the center lane, and slam into the side of a small car. Tragically, that wasn't the end of the horror. In the rearview mirror I watched it ricochet back into the right lane, spin around like a top, and pile up with two automobiles following it. It was chilling to read in the paper the next day about the passengers' injuries; I realized that if I had stayed in the slow lane, one of those cars would have been mine!

As it had been with the briefcase, the "move" information had come from somewhere in my head and made the same kind of impression on me as any person's verbal instruction might. I would have responded as obediently to: "Close the door when you leave," or "Hurry up, we're late." Typically, I hadn't reflected critically about whether or not it was possible to receive that directive to "move to the left lane." I was aware only that it had probably saved my life, and that I would have been in real trouble without it. That incident wasn't the first in which I had learned about personal danger early enough to change my plan, and thus to reshape the future. Rather than be injured, I had the opportunity to drive myself out of harm's way. Even in my innocence I had no doubt that this wouldn't be the last time I'd be forewarned.

That memory cinched it. I wanted to understand these matters better. Soon after our return from the Vancouver conference, I decided I'd practice paying attention to psi effects. With this decision, Phase One was under way with "psychic readings," as they were called. That was September. The next leap in learning came when opportunity knocked in mid-December. It was a startling eye-opener. On one particular evening, I found the evidence I needed to begin comprehending the reasons psi effects occur in our human world.

($\psi$-11) It opened with Jerry's telephone call at four o'clock in the afternoon. He was the leader of a southwest mountain search-and-rescue team. We had never met. He described how for several hours they had been looking for a small plane that should have landed at its destination before noon. There had been no radio contact since the pilot had taken off from Palm Springs, California. It was nearly dark. The storm, which had raged all day, was predicted to continue through the night.

The recorded plan indicated a short flight, traveling north-northwest over mountains from Palm Springs to Fresno. Everyone agreed that the storm must have forced the pilot to reroute. Although they had ideas of what he might have done, they wanted as much information as possible before searching further. Would I help?

I immediately was certain intuitively that the pilot was dead. I told Jerry this much information and promised to call with any further details. Within half an hour, I had a distinct impression. It was an obvious psi effect:

*Seized.*

It was only one word, and it meant nothing to me.

This particular search was the first I'd ever made for an organization. There still was so much that I had to learn about reporting the psi effects' information intelligibly. That was a red-letter day, largely because I made a cardinal error, one that so many other people have made: I tried to make sense of the word and decided the detail was unusable—because I myself didn't understand the meaning of the word. Instead of ringing Jerry, I tried to figure out: "What does the word *seized* have to do with an airplane in flight?" With this change in thought, my intuitive learning stopped. You will discover that it always does.

That day I learned, once and for all, that it is wrong to analyze information produced by a psi effect. It has its own true meanings. We must not ever interpret the data the way we might look for psychological significance in a mood or dream, for example. *Most* of these psi effects are literal. They always are factual. The information is transmitted from the event—called a phenomenon—in the environment and becomes a psi effect, the same way the traffic light on the corner becomes a visual effect. Both effects present authentic representations in our perception of the objects influencing them.

In this case I was fortunate. After an hour Jerry called to check on my progress. When he asked for news, I responded unreservedly, "No, nothing yet. I perceived only one word. It doesn't mean anything."

"What?"

"Seized."

His silence was deafening. Then he erupted.

"What are you saying? 'It doesn't mean anything'?" He was shouting into the phone. "Gail, an engine seizes up!" He became almost frantic. "Tell me everything else you know. Is there *any* more information than that?"

I began reporting words as I learned them:

*sunshine . . . south by west . . . seized*
*. . . spin . . . silence*

He sounded excited as he assured me these were precisely the details they needed. He also warned me pointedly never, never to doubt what I learned this way simply because I didn't understand the information.

He was emphatic: "Gail, *I* am the one who asked the question. So, it follows that *I* am the one who will understand. You are not the person out here in the snow and sleet looking for a plane." He continued, more gently, "You're our primary information resource. Your job is to show us our options. We'll decide whether they're useful, and follow up."

Using those seven words that I provided, the team correctly calculated the real sequence of events. The pilot had engine trouble shortly after takeoff to the northeast. He was returning to the airport when his engine seized up. His heading on the return would have been south by west.

Jerry's admonition proved to be correct. The information in my head had been accurate again; however, only he could follow through. It informed the searchers about a sequence of events that would lead them to another range of mountains they simply hadn't considered. Within three hours, they found the crash site. The impact had killed the pilot. In truth, he had not even flown near the storm in the north.

While they searched, I went back to thinking about the potential hazards to using intuition intelligently. Clearly, I had a lot more to learn.

## Reality and the Paranormal

That incident opened my eyes. Jerry's one comment about the psi effects' providing options for action made utter and complete sense of the whole phenomenon of learning this mysterious way. When we're stuck, like a truck in the mud, we can't move in any direction. In that moment, we need fresh alternatives. I now suspected that every time such a need arises, these effects would reveal authentic options for constructive, successful moves. It would do this 100 percent of the time, for each and every one of us. Therefore, we should consider them normal candidates for new, accurate information—when we need it. This proved to be true.

## Parapsychology

Now I was excited because I understood finally. These psi effects offered options for action—excellent options. Here was a new key that I needed to test. It was time to analyze what other people had learned. Obviously I wanted more material, some background facts. They were easy to find in parapsychology. Describing my next step requires a brief history of this fascinating science.

In 1932, at Duke University, a pair of young psychologists, Dr. Louisa Rhine and her husband, Dr. Joseph Rhine, established a laboratory to investigate paranormal phenomena, which they named "psi effects." Little did they know at the time that their experiments would spawn a far-reaching scientific revolution over what everyone agreed were indeed paranormal experiences, or experiences that went beyond what we understand as natural. Some people settled on calling them "anomalous," meaning they only deviate from what is expected. In plain English, the effects had everyone boggled. These experiences were an unexplored human behavior, and a corner of the field of psychology that serious scientists rarely visited. It would become "parapsychology." The Rhines persevered for years, directing rigorous research on the dubious behavior known as telepathy, precognition, and clairvoyance.

Perhaps it is not surprising that, although these are commonplace human experiences that have been observed and questioned throughout humankind's recorded history, from the day the Rhines began their work, hundreds of thousands of people have loudly proclaimed that parapsychologists should be doubted, even feared, and have commonly treated the psi effects more like dread diseases than possible human assets. In balance to the critics, probably just as many have sought answers to the seemingly impossible human experiences in spiritual teachings and study of the supernatural. I can't resist adding here that, though sometimes damaging, censure and dogmatism have neither destroyed the science nor stopped the phenomena.

Midst the distracting fray surrounding their work, the Rhines quietly hypothesized that the psi effects were evidence of some kind of sensory behavior; they categorized it as an extra sense. In fact, they coined the term "extra-sensory perception" to identify the effects they so wanted to explain. To their credit, the Rhines' meticulous research, which spanned three decades, contributed significantly to parapsychology's accreditation in 1968 by the American Association for the Advancement of Science.

Unfortunately, very little has been gained since that giant step into the scientific big leagues. Despite a profusion of interest and ceaseless attempts to prove their hypothesis of an extra sense, which would point to a concrete purpose for psi effects, the element of purpose most crucial to advancing parapsychology was still missing—and remains so at this writing. Without this basic knowledge, the now thirty-year-old field of science lacks clear direction. The disappointing result is that, at the moment, psi effects and parapsychology float in isolation, a science in search of its raison d'être.

Studying the Rhines' and others' impressive parade of rigorous experiments only highlighted the importance of explaining effects. I decided to join the endeavor. So far, I had positively identified five effects, including the three researched by the Rhines. Knowing by now that they occur in a consistent, orderly pattern, I set my sights on learning about their source—both the environmental and evolutionary reasons for their presence. I would focus on intuition, which I suspected would prove to be a vital sensory system functioning within our bodies.

I felt as if I was on solid ground already. It seemed to me that, if we are intuitively sensitive, that sensitivity would set up a natural purpose for the effects—as the means for detecting phenomena when they influence us. So it was that I opened the next chapter of my saga with my very small package of new information; it held two pieces of evidence: (1) psi effects have the capacity to influence our behavior, thinking, and/or feeling, and (2) they reveal options for action when we need alternatives that lead to success. It was 1977.

By 1983, I had found seven effects. Following is a brief description of how each one functions and the type of data it delivers. I have taken the liberty of including the nickname that I attach to each one, to depict its unique characteristic. The seven established psi effects, as I have categorized them, are Reflex, Instruction, Telepathy, Teleos, Clarification, Dream, and Déjà vu. (Precognition is classified under Teleos, and clairvoyance under Clarification.)

Chapters 7 and 9 delve more specifically into these phenomena, with real-life examples of each effect in action.

## The Psi Effects

### Category I: The Reflex Effect

This is a new category, although we've known about the effect for years. It is unique as the only effect that offers us no options for the moves it generates. It acts on us, causing us to do things involuntarily—frequently without our knowing it. This unintentional-movement feature led me to cheerfully dub this psi effect the "Bulldozer."

Reflex occurs when an interaction *needs* to take place somewhere and there is no time to lose. In essence, it must not fail. It behaves like a textbook physical reflex, appearing as your classic mechanistic response to a stimulus. For a familiar parallel, think of any reflex, as when your hand recoils from a hot object or when you spontaneously right yourself when you stumble. So it is with the Reflex psi effect: it produces a restorative movement to promptly correct an imbalance. Very often, however—in fact, most of the time—the correction it causes slips in with the activity of the moment and goes unnoticed. When discussing the Reflex effect, most agree that it produces no *apparent* change of behavior or moves, but instead results in some unobservable movements that manifest themselves much later.

When people speak of coincidence as an intuitive function, I suggest that they are referring to Reflex. In addition to coincidences, I am convinced that this effect is at the core of wellness, illness, and spontaneous healing, and of central importance to the studies we now describe in more general terms as "mind and body healing." This being true, I suggest that we can learn to use each category of these psi effects practically to heal ourselves from physical and mental ills and to sustain our state of health at optimal levels. I propose too that the Reflex psi effect is also at the heart of miracles.

## Category II: The Instruction Effect

Instruction is also a new category of psi effect. It tightly controls how you move, but, unlike pushy Reflex, this effect leaves the choice of whether to act to the intuitor. As stated earlier, it gives only peremptory orders, nothing more. "Pick it up." "Move to the left lane." Hence its formal name, Instruction. It issues specific information about two kinds of moves: direction and timing. The details always relate to our *very next* physical or mental move.

I've found that this effect demands absolute power, so much so that, as a lifelong sailor under command of many captains, I sentimentally nicknamed it the "Captain": On board ship there is only one captain, and that person has supreme authority over the vessel's every movement. Throughout a voyage, he or she is kept informed of variables that might affect progress to the next destination—currents, weather, the trim of the sails, health of the crew—and orders the sailors to do the work that assures that the ship will arrive at its port intact and on schedule. So it is with this Instruction effect. It's the captain; you're crew. It alerts you to make particular moves, to guarantee that specific interactions will or will not take place. Despite the fact that it is an order, with this effect you always have the option to follow through or not. Remember "Pick it up" ($\psi$-7).

## Category III: The Telepathy Effect

Telepathy has been recognized for centuries, and feared by many to be an intruder on our privacy. Rumor incorrectly has it that some people can read our every feeling and thought. The truth is that the Telepathy effect reports only our states of mentality, which are naturally limited to only some matters of the heart and intellectual activity.

I have nicknamed this effect the "Barometer" because it is so like the ancient weather instrument that determines the pressure of the earth's atmosphere to give us precise knowledge about present outdoor conditions. Telepathy, likewise, reports the external atmosphere, exposing here-and-now mental climates only, and no other—not yesterday and never tomorrow. We learn about others' passions of joy, sorrow, and grief, of distress brewing, of the mental calms following storms, of all current moods, of heavy concentration, and much more.

If we use it to guide our behavior, Telepathy's information enables us humans to interact wholesomely. I am convinced that all the people who intuited the Oklahoma bombing were telepathic to the predatory perpetrators' mental states of explosive rage and intense concentration on their plans. Had they known Telepathy's ways, these intuitive individuals could have taken immediate defensive action. As you saw evidenced in the two opening accounts, we always have to decide whether to take action on what we learn telepathically.

## Category IV: The Teleos Effect

Teleos (pronounced: "tea-lee-ose") is another completely new category and name. However, inside the classification you will find a familiar group of well-known effects, which report data from the past through "retrocognition," literally meaning *past knowledge*, the present, through "direct cognition," and the future, through "precognition."

Nature's efficiency shines here in limiting and specializing the functions she has created with this intuitive sensory system. You will learn while the Telepathy effect reports all current circulating cerebral activity, Teleos has evolved to cover every other unpredictable and unknown phenomenon, every other physical and mental event in space and time. This might sound preposterous, but it is as it is. Although its field of phenomena is unimaginably large and complex, I have discovered that Teleos can manage it magnificently. For instance, it

▲ produces pertinent information about the history of people we hire to work for us in our homes, offices, and nations;

▲ overrides deceptive advertising and reports any facts about the genuine quality of child-care centers, food in a restaurant, and the air we breathe;

▲ monitors developing environmental conditions, reporting when they are unstable;

▲ locates mundane missing objects and carefully concealed deadly ones (in the possession of one person *as well as* those stockpiled weapons of mass destruction in the hands of nations or terrorists); and

▲ predicts future outcomes of every process, from a short trip across town, to long-term projects on the drawing board, to physical well-being.

I've nicknamed this Teleos effect the "Periscope" because it introduces information that otherwise would not be available, much the same way a periscope stretches above the water and allows an observer to see what would be impossible to view without it.

## Category V: The Clarification Effect

"Clarification" is the second new collective name. I've assigned it to a group of historically well-known sources of intuitive knowledge: "clairvoyance," "clairaudience," and "clairsentience." Already mentioned earlier in relation to the Drs. Rhine, these are effects that have been recognized for more than five thousand years. To my surprise, close observations reveal that this group has a very different role from the one we've traditionally assigned it.

Conventional wisdom says that these sources of knowledge are stimulated by events in the environment, but this appears to be incorrect. I maintain that they are indirect forms of intuition, representing information produced first by Telepathy and Teleos. Like Instruction and Dream, Clarification is a secondary psi effect, a backup that swings into action whenever the intuitor misses earlier warning signals from those two primaries. It reports the same information, but in different guises. My pet name for this effect is the "Mimic," because this is exactly what it does.

## Category VI: The Dream Effect

The Dream effect is well known for foretelling the future, but it does much more. It has two distinct roles. First, it has the primary responsibility for covering all of the seconds, minutes, and hours during which we are not fully alert. This means we're intuitively sensitive even when we take a rest, during both night and day. Since it reports in night dreams and daydreams, we are assured constant intuitive surveillance, with round-the-clock access to intuitible breaking news. Second, like Instruction and Clarification, it plays a secondary role: It repeats during sleep time what we might have missed from the two primary effects when we were awake. For obvious reasons, its name of endearment is the "Lookout."

## Category VII: The Déjà vu Effect

People conventionally use the term *déjà vu* to refer to the feelings of having been in a particular situation before. I disagree with that usage and maintain that people are incorrectly describing ordinary memory to explain a mental experience that is not in any way related to our "past." A Déjà vu seems to be a display for display's sake of the microworld of nature that our intuition plumbs. I think Déjà vu is meant to be our first step on the way to the well-known "peak experience"—also called the oceanic, or religious, experience.

You will learn in following chapters that I think intuition gives us access to the biological and physical subsurface dimensions of life, which we might generally refer to as the microworld or as the evolving processes of life. Physicists probe its subatomic and supergalactic dimensions; biologists explore the cellular structures. We all tap into it personally with our intuitive sensitivity. Déjà vu's purpose seems to be to introduce this deeper natural world to us. A relatively rare experience, it roots us through a sense of being acutely aware of an element of the environment— a conversation, a room, or a person's face, for example. It fades as quickly as it came, leaving nothing to be analyzed, but we have certain knowledge that the Déjà vu occurred.

Its pet name is the "Museum." I chose this because the effect appears to be an introduction to the full complexity of intuition's information—an exhibition, if you will. In a single Déjà vu, we are able to gaze on the dynamic microworld as we might a work of art or a life-size model of the *Apollo* landing module. We do this in all museums, discovering the world as observers, encountering things from a different perspective. In exhibits we see in their canvasses what Monet and Picasso saw; in the lens of a scope we see the living cells a biologist sees; through a telescope we see the stars beyond our galaxy, which is the world of astronomers; and in a Déjà vu, one peers at the tiniest details of life. This is an exhibit of the territory that we help control once we harness our intuition. Our only responsibility in the Déjà vu experience is to perceive these systems and functions in the natural order that influence our intuitive sensitivity. It is our "How do you do."

## The Seven

Give a human an opportunity, and what happens? He or she nearly always takes it and runs. Why? We all want to live well— to make decisions that will lead to success, to solve problems completely, leaving no loose ends, to stretch abilities and develop expertise, and to plan a future that brings optimal opportunity. I shall say again and again, intuition is one more major ability in each of us that will help bring home all of these ideals. It is the best capability you have for taking greater control over your life. Simply use these seven to guide you, as outlined in the following chapters, and watch how they lead you to success:

▲ The Bulldozer pushes you when you're at the edge and at immediate risk of either becoming hurt or missing an opportunity.

▲ The Captain commands what your next move must be so that you will arrive, on time and unharmed, in port.

▲ The Barometer records any mental "weather" that is affecting your successful passage.

▲ The Periscope informs you with all the information you could possibly need to guide you along your way.

▲ In case you missed them, or doubt what you learned, the Mimic duplicates your familiar sensory systems to catch your attention, and then repeats any reports from the primary effects.

▲ The Lookout keeps watch when you rest and repeats reports, lest you miss or doubt them.

▲ In the Museum, you contemplate nature's fine arts.

Here you have them, a concrete spectrum for the psi effects, considered by nearly everyone to be mystifying. They empower us to make moves that ensure that life will not only continue to roll on, but also continue to be excellent enough in order for you, your loved ones, your neighbors, and, ultimately, all that exists, to reach full potential.

## A New Definition

A psi effect—synonym for a paranormal phenomenon—is an element of the sense of intuition. It reveals the factual information about interactions occurring in the environment that need a human helping hand if they are to come to an ideal conclusion. It will be noticeable either in a person's involuntary physical movements or in mental experiences. When an intuitor follows through precisely on a psi effect, the resulting move or moves will favorably influence the physical or mental behavior, or both, of either the person who experienced the effect, other people, or events involved in the interaction. Or it might influence all of them together. Through these psi effects we will meet and influence a staggering range of incidents.

# CHAPTER 3

# Nature Is an Optimalist

AT THE BEGINNING of sailing season, a group of us decided to have an informal dinner and get acquainted. Plates in hand, my husband and I wandered among the tables until we found two empty chairs. We smiled polite greetings to the people already seated and slipped into our places. Conversation soon flowed easily, between tasty bites of the usual potluck fare.

The introductions proceeded mechanically. "What do you do?" "And you?" The brief interchanges continued until a ruddy-looking gentleman mentioned a profession that captured the interest of a plump, sunburned woman. "Oh, you design houses? How fascinating! We built our home about ten years ago. . . ." With this, the group relaxed because now everyone was headed comfortably in the same direction, a flock of instinct-driven birds flying in formation. Once that subject was spent, the questions started around again, this time stopping with me. I said I was doing research in my field. "What field?" "Well, I'm analyzing human intuition."

Across the table a man named Clint perked up. "Oh, you're an intuition lady, are you? Tell me, what is it?"

I didn't reply to the question, but instead, ever the teacher, returned it to him. "What do you think it is?"

"Well, I'm certainly no authority, but it seems to me it's that feeling you have about something you should do or not do. My experience is that when that special feeling happens, telling me what to do, then that's what I should do. I've tried not paying attention and even just plain disagreeing with it—doing it my way—but I can tell you, that's not smart."

He hesitated. Everyone was attentive. He rolled on.

"I've heard a lot of people say they think intuition is something destined at birth, a way that only certain people can 'know the unknown.'" He made his voice quiver, depicting something spooky and on the fringe. "But, I definitely disagree because it's in my life, and I didn't do anything in particular to deserve it. It's just there. I'll tell you what makes it special. I think it's astounding: When the feeling pops in—no matter whether it's about business or family matters—I know it's going to head me in the right direction, and I might just as well follow its lead from the start!"

He came up for air, took a quick breath, and dived in again.

"It's kind of curious. Sometimes, when you have a bad time, you search for explanations; I suppose that's normal, because we're rational creatures. But when you have a bad time and you knew beforehand not to do it, you get so you don't go looking around later for the reason, you just know there was one. I think those are the times when I'm running on intuition—the times when I know what to do, or *not* do, beforehand."

Another pause. During this one he only shook his head as though unbelieving, in the way of someone inspired by an awesome truism. Then he stated, "It's always right. That's the amazing thing—it's *always* right!"

With this, he made his closing pronouncement: "When it comes to explaining this intuition thing, I think I'd say there are some facts you just know, that's all, and you know them because of it."

He took his first long breath. Everyone was nodding, obviously recognizing personal experiences in his example.

My investigator's mind was now geared up and running. I couldn't resist the temptation to ask him another question. "Have you ever heard of a psi effect?"

"A what?"

"A psi effect."

"Oh no, not me! I'd never touch one." He leaned back from the table, covering his face with his hands in mock self-defense. And then looking puzzled: "Is it one of those fancy words you scientists make up, so's you can talk privately with each other?"

"Well, yes and no. It is a technical term, but it's a reference to exactly the kind of experiences of 'knowing' that you've just described."

"People have a name for 'em? What do you say they are?"

"That they're connected with intuition. In general, they're the reporters of intuitive information. You use them to learn what moves you should make."

He looked thoughtful. "Are you telling me those feelings are something real, with a fancy name?" Bowing his head in feigned reverence he conceded, "I'll have to respect them more from now on." At that point, someone arrived with a delectable dessert. Our conversation came to an abrupt halt.

About six weeks later, I was walking along the docks to our boat when I heard, "Hey! Intuition lady!"

I looked around. It was Clint, on the run.

He called, "I think I've had a few more of those 'special effects' you were talking about." Before he caught up with me, he had launched into another account. He described how, soon after our conversation, he'd had a strong "gut feeling" about a major purchasing decision for his business. He'd figured that, since the intuition lady agreed that such sensations were always right, he would follow it. By now the proof was in—it was a splendid move.

He stopped walking and looked pensive. He wanted to know: Was that "feeling" one of those fancy effects? I confirmed. Shaking his head incredulously, he said that, since our conversation, he'd begun to realize he'd had hundreds such feelings in the past. By now he was enormously frustrated. For years he'd been fighting them, accusing himself of wishful thinking, and insisting on hard evidence before he made his moves. Now he spoke in a tone of genuine sadness. He'd begun wondering just exactly how many opportunities he'd missed during his lifetime simply because he didn't know that the "feelings" were something he could rely on. He looked at me, obviously hoping I'd reduce his confusion.

That was easy. First, I assured him he traveled in very good company. Untold numbers of people reject the psi effects daily, without understanding how much they're losing. Then, in answer to his question, I was completely candid. It was a pleasure to watch him begin to understand as I described how every time we deny a psi effect, we miss an opening to make a move that would bring some kind of benefit to us or someone else. I told him the story of my mistake with Jerry and the missing plane ($\psi$-11), and why I think any psi effect is a call from within nature's order for assistance.

I closed by saying: "Intuition is really only a terrific regulator, literally a biological mechanism within each one of us, helping us adjust to countless changes, maintain stability in our lives, and identify those situations and issues that are truly important to our well-being." I explained how it communicates with us through these psi effects, that when an effect reports to any of us individually, it's saying that something has changed, and *we* have the option to do something constructive about it. It's giving *us* the information because we are the ones who can turn the particular situation correctly, away from risk of failure and toward success.

By the time we'd reached the end of the dock, Clint understood. "Aha! I get it." He was almost laughing. "You're telling me that it puts us in the control seat for life, on the road to precise decisions and top performance. When we have intuitive experiences, we are getting a chance to shape our own futures ideally."

I nodded and added the last point. Yes, his idea was absolutely correct. Intuition *is* always right.

He groaned. I've heard that same low wail of frustration from people everywhere in the world.

## Intuition, the Great Stabilizer

One incident from years ago stands out as an illustration of that answer—and on this particular day, my stomach and I were both grateful for intuition's direction.

($\psi$ 12) Since I was mother to three, homemaker, and the only breadwinner in the family, time was more precious than ever. Illness of any kind was flat-out unacceptable. On this day, during a series of meetings at work, three colleagues and I decided to stop for lunch at a specialty restaurant near our offices. While we sat chatting and scanning the tantalizing menu, I noticed a psi effect—Teleos—informing me pointedly with a "sense" that the food was tainted.

I considered what to do and decided I simply would not eat anything. With the decision made, I asked myself for the quintillionth time, "Why did I learn this?" I looked around; visible signs belied my intuited fact. The restaurant was well established, and although it was new to me, these women had been there previously. Though a casual spot, it certainly looked sanitary, yet I knew I shouldn't order a meal. The downside of the situation was that our afternoon work was going to be demanding. I couldn't afford to run out of steam by not eating. And, quite naturally, I also wasn't eager to affront my well-meaning colleagues by not dining in their restaurant of choice.

It was indeed a frustrating dilemma. Here we were, sitting in a charming room, flooded with appetizing aromas, yet my intuitiveness had raised a warning, the equivalent of a quarantine flag, to alert me to some hidden risk. I would be senseless not to respect it.

But in fact I *wasn't* senseless. In this case, I learned later that I was beneficiary of a signal from the only human sensory system that could provide any useful information in that situation. Intuition was the border patrol for me that day, and I knew it. It identified hidden danger and warned me in plenty of time for me to prevent myself from falling into a trap. Of course I had to comply, for the same reasons that when my eyes reveal an oncoming car, I don't step out in front of it. The rule is the same from all the senses: We must honor their effects and do our part with their information to protect ourselves.

On that account, I decided to tell my colleagues about my insight into the contamination. While they were extremely polite about it, they made their views clear: This place had an excellent reputation. I had to be wrong. My effort done, when the waitress came, they ordered their entrees and I requested a cup of tea (which, according to intuition, was within the safety limits).

The general facts behind what I had intuited were disclosed early the next day when the husband of one woman of the group called to inquire after my health. Obviously surprised to hear that I was fine, he exclaimed that I was a very lucky lady and went on to say that his wife and the other two women who'd been with us were miserably ill—with food poisoning.

That strong "sense" of contamination definitely saved me at least one day of severe illness, so my life and full schedule weren't interrupted. But my peace of mind was disrupted because the question lingered: Why did I learn about that food? This chapter offers a solution to that question.

The simple answer is that it is possible to intuit spoiled food anywhere, well before our other senses can help—such as by smelling rancid odors or seeing mold. We can assume this type of learning is possible from the evidence of that incident. Our combined senses of smell and sight, and theirs of taste, failed utterly as safety nets, for none of us detected that contamination which my intuition caught effortlessly before I ordered. The situation would seem unbelievable if I didn't know intuition so well. We *all* had oohed and aahed appreciatively over the attractive presentation of the food and the tantalizing spicy aromas. And, while I sipped my tea, they innocently ate their meals with gusto without one clue that they were sitting ducks!

## State-of-the-Art Living

The precise, and more complex, answer to the question of why I learned intuitively that day is based in biology. Consequently, it is completely rational—but also somewhat elaborate. Nevertheless, despite the complexity, it is a crucial element to our understanding the importance and ways of intuition. And there can be no question that if you understand the purpose of intuition in nature's orderly plan, then you can truly respect and even enjoy the oftentimes inexplicable, other times wise, and still other times whimsical routes along which your intuition will lead you. What's more, whether you know it or not, you're too often at risk without it, as were my friends at that restaurant. And so, because all of us have been faced with difficult decisions, and will be again, we can benefit from learning the fundamental physical reason why this intuitive ability exerts so much influence over our lives, and should be allowed to have more.

The story of our need is not novel, but it is one that every one of us has to learn if we want to survive and flourish.

## Nature's Reason for Intuition

Biologically speaking, our bodies, known technically as *organisms*, are living systems. Ideally, from the instant life is generated, any organic structure should be able to grow and develop to the full measure of its natural potential as long as the component cellular systems are sound. Thus, as organisms, we humans fall within this rosy picture: We too are fully equipped internally to physically survive life in the universe. Why is this possible? Intricate control mechanisms work ceaselessly from the instant of conception to keep us on a successful course of action.

Most of these mechanisms hum in the background of life as we know it, keeping order in an atomic and cellular microworld where our unaided senses cannot penetrate. Were we to lose these controls, the orderliness would be shattered in one system after another. Preventing this is a ubiquitous mechanical process called the regulatory mechanism. It is the archetype of an infinite number of control mechanisms steering life and one of the great contributors to the way things function in the universe, including the successful evolution of our species. This regulatory mechanism appears everywhere in our individual systems, playing a significant role in helping each human being flourish mentally and physically. I propose that intuition is such a regulatory mechanism that this is its sole purpose for existence. Observation has convinced me that, in its way, our intuition continuously guides us to take actions that assure we will survive and thrive.

### Weak and Strong

When we or any other organisms fall ill, the interrelated processes that maintain the stability in our bodies begin to unravel, thus opening the way for a number of system failures. Amazingly, the laws of nature will continue to regulate the systems as long as possible; they will work assiduously to stabilize the parts and the whole. It doesn't matter whether the system is one cell only—which is considered to be a complete living organism—or an intricately structured group of cellular systems, such as are mammals (including human beings of course).

It's no surprise that an organism that is unable to meet its own biologic needs rapidly becomes handicapped. Think of the last time you had the flu: Did you work or play at anywhere near your peak performance? On the other hand, when any organism is more or less stable internally, it is free to move around in the environment and to satisfy its basic needs well enough to assure it an ideal existence. Using our species as an example, you know yourself that people who manage to stay in the pink of mental and physical health are able to take on challenges enthusiastically and can work at peak performance.

The principle here is a natural law: Life proceeds successfully for those organisms that have precise control over their internal environment. As the noted French physiologist Dr. Claude Bernard taught us more than a century ago, as long as the cells' milieu is held in proper concentrations, life will go swimmingly.

For most of us, perhaps the most daunting matter here is the total amount of interactions involved when we are speaking about an entire human body. How can we possibly meet the demands of every one of our quintillion, microscopic cells?

So many variables come into play in the physical universe. We have to be constantly aware of our delicate systems and neither throw them into excessive conditions, such as by overexposing our skin to the sun, nor deprive them of their vital needs for nutrients, fluids, and warmth. It is definitely a balancing act. Yet, we are so exquisitely designed and managed that most of us don't spend even a minute thinking about the health and well-being of these tiny crucial building blocks of our body tissue and systems.

But, don't be lulled into false confidence. Two major obstacles stand between us and that stability. First, when we use up supplies in our bodies, we run out of steam, so to speak. That endangers—even damages—our internal systems' balances and performance. The second looms as a result of this first restriction. In order to replenish those variable life-support substances and materials, we have to venture out into the environment and forage.

Alas, this external world where supplies await is big and strong—much bigger and stronger, in fact, than our physical structures. What's more, it is filled with predators. Obviously this disparity in sizes and forces makes us very vulnerable creatures while we seek the precious life-support materials. From this, we live a paradox: We face trouble by not keeping our bodies balanced and double trouble when we set out in the world to replenish them. With these adversities menacing our freedom to move, how have we managed to survive? The explanation: Granted, on one hand we are hopelessly vulnerable, but on the other hand, with regulatory mechanisms controlling the multitude of interactions, we are always provided for.

## The Regulatory Mechanism, a Miracle Maker

A poster I once saw goes to the heart of the matter. It featured the waiflike face of a child about eight years of age who was seated cross-legged with coloring book in hand and gazing sweetly at every passerby from its two-dimensional world. The caption read: "I know I am a wonderful creation. God doesn't make junk." This of course is true. The forces and elements of nature create one extraordinary life form after another.

We often take for granted that daily miracle of the world around us, abundant with life in everything from the songs of birds in the garden, to the colorful flowers that grow there, and on to the humans who move to and fro along the paths. We tend to assume that this exuberance in nature in all of its billions of forms will always take care of itself, for it seems so self-sufficient. In fact, the regulatory mechanism is at the center of it all. It appears at each juncture of interaction, at every moment in the processes of life, and at all stages of mental activity. We likely have millions of such controls within our bodies, helping us perpetually.

This is a deceptively simple process that operates for one reason. A regulatory mechanism becomes necessary whenever a system contains a substance, such as water, or a characteristic, such as temperature, that must be held constant. The regulating procedure goes into operation the instant any variance occurs within a system and throws it off enough to disturb its functioning optimally. For instance, if a person chokes, air is cut off. As we are utterly dependent on this substance for survival, the body's systems have reliable reflex functions in place that begin correcting the imbalance immediately. The most visible one is our gasping for breath in an attempt to gulp in air that will restore the proper amount for the body's health. The individual suffering from asphyxiation gets natural relief because of a regulatory mechanism.

This mechanism normally operates for one of two reasons: The system uses a material that must not fluctuate, or a necessary ingredient isn't always available in the environment. Examples are everywhere. For instance, human bodies need constant amounts of internal heat, but in winter the sun is at its farthest position from the equator and casts a chilly scene; this is not acceptable for the human body, which must have a more or less constant temperature of 98.6° F. When it fluctuates, either dropping down some degrees or rising above the preprogrammed point, we are at risk. We also need predetermined amounts of water and food to function at our best, yet our tissues consume both of these constantly in energy production. These are such critical commodities that death comes to any creature deprived too long of either water or nutrients.

The regulatory mechanism attempts to overcome these hazards. Its assignment is as simple as it sounds. In a machinelike fashion it governs the stability of systems by overseeing all exchanges of life-support materials and elemental operations. It is prepared to make corrections when they fall off and become endangered. This lifesaving mechanism consists of four essentials:

1. a substance, such as water, or an atmospheric condition, such as heat, that needs to be regulated—usually referred to as the *system variable*

2. the *set point*, or preset amount around which that supply system is regulated and functions optimally—like the 98.6° F human body temperature

3. a *detector* that is sensitive to deviations of the system variable whenever it rises above or drops below the set point—such as a thermostat on a heating system

4. a *correctional mechanism*, which is capable of restoring the system variable to the set point

We have imitated the regulatory process everywhere in our material world by inventing machines controlled by pumps to manage water, fuel, and air flow; internal combustion engines to power vehicles; autopilots to regulate the moves of planes and ships; thermostats to stabilize the heat in kitchen stoves—which cooks everywhere agree beats an uncontrolled, scorching, open-fire-pit blaze any day—refrigerators to hold a steady chill; medications to return our broken-down organs to correct balances. Why? Because this regulatory mechanism is so efficient. It corrects problems when they happen, at the sites where they occur.

An excellent example of a man-made regulatory system is a room whose temperature is controlled by a thermostatically regulated heater. The system variable is the air temperature in the room, and the detector of the changeable temperature is the thermostat.

This adjustable device can be set so that contacts of a switch will be closed when the temperature falls below the predetermined number (the set point). When that switch closes, the correctional mechanism begins by turning on the heating system to warm the room. The rise in room temperature causes the thermostat switch to open and turn off the heater, thereby stopping the correctional mechanism that it started. You'll find thermostats in the heaters and air conditioners that make your life comfortable.

Your foot is also a regulatory mechanism when you need it. On those occasions when you are driving, for example, the system variable is the speed of the vehicle; the speedometer becomes the detector; a set point would be the speed limit; correction is up to you. Your foot's pressure and release on the accelerator allow you to regulate the car speed. You pay attention to the speedometer for signs that indicate you are exceeding or falling under the speed limit. Look around you and identify other systems that work on this regulatory principle.

### Intuition as a Regulatory Mechanism

As I see it, intuition is following this same process. This, then, leads us to the explanation of why psi effects occur: They are our detectors. I consider intuition to be nothing more nor less than an ordinary regulatory mechanism within us, one of many thousands of assistive processes helping us manage our successes. I am proposing that as a mechanical action, intuition keeps us fine-tuned and safely interactive with every one of the universal systems and forces that circulate around and run through us. With it behind us, we can survive an unimaginably wide array of internal and external environmental threats and opportunities, even though we are such vulnerable creatures in a vast living universe. It helps us to find our direction and "turn out" perfectly, or simply put, to reach our full potential. To repeat: I say that this is the sole task of any person's intuition.

To confirm this conclusion, consider my proposition that the intuitive process is influenced by the elemental and cellular materials and basic forces of life. It would make logical sense, then, that by being intuitively regulated to interact with the microworld, we can have options for self-help that we never knew were possible.

Take the restaurant ($\psi$-12) as a case in point. Analyze what intuition accomplished there: It was my detector for that food contaminated by microorganisms. My being intuitively sensitive to the phenomenon that would throw my body off its set point more than likely prevented physical illness and untold amounts of mental consternation. Having the psi effect as detector that the food was tainted gave me that crucial opportunity to take preventive action. By introducing the detector Teleos effect, intuition, as a regulatory mechanism, was protecting my body—specifically the digestive tract. The effect's information was enough to stir me to a decision and ultimately to the frustrating but wise move to drink only tea.

This is an example of Clint's observation. I was in the control seat. Learning as I did from one of those "special effects," as he called them, I had all the information required to remain at set point. We know the strange ending of the tale: While those around me fell ill, I remained healthy and was able to proceed with life as usual.

As I see it, we have become intuitive because of our desperate need for the very specific kinds of information about the activities in a sector of the universe that will have the potential to injure our systems. We then have to ask how far into the natural order intuition can reach.

## The Regulatory Mechanism as a Universal Manager

Have you ever watched the growth process of a seed? Drop a carrot seed into the ground or a posy seed into a pot—a chrysanthemum, for example. Given adequate moisture, nutrients, and sun, a green sprout will peep through the soil in about ten days, and a vigorous carrot or posy is on its way into the environment. The carrot won't be a green bean. Neither will it be a chrysanthemum. It will be a carrot. Why? A carrot is what a carrot seed produces. To grow a bean, one must begin with a bean, likewise for a chrysanthemum. As long as the seed is allowed to follow its genetic code and to sustain the correct amounts of variable substances inside it, such as water and nutrients, the cells constructing the plant's systems can grow and divide ideally. Nature's processes assure that the seed is capable of reaching its full potential. This is standard natural procedure.

The same is true of human beings. As living organisms, we're preprogrammed biologically and are steadily guided by the laws of nature, which include the ancient regulatory processes. That internal work of cell growth, division, and differentiation all proceeds according to regulation laws. As it was in the beginning and has been up until the present, the basic human body structure is founded on the latest evolutionary model of your run-of-the-mill human being, with a head, limbs, a trunk, and so forth. The natural purity of genetic material has always ensured that biologic systems would have only human-based genetic information controlling new human beings' growth and development in both the womb and the world.

Note that the introduction of organ transplants and cloning means that this purely natural generating process will be changed forever, because no matter what kind words and noble purposes we use to prop it up, the fact is that by introducing genetic engineering, we're tampering with natural evolution. Thus, we have to qualify the discussion on the pureness of human life, saying that *up until the end of the twentieth century*, only the parents have ever added their special genetic touches to a new life.

## The Business of Living Well

We, like the carrot and chrysanthemum and untold numbers of organisms, have the ability to grow naturally from "seed" to become bodies with all systems and processes working so well that we are as able to be ideal creations as are the plants in the garden.

Knowing that this regulatory mechanism is a universal manager, it becomes apparent that optimal performance is the standard state-of-the-art living in the natural order and that the promise of ideal growth and development is true, *as long as* the mechanism can follow through on its task. The wonderful lesson of the process, then, is that nature is an optimalist. All the miracles of life follow from this fact.

## Self-Control: Nature's Invention

The controlled internal environment of an organism is only a portion of the picture. It's time to go out into the world around us. We all agree that it regularly destabilizes us. Remember the newspaper headlines in Chapter 1? Storms threaten our homes, which are our primary shelters from the elements. Germs lie in wait to invade our bodies; if they gain control, we're in serious cellular trouble. Clearly, we are not free to be ourselves, to move as and where we need, unless we have a steady flow of data about variables shifting the conditions in our lives. If we can become masters of the regulatory mechanisms controlling the information we learn, then we become masters of our own unfolding fate.

A poignant but astounding example of our vulnerability is seen in the odorless, deadly *E. coli* 0157, considered to be the "bad" strain. We need only ten to eleven cells of this strain to fall ill and possibly die. Ten to eleven! Think about that. Wouldn't it be remarkable if each of us could know before taking a bite whether *the villain* lurks in the food we are buying! This threat is so like my experience in the restaurant that I dare say that *E. coli* protection could always come from using intuition.

## Not "Tougher," More "Sensitive"

In the nineteenth century, physiologist Dr. Claude Bernard tapped into the importance of regulatory mechanisms when he described every organism's most elementary need as a "stable internal environment." He described how an organism that is able to hold its life-sustaining functions steady at set point would then be free to move about the world, even in hostile environments.* Bernard was stating this natural law: Not one of our interior systems' processes should fluctuate dangerously. We've seen that observation confirmed repeatedly in examples of hunger, thirst, and the like.

The *cell* is the precisely regulated unit structure of all plants and animals—a blob of protoplasm surrounded by a membrane with a nucleus inside it. Dozens of them would fit inside of this box: □. (Again, we need only ten to eleven *E. coli* cells to lethally infect our digestive system.) In our brain alone, we have 100 billion cells, called neurons.

It may be hard to believe that your life and every move you make is dedicated to cellular safety, that before anything else matters, all of your life processes—including the functional activities of your body, your sensory awareness, and your intelligence—are directed at supporting the stability of your cells. Perhaps it seems preposterous to suggest that without cell security afforded by the regulatory mechanism, humankind would not have created civilizations, sailed the seven seas, or stepped on the moon. Nevertheless, this is true. Humble though any single microscopic cell

---

*For a good account of Bernard's thinking, see N. Carlson's *Physiology of Behavior* (Boston: Allyn and Bacon, 1977).

might seem, the fact is that without our immense array of them, we simply wouldn't exist.

Note that in all the hundreds of millions of years of life on planet Earth, the evolutionary process has never produced "tougher" cells to cope with hostile environments; instead, it has increased the sensitivity of the organisms by evolving more sensors, thus allowing a creature to travel more extensively.

And human beings have followed suit. Whenever we decide to explore new territory, we, too, increase our sensors. For instance, we have discovered that it would not serve to put a deep-sea diver in a heavy suit of armor for the descent into the watery world. Tougher outer layers do not solve the problem created when a delicate human respiratory system enters the compressed atmosphere deep beneath the water's surface. Instead, we add sensors in the form of regulators on the tanks of compressed air; these will go further toward preserving life. Such sensors measure increasing and decreasing pressure on the lungs while the diver descends and ascends. Without this extra sensitivity to identify the conditions, a diver runs the risk of surfacing too quickly from the deep-sea environment and creating perilous pressure imbalances inside his or her lungs.

Inevitably, as the number of information messengers increases within an organism, more interconnections are organized to improve communications and assure safe passage in the environment. Nature's way has always been to increase the organism's sensitivity, thus more finely tuning the organism to its interactions with the environment.

The result of increased sensitivity is visible today. Living systems have changed fantastically since life formed on earth, but amazingly the ground rule remains constant: Regulate. Regulate. Regulate. Looking back along the seemingly endless evolutionary pathway, we can see that this miracle mechanism has performed its task so stupendously that life *was* able to grow and develop steadily. From those first days when the brainless, witless single-celled blobs of protoplasm hunkered down for a good long wait to begin moving, to the twenty-first century in which sophisticated intelligent mammals like us can voyage gleefully among the stars, regulated self-control has worked.

*Intuition is a regulatory mechanism.* More than a decade ago, I fixed this observation at the center of my thinking and identified it as the purpose behind my personal use of intuition. It brought together the loose ends of my observations. First, it explained the psi effects. They were the perceptible detectors of the background activity of my life, and that of all other human beings. This deduction exposed the fundamental sensory process and anointed intuition with the reliability it needed to be more than merely a paranormal happening. For this reason, I am suggesting that intuition is a purely sensory process, and a crucial one at that. Having conducted my search for understanding from back to front—observing the behavior in psi effects first—I can say that it was more than a little gratifying to identify their first cause. Knowing now that intuition is one more specialized regulatory mechanism to help us learn and adjust to living situations, I suggest that we have found the fundamental reason at last for its evolving into our species.

The list of phenomena to which we are intuitively sensitive seems to me to be endless. This ability will become blatantly obvious as more people identify it in themselves. Nevertheless, the function never varies. When a system is off set point, or is about to fall off, your intuition, or someone else's, will begin to work immediately to prevent the quality of life from slipping, as happened that day with the contaminated food, or to restore it if it has become rocky and is in danger of missing the turn to optimal performance.

The next question is: How do we make the system work for us? You are about to discover that this is a two-part process. First, we learn from the detector psi effects the facts we need to know, and then we have the responsibility for following their lead and taking real action. You will discover, too, that without this second step, you relinquish your option to make intelligent corrections. With it, intuition will always return some phenomenon to set point and thus have a beneficial effect.

# CHAPTER 4

# Follow the Lead

(ψ-13) JOSEPHINE WAS driving along a clear four-lane highway that meanders through the foothills of the Blue Ridge Mountains, en route to delivering a group of her framed paintings to a doctor's office in Washington, D.C. The trip would be an hour and a half. With her left hand on the wheel, she leaned over to the floor on the passenger's side for a bottle of drinking water. Alas, the bottle had slipped under the seat; it was almost, but not quite, within her reach. She stretched farther, intending to grab for it. By her account, at that instant she "heard" a definite instruction in her head:

*Don't get it now.*

Because traffic was light, she ignored the warning. She'd used the lunge-and-grab technique successfully on previous occasions, so in spite of the Instruction effect's repeating several times, she continued hunting for the evasive bottle with her right hand while steering with her left. The rest of her story has many parallels with others' who also have not followed the lead offered by intuition.

Suddenly the car slid over the road's edge and onto the gravel shoulder. The molasses-like gravel grabbed the wheels, throwing her out of control and making her victim to the forces of nature. The car rolled crazily to the right. Somehow she was able to steer it back and prevent it from flipping. It then swerved, spun to the left, and like a child's top made a 180-degree turn across all four lanes. It threatened to roll over again, but she held tight, guiding the runaway chunk of metal until it finally stopped. When it settled, she was headed in the wrong direction, with the front tire one short foot of a menacingly deep ditch—without a guardrail.

Almost as soon as she stepped out of the car, a truck driver approached her. He'd seen the whole wild ride. He said, "Ma'am, I was watching you work that car. All I can say is you're darn lucky. By all rights, you and it should have rolled."

Today Josephine knows that the phrase she "heard" was an Instruction psi effect. In the same way that my dinner companion Clint learned he should act on the "feelings," she too appreciates now more than ever that she ought to have acted on the explicit Instruction to control the circumstances, even though the reason was concealed in the future. In her account, indeed in each account about intuitive experiences, we can identify intuition's broad purpose. It will always empower us to shape our own future.

## Knowledge Is Almost Power

Josephine's and Clint's experiences underscore the potential effect of our intuition. In uncountable numbers of situations, there is that critical juncture, which I introduced with the mathematician ($\psi$-7). It is the crossroads in space and time where an unfolding chain of events desperately needs the helping hand of a human action.

Both Josephine and Clint were at this juncture, but they were handicapped by not knowing exactly what to do with their information. Neither understood that this was the time for making a move. If there were to be an explanation, they would discover the reason for the effect only by taking action. (Of course, in Josephine's situation the result would have been invisible because, had she acted, there would have been *no* danger.) Why? Because they would not be able to outwit the knowledge they had received. It was no time to argue with their limited logic on the matter. Rather, they should simply follow that Instruction and feeling, knowing that the details would be accurate. It is the same situation as described in the search for the missing airplane, when intuition had more information than I had ($\psi$-11).

This expectation of an explanation before taking the assigned action is the same demand people have always made of psi effects. It's part of our intellectual heritage. For 2,500 years, humankind has been building confidence in rationalism, as the Greeks introduced it, and that conviction is confirmed daily by the knife-sharp precision thinking we've watched evolve as a result of scientific method. In short, we have come to "trust" reasoning.

All this is well and good for rationalism but not for learning what comes with psi effects. Fighting the facts that inevitably accompany intuition's effects renders the sense powerless to turn a situation because chances for success exist only when the intuitor makes a decision, based on the psi effect's information, and *follows through with definitive action*. Only then, with the movement, does that knowledge become power.

Ask yourself what you would have done in Josephine's situation: You recognize that the Instruction was a psi effect and obviously a directive. Would you have followed through? Why didn't she? Her answer is that, as with Clint, she had no idea that intuition is always a two-part process. The detectable information appears first, to report the system variable, but then it must be followed through—to make the necessary corrections to the variance so that the system can return to set point. This correction, as was explained in Chapter 3, is one unalterable element of the regulatory mechanism's process. It is so important that, until the intuitor makes the move, the intuitive process is incomplete, making intuition ineffective in changing that particular system fluctuation.

This example highlights another crucial point about our intuitiveness: Excepting Déjà vu and the Reflex effect, the intuitor *is always required* to make this decisive move. Let me explain. The new definition of intuition describes it as a sensory ability to attain "facts." Psi effects are the "reporters" of those facts. You can see that in each intuitive interaction the process produces free information, but that is the only product. And this is the component of intuition that both Clint and Josephine experienced, that anyone experiences, up to that point in the regulatory process. The variable is detected, nothing more. Decision and action are the next and final steps. These are our responsibility.

Now here is a surprising twist of nature: Even though some kind of responsive move is required for the correction, in five of the seven psi effects, *we always do have the option to not follow through.* (The exceptions are Déjà vu and the Reflex effect, which is imperceptible and therefore is not included in this context.) This means that the factor of correction that assures intuition's success as a regulatory mechanism is dependent on the intuitor. If he or she wants to benefit from the facts that intuition reports, decisive action is the *compulsory next step* in the process.

Conventional wisdom says that knowledge is power. However, like it or not, knowledge is only information. It's powerless without the vitalizing moves that follow. We can have all the details in the world, but if we don't make that corrective adjustment that uses them purposefully, then invariably they will never be anything more than a potential force waiting to be applied. (Note: This optional feature is one of the reasons intuition has confused us for so long. This optional factor is exemplified in the food poisoning incident—times four ($\psi$-12). The Teleos effect oriented me, allowing me to know about the danger and thereby offering me control over my future. I initially resisted the obligatory next step because I preferred to not insult my colleagues. Fortunately intuition prevailed, enabling me to expose myself to the embarrassment. They elected to disregard my forewarning, and you know the outcome. Although intuition may put us in awkward positions, I have learned from experience that opting for the correction always creates an advantage.

Above all, you need to remember that intuitiveness is an ordinary regulatory mechanism in action. Detection always demands correction, to return the system's variable back to set point. Simplifying the sequence: If you detect it, you correct it.

This procedure is ritual for all of our perceptible sensory processes. When you see the bus coming, you step back from the curb, if you decide to do so. It is similarly your decision whether you go swimming in water where sharks have been reported, isn't it? Likewise, should you feel your skin getting toasted, you always have the alternative to stop sunbathing. The option to act is a universal law of sensory systems. Their information empowers you to help yourself or another condition.

When perceptible sensual effects are involved, you will discover that you always have the choice to not take action that brings change. If you don't go through those three paces of detection, decision, and action, then any knowledge, whether gathered from a sensory system, including intuition, or rationally calculated, will become only another memory stored in your mental bank of historical events.

The lesson in this story of perceptible sensory information is that when we have powerful knowledge, and want its power, we must *do* something with what we learned through it, for action converts knowledge to power. Likewise intuitive information gives you authority to act, but you must use it intelligently to be powerful. The final lesson is that no intuitive information should be stored. It should be taken seriously, and used intentionally, as an opportunity to shape the future ideally.

## A Good Example of "Knowledge Is Powerless"

($\psi$-14) I poured a bit of olive oil over the salad and absentmindedly pushed the bottle to the side of the counter. At the same time, I had a strong mental impression:

*Tighten the top.*

However, I made no move to do so. I thought instead, "Why bother? I'll need more in a minute." Well, I definitely should have followed the order. When my husband came into the room a few minutes later, he threw open his arms to embrace me with a hug. In the process, his hand clipped the bottle and sent it flying. The sticky oil instantly carpeted the kitchen floor.

What caused that impression I detected? Obviously it was advising me to do something very sensible. I knew it was my sense of intuition. I was being forewarned through the Instruction psi effect. What did the instruction accomplish? Not enough, but that was my fault, not intuition's. *I had the option to follow its lead.* And why didn't I? I simply didn't want to be bothered. Who suffered? Only I!

Trivial as it might seem, by returning to that bottle and giving the cap one more twist, I could have changed my future for the better. I would have saved myself time, and half a bottle of perfectly good olive oil, and had a wonderful warm moment with Gayne, which also was lost. Again the moral to the story is: No matter how trivial the situation might seem, *follow through*, and return the system to optimum conditions.

# Process: A Series of Operations Advancing to an End

Nature works in a few simple patterns. Consequently, it's no coincidence that we discover a pattern in all of the sensory systems. First, the familiar three-step empowering process is at the base of them all. "Detect. Decide. Act." Intuition follows their pattern. And you shouldn't be surprised to discover that the three-step process is in reality a regulatory mechanism with its four essentials: It begins when the system varies off set point. A message is transmitted from the detector sensor to you via that system's effects. All of them come to conclusion when you make an intentional correction.

We've established that intuition is a regulatory mechanism. Now we move to the question of its being a sensory system.

To confirm the similarities between intuition and other sensory systems, look for the patterns in Josephine's account. The set point here is her completely safe driving. The system variable is the quality of her driving, *in that one situation* of chasing the bottle. The detector for her is the Instruction psi effect, reporting the change that activated her intuitive sensitivity, "*Don't get it now,*" which made her aware that the situation was unstable. As is always the case with the Instruction effect, it precisely described the correction to make. Remember the Captain who gives commands? Typical of intuition, which is always efficient, it gave her precisely the amount of information necessary for her to adapt her behavior for her own safety, and not a farthing more.

Regardless of the event taking place, sensory intuition is absolutely consistent; it triggers a complete regulatory mechanism.

# How Do You Learn?

We generally think of *learning* as a formal task. We picture ourselves sitting in a classroom and listening to a teacher, or putting our nose in a book to study structured information. However, this description overlooks the internal learning process, which is our natural experience of it. This process is a highly valuable way to reach understanding, even preferable because it is the purest orientation available, that of personal participation.

Our failure to teach ourselves to be aware of the actual physical way in which we *gather* information from sensors in our bodies works against us while we're struggling to break the codes of our own intuition and learn to use it brilliantly. The outcome is that we don't trust our experience of the effects, and thus find it difficult to identify how we are actually physically *getting* information from the psi effects, or from any other experience for that matter.

Since knowing how people learn is important to discovering one's own intuition, it helps to go back to our beginnings so that we can answer the question: How are we *learning* intuition's information? Where do we find the information that we "know"?

The complete answer is consistent for everyone. All of the fresh information—call it breaking news— that we receive from the environment enters our systems through sensory cells called neurons, which are distributed throughout our bodies. Those sensory influences, which we actually detect and have the option to use, travel along our nervous system all the way to our brains and are distributed to various areas within it. There they give rise to the perceptible "experiences," or effects, which we all detect *in our heads.* This is a significant point to understand when you are discovering the psi effects of your intuition. With the exception of the Reflex psi effects, we all learn about every one of our intuitive encounters "in our heads."

As you begin to find your intuition, you'll note for yourself that it doesn't matter whether the effects originated with a phenomenon somewhere in the interior of your body—say, a group of cells becoming chaotic—or with the exterior environment—such as a child's panic—you will learn about it up there *between your ears.* There is a basic biological reason for this, which is important for us all to know as we begin to include intuition in our lives.

The next pages document my observations of the pattern in the development of sensory systems and demonstrate the correlation that, I think, confirms intuition as a system laid down through the epochs as a primary sensory system of the highest order. Typical of natural processes, it is elegant in its simple purpose. It began in antiquity, long before evolution had produced mammals.

## Intuition in the Brain: The Big Picture

The story of intuition seems to me to be inextricably tied in with evolution of the nervous system. I propose that because we are aware of psi effects, we can assume that this new sensory system is a primary system that we can learn by and respond to intelligently.

To demonstrate this principle, let's begin at the dawn of life itself. In his 1859 *The Origin of Species,* Charles Darwin reported a correlation in adaptive growth in animals that he had observed, and which I have found in our intuitive capability. His point was that the whole organization of an organism is so tied together during its growth and development that when variation, however slight, in any one part occurs and accumulates through natural selection, other parts become modified. I am convinced that this phenomenon of modification is related to our intuition, which has emerged in the human system as the regulatory mechanism that protects us from our own potentially hostile mental ability to reason.

Regulators, after all, are nothing new. They existed eons before brains evolved on the primeval scene. When life consisted of single-cell organisms living in the primordial waters and materials of earth, these, too, were required to keep precise control of their internal stability. The story of our intuition begins with their carefully regulated dynamic interaction with the environment.

Before attempting to explain how this basic structure could lead to Josephine's intuiting that she should not reach for the bottle, or my learning about that poisoned food, or why any other intuitive information helps us shape our futures, we have to step back into our most ancient history and find intuition in the evolutionary picture. We want to know about the roots of this system that delivers factual information that no other known internal system provides.

We know that the human body is composed of cells and cellular structures, one of which is the nervous system. Its cells are classified as neurons. We must reach back to the origin of this extraordinary structure with its billions of neurons, and review the role it has played in the modification of life as it scales the evolutionary ladder.

As "sensors," neurons are delicate little communication devices that respond to specific physical phenomena—heat, pressure, light, magnetism, particular motions, odors, sound, and much, much more. These are continuously influencing humans; we feel the sun's heat, feel pain when pinched, smell dinner cooking, watch a sunrise. Each individual neuron is under the management of its own internal regulators and is built to carry out specialized functions, like a skilled technician. Neurons perform a broad and fascinating array of functions. Some can argue, others reach decisions, and still others produce muscular movements, store information, and retrieve it—even years later.

The early single cell's life hundreds of millions of years ago wasn't much by our modern-day standards of enjoyment. It would have lived in the water—where life began. To meet its nutritional needs, it merely made exchanges with the external environment by passing substances back and forth across its membrane in a process called "diffusion." Simple though the process might be, these little fellas did have absolute power over which materials entered and exited their bodies.

And then an exciting event occurred: When some tiny cellular bodies living in water were unable to regulate their fluid world around them—the temperature of the sea itself is one example—they made a giant adaptive leap for living systems. They evolved the ability to change their buoyancy spontaneously, and ascend or descend to regions with a more favorable temperature. That day life began to bob. It also began to swim a little.

Time passed. By dint of their bobbing and swimming movements, the cells entered new territories. This forced modifications. Additional self-protection evolved because the different environments varied and, as a result, threatened the stability of the cells so accustomed to one type of environment. Nature solved the growing problem by producing more sensory awareness, more interconnections, and more types of movement. For example, think of plankton, which we know as the basic diet of the whale. These move by drifting on or near the surface of the water, depending largely on tides, currents, and winds. By design the plankton were too small to swim against currents, but the crustaceans that soon followed could swim and crawl in moving waters. With sensory antennae and, now, eyes to inform them, these creatures—such as brine shrimps, the tiniest mussel shrimps, and krill—could find their way better, and began to travel the watery world in all directions.

You can already see the pattern: increased movements allowed the organism to roam farther afield into other regions, and to face new threats. The sensitivity was augmented, making the creature still more complex, and hence more mobile. Consequently, the need for modification arose again to upgrade sensor systems.

Time passed. As more intricate organisms evolved, they began to require the regulatory mechanism. Now creatures, such as crustaceans, had multiple internal systems, which needed to coordinate. Sensory cells began to organize into ensembles, or circuits, that processed specific types of information—and with this new internal cellular communication, the nervous system was on its way to life.

The earliest circuit was like a simple reflex—the equivalent of your knee-jerk response. Sensory information was allowed into the system, transmitted along the circuit through the organism, and motor reaction resulted. Now a neuron could produce movements. Of course, these early actions were brainless, witless affairs, not fine-tuned precision moves like a prima ballerina but instead involuntary reactions. The lobster is an excellent example: think about its gawky appearance and clumsy way of crawling.

Time passed. Growth and development continued. Sensory systems organized further, changing from mere message-in-action-out circuits, to carry the messages into the first signs of a collection center—the first brain. This structure amounted to a spinal cord with a stem at the top. The stem comprised an ensemble of neurons that served as communications central, controlling an increasing array of the body's interactive internal systems, which developed first into digestive, circulatory, respiratory, and excretion systems.

This brain stem put the organism on automatic control, by flowing vital substances through the systems to specific sites of need and removing wastes to prevent contamination. Human beings have this automatically regulated service in our own bodies today. No learning was, or is, involved. The organisms operated on a course of preprogrammed behavior, functioning robotlike internally and externally, in ways that ensured survival. Lines of creations were appearing in what we classify as species of creatures. Among them were the crustaceans of the sea and now reptiles, which had evolved with the ability to leave the water and rove the land.

Time passed. Next to appear was a dedicated sense of smell, with its own external organ—the aardvark's snout, the elephant's proboscis, the human's nose. Its sensory cells collected in a new lobe on the brain. The creatures were still concerned only with survival, still lacking learning capabilities; however, the innovation here was an ability to sort and analyze data, and to send back cell-made decisions regulating the creature's very basic behavior. Although the creature certainly had no fine-tuned intelligence for planning, with this new chemical-sensitive smelling ability came the first organized control instructions for our most basic reactions of attraction and repulsion—all according to odor.

Time passed—millions of years. Finally, land-dwelling mammals evolved on the scene, with new needs. A different group of interconnected deep-brain structures developed. It introduced sexual drive, arousal, attentiveness, fearfulness, and defensive actions. This was the limbic system.

What an evolutionary leap occurred. With its new sensory structure came new sensations. Creatures felt "motivation" for the first time on earth. These sensations were strong, so strong that the mammals could be caught in their grip. Being held in these states, the mammals had opportunity to learn and could recall later what "feelings" they'd experienced.

This limbic system pushed us beyond robotic brain-cell decisions by introducing learning and memory. For the first time, selection of behavior was controlled with internal mechanisms accompanied by mental states that also became involved in the selection process. Some would call these feelings "emotions," but I prefer to categorize them simply as mental states that allow self-awareness. At last the creature was learning within its head; it was transcending its eons of witless single-cell "smartness." Being caught in the grip of sensations, or inner feelings, the creature could detect them and had time to make decisions about how to respond.

For the first time, nature's order had a creature with fine-tuned "knowing"—whether to drink that foul-smelling water, for example. It could discern gradations rather than be chemically controlled with all-or-nothing reactions. It could "feel" all good or completely miserable, but it also could be somewhere in the middle. Now there were strong internal sensations about life and the environment that touched the creature. It would recognize pleasure and pain, desire and distaste, care and disinterest. This new ability created a different pattern: Mammals regulated their moves according to these feelings. They could *select* their behavior.

Time passed. While larger territories and complex movements were putting new demands on existing systems, nature was keeping up by designing and connecting additional cellular systems. Was it inevitable that one of these systems would eventually evolve into a region that would interconnect and organize the welter of new experiences, processing what goes on between the sensory input and motor output? It did come to pass. The brain developed the neocortex. Now creatures could be self-critical and think intelligently about what was happening in their world. With this powerful tool, they acquired an immense variety of options for fine-tuned self-control. By so doing, life took one more giant step in evolution.

We had the power of reason in our brains; it would allow us to regulate the information we learned, to think and make decisions with the sensory details that our brains were producing. We alone would be able to perceive the various effects coming from the sensory signals—visual, auditory, and the rest. We could associate them, filter and sort them, intentionally ignore or revel in them, draw conclusions, take risks. Our thinking ability was of course unrefined at first. This human with its undeveloped ability to think was like a newborn colt on its wobbly legs.

Time passed. While creeping through the epochs, we slowly organized the internal chaos of data passing through our cortex and tried to find answers for phenomena we didn't understand. For instance, we developed the ability to make up myths about why we had those limbic-based feelings. Storytellers went from town to town repeating what others had experienced of the forces of nature and explaining which gods were responsible for both the bad and the beautiful events. Lacking knowledge, they found their own ready explanations, and the masses believed what they were told.

Clearly, our rudimentary new thinking capability needed to be shaped into reliable working order. For this, there was time, plenty of time. Evolution was working.

In those early days of reason, getting the details right was not important. The fledgling rationalist was only exercising the new ability and slowly assimilating it into human behavior. The brain was wired to "think," but the brainy people had little "experience" with thinking. We can only imagine how slow the progress was. While that understanding was building, people no doubt were beginning to control their lives in small ways with this thinking ability and were able to help themselves because of it in a still overwhelmingly perilous environment. But the day did come when we took a leap in learning.

For this development, we can thank the ancient societies who started asking questions. Around 2500 B.C., the Chinese developed pharmaceuticals and medicine, including a medical text. Two thousand years later, in the fifth century B.C., the Greeks produced the Sophists; these were itinerant teachers who taught for a fee. Their pupils learned skills useful for achieving success, particularly in public life. Socrates appeared on the scene as an independent thinker who spent hours in the public places of Athens, engaging in dialogue and argument with anyone who would listen. By the Grecian era, we were well on our way to the possibility of controlling the flow of information that moved inside the human brain.

Time has passed. We leapt again, in 1620, when English philosopher Francis Bacon introduced his technique of inductive reasoning; it ultimately led us to the use of the scientific method for learning, to a new art form, and yet another giant step for humankind. Today we think of human intelligence as evolution's high point and of ourselves as the capstone of her parade of species.

## The Rational Destroyer

Looking back through recorded history, we witness the natural order marching on, with its systems, including the nervous system, growing and developing nicely. When analytic abilities evolved, nature pushed Homo sapiens out ahead of the animal kingdom, making this species the supreme creature, the most complicated, self-regulating, rational organism in existence so far on earth. From the single-celled blobs of protoplasm clinging to a rock beneath the sea, organic life had come far enough to be able to think creatively. Odd that out of all this welter of life, only one creature could put a mirror in front of itself and observe its living inner world. This means that we alone can describe the experiences of the activity within our brains.

The bad news is that, for all of its wondrousness, reason has led us to a hoary problem that critics forewarn and doomsters promise will result in troubles of the magnitude loosed by the mythical Pandora. Legend has it that a box was sent to her by the gods who forbade her to look inside. She ignored their wishes and opened it out of curiosity. By so doing she was responsible for releasing a swarm of evils upon humankind. Evidence is coming in from numerous rational explorations that in recent generations we have been using intelligence and planning power without enough restraint and have broken into the most delicate structures of nature—the fundamental forces, elements, and cells. We are roaming these new places, tinkering excitedly with life, altering the elements with their unimaginable forces, and remodeling cells and their structures. Lately we have begun to question what horrors we, like Pandora, have released. While it is a great adventure, we don't fully understand the repercussions of turning the courses of nature away from their set points. By so doing, we have taken one of the more dramatic turns in our two-hundred-thousand-year history as Homo sapiens. We do know that we have become a threat to life on earth. The possibility of an evolutionary failure looms in the natural order—unless a correction comes very soon. We also know that one simple corrective solution for regulating this creature, man-turned-predator, would be to eliminate the problem from the natural order altogether with a cycle of human self-destruction. Of course we consider this unacceptable and have begun to wonder how to save ourselves.

How we arrived at this juncture seems quite obvious. We uncovered our formidable powers of reason and released them to think and be creative. One great discovery was the fundamental regulatory mechanism. Although records show the Chinese incorporated it into their engineering more than two thousand years ago, the real explosion of inventions occurred in the eighteenth century with the Industrial Revolution. We went wild developing mechanical implements—furnaces, water mills, and windmills were only the beginning. The revolution and humankind flourished, in part due to the highly versatile regulatory mechanism spreading across the land, turning up everywhere in science and technology, psychology, medicine, war machines, and of course computers.

On the evolutionary clock, it took what seems like a nanosecond for us to apply our new rational ability to harness the power we'd discovered in our brains. The revolution that began with attempts to enhance our adventures and comforts has culminated in the first example in the history of creation that an animal could augment nature's regulatory mechanisms. This has not been an altogether good development.

What has happened? At the dawn of our existence, we discovered a method of simplifying our labor with tools of stone, bronze, and iron. In those early efforts, we were looking for ways to get along with the forces of nature. Lately, however, we have been less content with nature's line of products. Now we actively pursue ways of perfecting her multitudinous methods of running things. We've learned ways to attack what we dislike, and to rush matters when we're impatient to have what we want. Using everything from global warfare for annihilating life to genetic engineering, which should perfect it, we figure out how to create a bypass here or override regulated processes there, when we decide to make natural systems more "efficient" and "effective."

## Detection

All this has led to our taking control of natural law, tampering with systems and abusing processes. By now we have ample visible evidence in large systems' breakdowns that we've been playing with very high stakes. In the centers of societies where ideas are forged and driven to action—commerce and industry, academia, law, and politics—it's common knowledge that all too often we've made our adaptations *before* identifying the consequences that we set in motion. In our tracks across the sands of time we don't need to look far to detect innumerable environmental breakdowns and a species that has been seriously damaged along the way.

## Correction

Despite our extraordinary capacity to ignore it, the evolutionary mandate still stands strong: "The internal environments of cells must be precisely controlled." If we ignore this law, we too will surely fall off our set point and lose our strength to survive. The rationalist will destroy itself.

I suggest that we find the correction to this threat if we return to what seems to have carried evolution thus far: not "tougher" but more "sensitive" cells and cellular structures. Since we are living under that same rule, the evolutionary process appears to have provided us with a regulatory mechanism that assures that we can be safe and can survive in our new rationally created environment. Let's review the argument.

Since our reasoning has set us free like birds released from captivity, we have been celebrating wholesale our new freedom to learn and create. Threatened now as we are by the products of our own mental capability, coupled with a will to use it unchecked, the time is ripe for a new sensory system, one that serves as a regulatory mechanism for us, to set us free once again in our dominion of reason, but this time advising where we can and should not go, so that we can keep safe and out of trouble while we stretch our wings further and gain safe passage among those most delicate and essential fundamental structures of nature's order.

Time has passed. We have been getting acquainted with this intelligence for about two and a half million years. Analyzing recent history, there can be no question: We do need controls. Perhaps an evolving sensory system is the answer. I propose that this intuitive sensitivity is standing by to serve as the regulatory mechanism to help us into the future. Its task is to guide our intelligence safely through the Factors "U" and to send signals promptly when our information and reasoning are faulty. Having its precise information about the infinitely complex and close-fitting systems in the microworld can open the window of opportunity that we desperately need to be able to know where to lend a hand and begin correcting their imbalances.

I contend that as soon as we understand that *intuition does report in our brains*, and that part of its purpose is to protect us from our own rampant rationalism, we can be safely on our way again, evolving cooperatively with this diverse, interrelated, and precisely operated living universe.

## Intuitive Power Is the Win/Win Power

($\psi$-15) My eldest son, Jeff, had a stunning intuitive experience while he was serving as a first lieutenant in the United States Army. His assignment was to lead his platoon of men and equipment on a three-day maneuver. They were ordered to depart the base at dusk on a given day and arrive at the first checkpoint by the following noon.

It was a steamy July. Heavy rain had been falling steadily for several days. Around one o'clock in the morning, my son and his men reached the designated point for turning north. As he stepped from his jeep to confirm their position, he was seized by a sense of foreboding. This, he knew, was intuitive. Something, somewhere, was terribly wrong.

Without a word, he returned to the jeep to review his orders. He had to be sure of every detail, because turning back was virtually impossible once they were on the narrow cliffside road. Maps indicated that the route had no obstacles and was adequate for heavy vehicles. His orders and the platoon's current location matched. Although it was muddy, the road was in good condition as far as he could see with his binoculars. Everything checked. Nothing should be wrong. Yet, the foreboding lingered.

Because of it, he decided to stop the platoon and send out a patrol to check the route. According to his calculation, this would take two hours. Meanwhile, he returned to his maps. Before long he sent out a second patrol to mark an alternate way to the next junction. He instructed them to return within two hours. This would risk being late to the next day's noon rendezvous but would be better, he decided, than endangering the lives of his men.

The first patrol returned in an hour with news that a section along the road had begun to erode, probably due to the recent rain. Under the weight of vehicles and men traveling over it, they speculated, part of it could collapse and drop into the chasm below.

Aha! Here was the peril he'd intuited. With the foreboding confirmed, when the second patrol returned, he ordered the platoon to take the detour. They moved out immediately, arriving that morning at the checkpoint with little time to spare.

A question: Would you have known what to do about that "foreboding"? Imagine yourself in this young officer's position. Under the time constraints of the assignment and rules of professional accountability, would you have had enough confidence in *it* to hesitate as he did and design a time-consuming plan to follow up on the "feeling"? How many people would? And then there's the top brass who devised the master plan: What would you have reported to them if you had arrived behind schedule, and they had demanded an explanation? Think about the bigger arena of the world, such as medical services, public education, businesses, and governments: how would *anyone* justify such a "sense" when explaining such a decision to administrators?

On the other hand, what if you, or he, had *not* followed through on the "sense" but instead had stuck resolutely to the orders? How would you have explained to your superiors, and your platoon, the inevitable dire consequences of the road's collapsing? How could you have lived with yourself? The fact is, when individuals ignore intuitive knowledge such as this, and disaster does follow, they suffer terribly. Usually they remember that they did have accurate information, and they don't understand why they didn't pay attention.

## What You Discover in Your Head Does Matter

Obviously, the very private phenomenon of learning through events that occur in our mental world is nothing new. From morning to night we actively perceive sensory facts and make decisions in our heads. For example, when you're approaching the traffic signal at the junction, you are mentally aware that "the streetlight is red." Turn on the radio: you hear sounds that you can identify instantly as "music" or "someone talking." If you dislike the noises, then you might have the idea to "change the station," which you do by physically pressing a button or moving the dial. You can almost "feel" the decision happening in your head. Every schoolchild knows the sensation of "arriving at a solution," "coming to a conclusion," or "settling on an idea." These are normal *learning* experiences. They have their own perceptible sensations.

Ask yourself: What does it feel like to "see" an object, "hear" a dog bark, or "feel" an ice cube in your hand? You know those sensations because the sensors have delivered the information about each experience to the proper areas of your brain and converted them there to perceptible visual, auditory, and tactile effects that you detect easily. When they arrive, they're decoded and available to us, via the specific sensory effects, for our consideration and application.

Those effects introduce "free pure information." Without changing them at all, we are responsible for thinking about them carefully and using them, if we'd like, to reach a suitable conclusion, opinion, or decision. For instance, if that noise is grating, there is not much point in pretending it is otherwise. Grating is what grating is. The effect is reporting accurately; it cannot be changed because it is a sensory report.

The phenomenon, however, is a different story. When the brain reveals that you are experiencing the particular contact, you can readily decide how to interact with it.

Sometimes we encounter conflicting phenomena in our heads; then we consider those effects in order to "weigh" decisions. We call this thinking. You may deliberate about a departure, thinking, "I'd like to leave for the office now. Well, on the other hand, seeing that the rain is falling so heavily, perhaps I'll wait five minutes. On the other hand, stalling might make me late. Hmmm. Better leave right now." Just as any sensory effect is detectable—visual, auditory, or olfactory—so is the experience of thinking. By paying attention to what is happening inside our heads, we can begin to recognize the signals unique to each effect. You have been receiving, learning, and thinking from them since you were a tiny tot!

## The Psi Effects

The signaling circuit is identical with intuition. If you can understand this, you're halfway to being empowered by it. There really is nothing to learning that psi effects exist. If you have a "feeling" that you should "leave a room," then that would be an intuitive effect; it should be enough to make you analyze in your brain, decide what to do with the information, and take action, just as you would if the effect were a visual impression of a red traffic signal.

Think about what the lieutenant experienced with his sense of foreboding. Using intuition as a guide to movement begins with an intuitor's being aware of these psi effects. You learn what you experience in your head. It might be "a sense of" something, "hunches," or "feelings," including "gut feelings" as well as "a feeling of certainty." You could discover that you have "known absolutely" what to do in some instances, by a "sense" of words and phrases spontaneously "coming to mind" such as I have described in my accounts. A "sense" of remote images is common, as is the "impression" of "hearing" as described by Josephine. All of these are solid descriptions of psi effects. They are the mental experiences that alert us to action, protect us when reason might not be enough, direct us when the immediate situation is simply too confusing, push us when we are uncertain.

Begin to keep a list of the psi effects you discover. Identify how they catch your attention. This is the way to start learning intuitively.

## When to Wonder, and When Not

Kipling said it for us: "Ours is not to wonder why. Ours is but to do, or die." You now know that by the time you perceive a psi effect in your head, the regulatory process is well under way. This is not the point where you, as the intuitor, begin to question. It is not the time to wonder "why." Now is the opportunity to *do*, or something will in fact be diminished, or even die. Clint, Josephine, Jeff, and I all agree that here is the place where action is in order. The psi effect alone is confirmation that you have encountered a phenomenon that is influencing you. You need to act confidently. The rule of use is simple: When intuition sends its psi effect, you can rely on it and follow through.

## Laws of Intuition

One difficulty with our intuition is finding a routine for using it reliably. I started with the same challenge but ended up discovering that we simply follow the pattern we use with all of our sensory systems. It's the old familiar "stimulus/perception/response" formula; simply put: Learn from the effect, and take action. Normally, if it is a positive influence, we stand by to benefit, but if it is damaging, we then dodge it.

Likewise with intuition: An intuitible system varies (stimulus) which you detect via the psi effect (perception) and then correct with a decision and move to return the system to set point (response). Look carefully—this is the ancient, unfailing regulatory mechanism. It is the system variable/detection/correction mechanism.

The laws of intuition as I have identified them follow precisely the established stimulus/perception/response regulatory sequence.

▲ I call the first part the *Law of Information*. The "perception" segment of the intuitive process transmits two classes of detectable information: (1) *it introduces us* to purely factual data—"A lot of people are going to die," and (2) *it gives instructions* about how to move—"Pick it up." Hence, the Instruction psi effect.

▲ I call the second stage of the intuitive process the *Law of Action*. This part draws us into the activity by giving us options to follow.

The outcome of obeying the laws of intuition sequence is that we take control and regulate a threatening fluctuation back to its set point. This will return the precious stability that sets the system free to move about in the environment, just as Dr. Claude Bernard indicated.

## Detectors Come in Every Make and Model

The next account illustrates two of the most common reasons that people do not follow up on their intuitive leads. First, it might be awkward or embarrassing. Second, the information doesn't make any sense. You will learn with experience that neither is a good enough excuse to deny intuitiveness its benefits.

The first difficulty is to be expected. How many of us are taught as youngsters that individuals must be on their "best" behavior in company? And what a collection of social codes we have. An amusing one from my childhood is, "Don't scratch your skin in public. Scratching is for monkeys!" Think of the dozens of reasons every human being scratches. Mosquitoes? Poison ivy? Dry skin?

Rules of etiquette were devised to discipline our behavior and make us conform. Unfortunately, they can cause individuals to lose that essential ability to respect natural cues offered by the senses. Among them, of course, are those coming from intuition.

While human social codes should never have gained the power to obliterate our freedom to make a move, they have somehow loomed as direct challenges to it. Even iconoclasts occasionally fall into their sway and stunt their self-awareness. Let me warn you once: Intuition knows nothing about human social conventions! It is doing its job helping to run a world. Even if it interrupts a party, its rule is that you should take action. This demand can lead to some strange mental conflicts indeed.

As for the second point—its not making sense: We have to allow intuition into our daily lives before debating this point seriously.

These two bothersome conditions came into play one evening not so long ago. This account illustrates again that intuition will protect us from most basic perils—in this case, the threat was fire.

($\psi$-16) Your average smoke-and-fire alarm system is designed to detect when a fire starts in a prescribed indoor or outdoor space and to set off a deafening wail to alert us, thereby preventing damage to life and property. A most clever device. People certainly sleep better knowing they are so protected.

Although installing such a reliable mechanical device is a sensible thing to do, in the past few of us had the luxury of a fire alarm system in our homes, until the advent of smoke alarms. My house certainly didn't have one at the time, unless of course intuition could be counted as the equivalent.

While we were playing cards with friends about 9:30 one night, a peculiar impression entered my head:

*Go brush your teeth.*

I knew it was an intuitive instruction, which I should follow.

It would be less than honest to say that I was delighted to do so on this evening. Why? Because the instruction was absurd. Wouldn't it be disconcerting to you to be invisibly but firmly advised, in the middle of a pleasant evening, to jump out of your chair like a jack-in-the-box and inexplicably dash from the room, simply to brush your teeth? But, rejection was out of the question. Intuition was signaling. Something, somewhere, needed my attention, and it was more important than our good-natured company and a light-hearted game of cards.

Amused by the thought of how bizarre the next move might seem, even to close friends, I excused myself politely, without explaining that this was an assigned mission—which I immediately named "Operation Toothbrush" for my own amusement. I walked down the dark hallway, turned into our bedroom, and headed for the bathroom—domicile of said brush and apparently ground zero for this mysterious exercise. Before I was halfway across the room, I saw a faint shaft of completely odorless smoke rising around the lamp on the bedside table. Moving closer, I discovered a decorative pillow pressing against a hot lightbulb. Its heat had ignited a small ring of embers that were rapidly eating away the fabric. Aha! This was the reason for my puzzling exit!

I stopped dead in my tracks. Here it was again. Solid evidence of intuition's unfailing accuracy. And it followed its own pattern: it's always right!

This, I realized suddenly, was not the time to become intrigued with intuition's operations. Reality demanded my attention. This was a fire! I'd better move! I grabbed the smoldering pillow and drenched it under the shower—to ensure that no ember survived. With that, I knew that Operation Toothbrush was successful. I returned to the table. No one asked where I'd gone.

Of course, I really didn't need to brush my teeth at that moment, as intuition instructed, but by sending me to the only place where this was possible, it pointed me in the direction where I could detect the developing crisis and correct it. Intuition had converted me to a highly effective human fire alarm and sprinkler system.

The challenge confronting a body becomes clear. All of the sensory systems give us fair warning of variables as soon as they are affected by a phenomenon. But we see here, as we did in the food poisoning episode ($\psi$-12), that intuition was the first one among them to send an alert. This is its way. Intuition is the pathfinder sense shepherding us through elemental and cellular events, the one receiving from deepest space with its scores of unfolding activities. To the extent that we need to know about them, and are able to recognize the alert, intuition will be the first to report distinctly *in every case*. Why? It probes creation's complex chains of events from their inception.

## Intuition in the Next Generation

And so we conclude with the answer to why I learned about that tainted food, why Josephine was forewarned about the bottle, and why Jeff had that feeling about the road. The definitive clue to the mystery of intuition has come from biological processes, which evolved a four-element survival mechanism eons ago. Intuitiveness is yet another regulatory mechanism in us, working toward that same end—that humankind might perpetuate in nature's grand design. I am sure we have another chance to restore stability to earth's life by using this new ability. As we go more and more out of control with our reason—tinkering with elemental atoms and twisting our cells' chromosomes—this potential for a new kind of regulation has urgent appeal. At the same time, it emphasizes our need for further study into the intuitive process as a constructive force of social change in our world where both disaster and great good is always at our doorstep.

Since this is not yet a household behavior, probably it is difficult now to imagine intuition's normal scope and power. Time and experience will bring them to light, however, making intuition visible at last and as inspiring as it is astonishing. It will be very much like any fine mechanical invention in our recent history—railroads, electricity, telephones, computers; when we devoted ourselves to making them part of us, they very quickly played a crucial role in interconnecting the entire globe, thus reorganizing our species. Likewise our rationalism. When we awakened it, reasoning certainly gave us the opportunity to set a new course on the evolutionary compass and deliberately seek success that we could not even speculate 2,500 years ago.

We stand now on the frontier of a new millennium. What will we be saying in the year 3000 about our discovery of intuition? We can only dream what potential it will release. Right now the best thing we can do is set the next new course for humankind, and turn spaceship Earth toward its new port.

# CHAPTER 5

# Roller Coaster to Reality

DURING PHASE ONE of my learning, all was not well on the home front. When I first went out in the field, chasing the butterflies that were my flitting ideas, half of my friends of scientific leanings were sure I had departed earth's reality altogether—accusing me of thinking too little. The other half, bent already toward a staggering array of wispy notions about what life should be, charged me with thinking too much. Fraying edges of solid friendships notwithstanding, I found excellent company among the pages of a small collection of ancient and modern books, which I began to study. Meanwhile, the battle lines were drawn: I was fascinated, and digging in deeper, while those around me were undeniably nervous and digging in their heels.

By now it was 1979, a time when people spoke in whispers about the mysteries of the occult and of shadowy characters called "psychics." The word "intuition" appeared only occasionally; "ESP" was the popular collective classification. Parapsychology was a fledgling science to be questioned. It dared to investigate such matters and people. Parapsychologists wanted to link inexplicable phenomena with our human behavior. According to many logicians and theologians, and multitudes of others in the general population, that was a very dangerous idea.

Yet, despite the forbidding climate, people everywhere in the world claimed to use ESP. Some earned their livings with their ability, classifying themselves as psychics, sensitives, clairvoyants, mediums, and channels. They spoke of "seeing," "hearing voices," "gut" feelings, and "simply knowing" about events, of life in different dimensions. They offered time-honored wisdom. Numbers earned their living by their ESP, classifying themselves as "advisers" and "consultants." Community and religious groups in large cities and outlying towns hastily labeled them "charlatans" and theirs as a fraudulent occupation. Public censorship notwithstanding, most of the practitioners continued undaunted, spinning out their information confidently, even though they had no basis of proof to support either that information or their confidence. They offered a rich variety of explanations for their learning by ESP. Many made no logical sense.

It became easier for me to spot what I had by now concluded was intuition. It appeared not only in those skilled with their ESP but also in natural everyday behavior. Some people used it involuntarily as I always had; others—like the practitioners—could regulate theirs to different degrees. The evidence of psi effects was extremely persuasive. At long last, I began to realize how profoundly intuition might influence future human conduct.

Now in the fifth year of consulting, I became involved with a small controversial group of friends who decided to gather weekly to discuss openly the impressive variety of paranormal phenomena and develop our own ideas about everything from healing to spooks to UFOs. Even though we agreed right from the beginning to draw the line clearly between innovative thinking and our imaginations, each of us would have to admit that the line was often extremely vague.

In due time, my relatives' mildly curious questions about my outside interests turned to manifest hostility against my growing involvement. Without ever challenging my reasons for the quest, they were beginning to think I was losing touch with our salubrious university life and, even worse, jeopardizing my sparkling six-, nine-, and twelve-year-old children.

Meanwhile, I learned that another resistance was growing vigorously outside our family walls. The town grapevine, always heavy with ripe gossip, crept back to my unbelieving ears, bearing dark reports. Apparently I was "dabbling with the occult" and "practicing witchcraft." At parties, I noticed that when I appeared, several of the women moved discreetly to the other side of the room.

Finally, at one particular social gathering my frustration peaked to overload. It was time to cut back the creeping tendrils that were running wild and damaging my private life. I decided that it was my responsibility to be the gardener, so I intercepted a pleasant woman whom I'd never met. It was obvious that she had spotted me when she came into the room, and she was headed for the other side at Mach speed. I introduced myself casually and commented on the unusual size of the gathering. It would have been impossible to miss her obvious discomfort—indeed, paralysis—but I was determined to make my assault and start pruning back those rumors. Someone would have to speak directly to me so that I could learn, once and for all, how I was being publicized among the hoards. Not a minute into my monologue her face reddened, obviously in anticipation of what she was about to say.

"Mrs. Ferguson, if you don't mind, I am extremely uncomfortable talking with you. Would you please excuse me?"

"Actually, no, because I'd like to ask you why."

"Well." She hesitated. "I've heard what you do."

"I presume you mean that I'm interested in paranormal phenomena. Would you mind telling me why that's so disturbing?"

"All right. To put it bluntly, I'm afraid that you're standing there reading my mind! I don't like the idea at all. It frightens me."

I could hardly believe my ears. Reading people's minds was the last thing I would do. Shocked at her naïveté, I gave my reflexive reply.

"Mrs. Flint, may I ask you a question?"

"I suppose so."

"When you read a newspaper, do you read every advertisement?"

"A strange question. I never thought about it, but, no, naturally not."

"Why not?"

"Probably because most of them don't matter to me."

Her answer was perfect. I had bagged my quarry. Perhaps I could turn back the wild growth. I explained my question.

"Possibly you can understand that I'm the same way with people's minds. Yes, I use my ESP to help some know their own mental states, but when I walk into a room, I don't start at one end and go to the other, "reading" them. That isn't what an intuitive person does. Even if it were possible, it simply wouldn't be that interesting, not any more than your reading all those ads."

She smiled wanly but of course didn't believe one word I'd said. When she scampered away at the first opportunity, I knew full well that she had determined, long before we met, that I considered everyone easy game for my personal gossip column and would unscrupulously probe anyone I pleased. I assure you, she was completely wrong.

Hers is a searing fear that many people harbor. They have the notion that intuition means "reading" everyone's private thoughts. This is completely incorrect and not at all the way the intuitive process works. Taken in the context of the regulatory mechanism, ask yourself: What could such behavior possibly correct? The matter will become apparent in a later chapter discussing telepathy, which explains why intuition could never be random mind reading. Mind reading is today and always has been only an amusing parlor game, designed for pure entertainment, with the hope of sensation. It has nothing whatsoever to do with true intuitive behavior and should certainly not be taken seriously.

Back to my attempt at pruning gossip. How little I knew. This woman's angst was only the tip of the public iceberg. I was about to discover a great deal more—from my children. To my chagrin, parents had started to freeze them out by laying down the law that my youngsters were unwelcome in their friends' homes. I learned the sad news when my youngest son, who didn't tell me until weeks later, finally broke down in tears of frustration and recounted a pathetic story about his little friend's mother. She had made sure he would know he was unwelcome at a large birthday party for her son. I wept that day for my innocent children and for the crude people who would dare to hurt them, just to stop me. Ever aware that my sole purpose was to find constructive forces of life, I explained as best I could to my young trio and continued investigating, despite the tightening ring of resistance.

## To Reduce Apprehension, Open a Door

Traditionally explorers and innovators have stepped out of the population, and out of their private circles, thinking only of the pursuit of a future change that seems useful. Causing others to suffer couldn't be further from their thoughts. Yet, skirmishes frequently erupt at the borders. Where challenges lure, repression invariably surfaces simultaneously, and this, no doubt, is natural. Frontiersmen and women usually lose far more scuffles than they win, but this doesn't imply that they are crippled by it. They know that the courses they follow are not to conquer the past but rather to move out and enrich the future.

The history of human expansion confirms how fortunate we are that many have persevered, even when, as so often happens, the all too unreasonable forces of opposition attempt to shut down the borders and keep the rascals in. Why the opposition? When the specter of a new development looms, traditionalists fear that their established beliefs will crumble. It is not a rare phenomenon to see that, in the desperate need to be secure, they are even willing to put faith in beliefs that will stifle advantages for life.

As I advanced on the intuitive unknown, I was unaccountably fortunate. In direct contrast to my becoming a lightning rod for condemnation on the home front, strangers from everywhere inadvertently began to play the role of coexplorers. This isn't to say they weren't apprehensive. They were. Nevertheless, their need overrode their fear, thus forcing them to open the intuitive door to new options. With their help, I had occasion to meet firsthand some of the dreads causing the widespread fears of my ability and others. I had the privilege, too, of watching some resisters sway in the defining moment when the facts came home.

The coexploration with strangers started because they'd heard that others had benefited from my help—but, as already explained, those who led the parade had been friends and acquaintances. Since mine was a personal quest for answers, I hadn't thought about where this new expansion would lead me. However, after a while, the combination of people wanting insight and my wanting to understand forced me to organize myself—to separate professional propriety from personal fascination. I gave myself rules for both intents. When a stranger came, I would be the teacher, serving his or her interests. And, for my part, I was the student, observing this nimble intuition, delighting in new exposure to its scope and promise.

Creating that divide provided a great advantage. In this cross-domain of purposes, I came face to face with the enigma of intuition that drives most people's fear. The core problem in resorting to intuitiveness was that each of the people who sought me out wanted to take control over his or her life in a way that was consistent with the individual's beliefs, but all too often, intuition did not meet that criterion. It was spooky stuff and, in their more traditional worldview, not a reasonable solution to finding answers.

It took months for me to figure out what was creating their internal conflicts, but I finally arrived at the obvious: All these people were calling on me *as a last resort*. This meant that none of their personal methods of solving problems had worked, including their religious belief systems. Naturally, they might be afraid of anything, from my integrity to censure from the church, because, as far as they knew, they were looking over the edge of common sense and reason into an abyss. Psychologists would agree that though these coexplorers might not want to resist, their mentalities would fight like the warriors of Henry V on Saint Crispin's day. Thus, my responsibility was to not overwhelm them—neither to interfere with their faith nor to force them to approve my ever-strengthening premise about intuition's value.

Over and over, they came through the door, trailing Old Friend Fear with them. The problem they relayed was always so innocent and natural: On one hand, they needed information they lacked, which they had heard I could deliver; on the other, they wanted to be true to themselves. If we were successful with the first order, that might force them to question their worldview. In the end, their challenge was never going to be a question of tolerating me, but rather of winning the war within their psyches. Of course, it stresses people to test their solid convictions. Yet, hundreds of brave individuals resorted to intuition for guidance, because nothing else had worked.

I finally was able also to define the main reason for the gossip-vine. We belong to a linear society, one that believes in reasoning logically and fosters fact-finding. By facts, we mean information that can be proved and that will bring correct results. We also tacitly agree that when facts are lacking, we have two possible solutions to problem solving. First, and perhaps most difficult, we should admit that we don't know and follow standard research procedures, Second, many people, but by no means all, turn to their religion as the provider of answers and release. Intuition was obviously forcing a face-off. It did not fit into either of these categories. The intuitive person "just knows," and that is totally unacceptable!

A typical example of people on the horns of the intuition dilemma is police departments. They certainly need as much precise information as they can gather, but from a "psychic"? Well, that's always dicey. While some law enforcement officers will look to intuition for solutions when public safety is in question, others think the idea is preposterous. Such was the case with one metropolitan department that contacted me.

(ψ-17) The issue was a madman. He was driving a frenzy of fear. It started with an angry male voice on the phone at a police headquarters in California. He announced that he would be in the civic auditorium at a rock concert that night. He planned to kill the lead singer during the pyrotechnics display. Such threats always hit their mark of police nerves, for all the right reasons. In this event, the concert had been sold out for weeks. Six thousand eager fans would arrive after dark, expecting to be aroused. The police would be challenged even if they could call in a thousand cops to control the wild herd of screaming, stomping fans who would pack the foyer, block the aisles, and jam the rest rooms.

Surveillance was a nightmare at best, and while the department met the highest standards of law enforcement agencies, they knew their squad was not sufficient if the caller planned to follow through. As if their internal frailties weren't enough, the band members had refused to cooperate with the department and insisted that the pyrotechnics should be in the program as advertised. They would risk the lead singer in order to rock the house.

I received the call around 7:30 A.M. Would I please meet the police at the auditorium as quickly as possible and help them in any way I could? When we were all gathered, I was introduced to a team of four men and listened quietly while the leader explained the reason for my being there. I would be the "psychic."

The word was no sooner out of his mouth than one of the strapping young officers, Rick Jamison, stepped back in obvious alarm. He didn't believe in psychic people, he told the group. And they certainly had no place here. This was a law enforcement agency, not a place for mumbo jumbo. If I stayed, he would leave. His church taught that people like that lady (nodding in my direction) were dangerous, not to be reckoned with. Then, he addressed me directly: "I've heard about people like you. I have to admit, I didn't think they'd look like the rest of us, if ya' know what I mean. I expect them to be all gussied up in glittery stars and moons. I'm sorry to have to say this, ma'am: You might look like a well-bred woman, and appear normal to some people, but as far as I'm concerned, if you do that stuff, then you're no ordinary female. You're going to be a weird, weird lady, and I'm not stickin' around to find out how." With that, he excused himself and departed. Those of us who remained took a deep breath. The others agreed that, "weird" or not, if I could help in some practical way, they would be more than grateful.

While we four walked together through the riddle of aisles in the cavernous hall, they told me what they knew about the band's leader and his angry reaction to the grisly forewarning. Yes, he had at least a dozen solid enemies. No, he'd never received such a menacing threat, but he didn't care. Let the animal rage. He was going to have his time on stage, with or without police approval.

We were moving along a wide walkway behind the first tier of chairs when I found myself peering at one seat three rows from the back:

*If that one is empty, all is well. If a man
takes it, keep him in sight constantly.*

I repeated it for the men. After confirming that the seat had been sold, we spent half an hour investigating what intuition knew about the would-be assassin and the adequateness of their surveillance operations. We worked well together, exchanging a dozen or more questions and answers. When they were satisfied, and visibly more relaxed, my part was done. We left the hall and said our good-byes.

Early the next morning, the head of the squad called. The house had been packed; the crowd reckless. Only twelve seats were unoccupied throughout the performance, including the one I had designated. They sounded enormously relieved.

Over the two years that I frequented the department, Rick and I encountered one another on several occasions. Each time, he only shook his head despairingly. In his eyes, I was obviously hopeless.

What went wrong between us? Here were two socially concerned individuals, working for the same result. However, we differed widely in vocation, social background, and gender, but especially in opinion about intuitiveness, which unmistakably challenged our effectiveness.

This forced division-by-conviction took me on another revealing journey of analysis into just what happens when people blindly disagree. Rick and I had no hope of working together, because he refused to expand his experience and viewpoint. This choice was his, of course, yet his convictions that declared me dangerous could never confirm that he was right. On the other hand, if he would test it, I could demonstrate that a woman of ordinary appearance did in fact have command of a superb resource. Given a chance, it could produce the pieces to a puzzle, that he himself wanted to finish. But for him proof was not required. Because of his fixed beliefs, he could simply draw a line between two people and stop a chain of beneficial events that would come to the result we all wanted.

Based on firsthand knowledge gained over the later years, I can say that whatever our ultimate goals might be, when working together in any endeavor, we'd best begin by working out personal relations with each other. To his credit, Officer Jamison made his position known, and not disrespectfully. Alas, time proved that when we needed to cooperate, the outcome would have been gravely affected.

His reaction so embodied the public viewpoint that it galvanized me to set some new goals as an explorer. I determined that I would find a way to reduce the fear. Ultimately it led me to teaching people to use their own intuition. I preferred this approach to that of being the middle person, the one giving guidance, the "psychic." If people would only learn to use intuition, they would convince themselves.

On another occasion, a need for a solution overrode religious dogma, and the story had a happy ending:

($\psi$-18) The wife of a commercial airline pilot called on a Sunday evening. She wanted me to find his wallet. He had it in his hand the previous day, minutes before he took off on the London-to-L.A. flight. When he arrived in Los Angeles, he left the airport and drove sixty miles directly to their ranch home. On that Sunday morning, he dressed for ranch work. During the day, he tilled fifteen acres of soil using a disc harrow. Toward evening he looked for his wallet. It was nowhere to be found.

She said she knew she could never figure out how to find a wallet somewhere between the Heathrow airport and fifteen acres of earth. But perhaps an intuitive person could. Would I help? I agreed and said I would call as soon as I had any information. She thanked me, then added cautiously that she would prefer to phone me. Her husband shouldn't know she had contacted me. She would call in three hours.

She didn't elaborate the cold facts behind her statement; I knew her reasons. They are members of a church that frowns on paranormal practices. As usual, in order to respect his faith, I didn't argue and simply complied with her request.

In half an hour I intuited the phrase "five furrows in." Even to my unpracticed ear it sounded agricultural. I continued intuiting and, in a few minutes, learned the information. It was the Teleos psi effect—specifically, what I call direct cognition:

*five furrows in . . . north/south run . . .*
*arroyo-like gully . . . six to ten inches under*
*. . . deep slash across*

When she rang, I reported these phrases exactly. She was quiet for a moment, then said quizzically, "I am sure there was no north/south run. You must be wrong."

I replied with the certainty that often accompanies intuition. "Yes, there is. You look in the morning."

The telephone rang early.

"You are right. He plowed a long section north to south. I don't see any gully though. Are you sure about that?"

I told her I was.

She was silent and then continued, sounding frustrated. Couldn't I tell her more? There was so much dirt, too much to dig alone.

"Dig? By yourself?" I was amazed.

"Well yes, of course."

Her pointed reply reminded me of her differences with her husband. She had to search alone because she dared not reveal her source of information. I told her adamantly that the information I'd given her was adequate to lead her to the wallet. Intuition had done what it could. She had new options now, hence an advantage. She was responsible for further action.

Later that afternoon, she called again.

"We found it." She was crowing.

A little surprised, I inquired what had happened. She told me that in her frustration, she ventured to speak to her husband about our conversations. Although not happy that she had contacted me, he was glad for a new lead, so he decided to test the information. He attached a harrow with five teeth to the plow and invited the neighborhood children to follow as he drove. She walked with them as they moved slowly up and down the only north-to-south run on the acreage. At the fifth turning, she spied the small dry wash that she had been so sure did not exist. Immediately after they passed it, one child called out, "There it is."

In that instant the wallet had turned out of the ground. It had a new deep diagonal gash.

The twist in this story is that her husband was the only one with the accurate knowledge. We needed him in our search team because she wrongly assumed "five furrows in" to mean the groove cut in the first run by the fifth disc, whereas using his method of counting, it would be in the fifth pass up and down the field. She laughed at herself later when she realized she had looked in the wrong place for the predicted gully. And, if left to simple logic, I would have been even more lost. I knew nothing at all about harrowing fields.

Within a couple of days, he arrived at our door with a magnificent bouquet of flowers, a true celebration of color. He wanted to know: How had I done that? Now he was quite fascinated.

## The Church

The foregoing success set me out on another eye-opening course and threw me into a massive entanglement with my church. I must preface this account of the reshaping of my understanding of religion with the fact that I grew up in a small town, in a modest home, where Sunday was the Lord's day, virtues were defined by the Bible, and performance of any kind was to be molded by the Protestant work ethic. Our Sunday worship and regular church social gatherings prepared us well to think for ourselves, to set our own demanding standards, and to meet others' principles with open interest.

With this as my childhood foundation, I regarded the church as the school where we learned the highest spiritual laws. It was a most persuasive foundation and, I knew, a major contributing factor behind the gracious lifestyle that had endured, essentially undisturbed, in both my tiny three-hundred-year-old seaside village and my own family history, which goes back more than a thousand years. The Golden Rule encapsulated it precisely and made decision making easy. Perhaps this is the reason that, as a youngster, I had no doubts about the importance of faith as a strengthening force for us. Fairly typically, I asked no profound questions, at least until I left home at age seventeen, when I began to venture outside my secure adolescent world.

Like most twentieth-century churches, ours centered around a Supreme Being—God, in our case. We devotees are taught that we can turn to that invincible Almighty for help in times of need. The teachings profess that through his grace (yes, his), we can experience miraculous healing and protection from suffering. In general, followers learn through religious lessons that the faithful have an ultimate caretaker.

This doctrine has an extraordinary consequence for uncountable numbers of people. It invokes a powerful way of thinking that is not easily changed. Most fascinating to me is the fact that once this position of turning to a divine source is fixed, numbers of followers lose the freedom to convert the belief into the sound rational knowledge that we do have personal control over some matters in our lives. This loss being so established, followers of traditional church dogmas often are less independent than others who do not belong to the organization. This fixed position remains, then, either because the believers cannot convince themselves that there is another way of action, or because that fact of freedom might work, and that could upset the apple cart of a comfortable existence. In the eye of the believer, it is enough to know that the Supreme Being upholds the standard and makes the improvements. In short, the anchoring viewpoint is that all things rest in the hands of the Maker. Life flows on from this thought.

When I began investigating the marvels of intuition, I held a position on the church Board of Deaconesses, sang in the choir, and taught children's Sunday school. My own children were learning Christian rituals and teachings in the church simultaneous with the principles of unembroidered self-sufficiency and independent thinking that my husband and I could offer them in our adventurous lifestyle. We expected that they would choose their own spiritual paths when they reached the age of decision.

Perhaps I shouldn't have been surprised when, after that wallet turned out of the ground, I fell out of favor with the church. Almost overnight, my religious affiliations changed dramatically. It began with my friends' fascination with their own experience. They went to their adult Sunday school and explained how they had recovered their wallet. And that started it. Like a gazelle in the wild, the story leapt over the walls from their church into mine. Once it arrived, I was caught in a struggle I couldn't possibly survive. The news produced a nuclear reaction among some of the members. Within two weeks, the ladies on the board quietly suggested I resign my position and leave the choir. I did so, without an audible whimper, and the next week set my sights on Phase Two.

Were the devout church members courageous in the way they protected their institution? They certainly had the strength of their convictions behind their actions, possibly even were strengthened by them. I know today, as I knew then, that this kind of circling the wagons is not the way of the noble teachers who inspired the world religions. To the last, the great teachers—like Jesus Christ, Muhammad, and the Buddha—were proponents of individuality and self-sufficiency, of inventing new ways and marrying them with the old, of being a living example of the Divine creator. I left that church, for its sake. It was time to explore modern science and ancient history. There was still so much to learn.

## True Teachers

I decided to return to religion through history and discover the simpler nature of faith and religious practices. I couldn't go on without pursuing this contradiction between religious enlightenment and facts of intuition. Did they really conflict? I vowed to dig to the roots to find whether human intuitiveness ever appeared around the great teachers. I wasn't disappointed.

Notable among the great are three real people whom we all know, at least by name. The trio comprises the sons of: a feudal lord in a warrior caste, an impoverished man, and a carpenter. They are, of course, the Buddha, Confucius, and Jesus Christ. We call them great spiritual leaders and know them as men who did outstanding work for rich and poor people alike. Each one is the figure behind a world tradition—two religious, one a philosophy, which some would say became a religion. All three practices have survived at least two hundred centuries. History says that each man taught a new perspective on living that was appropriate for the times.

A couple of points of caution must precede the discussion of these towering figures. First, the scope here is restricted to their intuition. My goal is to highlight these men as consummate teachers, whose intuition not only helped the people they served but also became a component of the exercises they gave their followers. Second, I am well aware that many critics believe that religion and the psi effects, which I bind to intuition, cannot coexist. These people and organizations even declare that a solid barrier separates the two. The implication is that religion is "good"; the psi effects are "bad." I have been reminded countless times, by kindly church people, that Western religion on the whole does not acknowledge psi effects as being normal or as having value. And they aren't the only critics. Numbers of people who have chosen to follow spiritual paths in the Eastern tradition believe likewise that psi effects represent dangerously manipulative dabbling with the supernatural. Rather than attempt to remove this securely established obstruction to open-mindedness, my goal is to demonstrate where psi effects appeared in the presence of these three venerable world teachers.

Although accounts of their lives are a sticky mixture of facts and legend, I think there is enough evidence for our singular purpose of understanding whether the Buddha, Confucius, and Jesus knew how to use their own intuition and if so, how.

Before considering each of the three in succession, let's review what they had in common. First, each led his people to understand how self-sufficiency and wise decisions optimalize any individual life experience. Each also, in some way, helped the poor and downtrodden in their day-to-day existence and made his contemporaries think in new ways. The result of their efforts was that they greatly enriched the human condition around them and improved the social order where they lived. (In all cases, the governments of their countries or provinces were chaotic at best.) Each likewise lived by the principles that he taught. Finally all three have made a considerable impact on human history, because a creed grew out of each man's teachings that affects the lives of billions of people today.

## The Buddha

When people asked the Buddha what kind of person he was, he responded with three words that define his entire message. "I am awake."

Buddhism is the oldest among the three traditions. It has been in existence for more than two thousand five hundred years. Siddhartha Gautama Buddha, born in India in 563 B.C., was to become a teacher. (Note: The rationalist Socrates was born in 470 B.C., about one hundred years later.) The Buddha lived in terrible times. Leaders of states, who were unashamedly corrupt and degenerate, thought nothing of the terrible injustices they dealt the people they ruled. India's religion was steeped in superstition. He couldn't agree with the religious teachings, or with beliefs in the supernatural held by his people; he knew how the dogmas smothered his people's discrimination and dulled their personal judgment.

The Buddha has been described as being the blend of "a cool head and a warm heart." His "cool head" made him one of the greatest rationalists in history; the "warm heart" balanced it, making him exquisitely compassionate. This mix resulted in what we know best about him—that he could neither be drowned in sentimentality nor numbed by indifference. The outcome was that he could act on the extraordinary enlightening insights for which he is remembered and revered by his followers.

This insightfulness—a word synonymous today with *intuition*—seemed to be his great gift. For example, he could learn on first encounter what qualities and actions were genuine in a person or situation and then work with them constructively. In his teaching, which is pragmatic to the core, it is obvious that he understood that people needed to develop this insighting ability in themselves. Evidently, he knew that if they were to make their own way to success, they needed to draw on the same developing sensory system that he had discovered in himself, which would make them as discerning as he. Judging from the descriptions of his teaching principles, I would call this ability their intuition. He taught his followers to develop this capability. One solid cause he could hold up as he spoke was the government's exploitation of his people's freedoms. He knew they should, and could, be free. By his lessons he led them to find wise decisions.

The result, which continues today, is that Buddha's simple teaching about insightfulness empowered individuals to break away gracefully from the paralysis imposed by social and personal systems when they stifled their lives. Although he stood ready when they needed him to help and give guidance by using his own insightfulness, he stressed that once suppression lifted, a person would be free to return to using his or her own mentality and decisions. His guiding principle was a practical one: "Be lamps unto yourselves."

I'm convinced the Buddha was speaking about his intuition when he stated so clearly, "I am awake." "Insight," "awareness," "mindfulness," "discernment," and "perception" are all specific words we use consistently in contemporary society to portray it. The lessons he developed are a form of what he learned when he wandered alone as a young man in search of his life's work. Human beings are born with the ability to perceive life as a matter of continual change, an ongoing event comprising events or chains of events. This insight was the path to a different way of life for his followers, as it had been for him. His message that "one had to be awake to travel through life" demanded developing insightfulness, for by being "awake," humans can lend stability to this complex but interrelated universe.

He taught that the result would be threefold: (1) Any individual who learns through awareness what he or she needs, and acts on it, will be able to stop suffering. (2) It would then be possible to function optimally, because all internal suffering is destroyed. (3) When we all are at our best, inevitably the entire world will be rid of suffering. He emphasized that the outcome could be an ever-changing world in optimum balance and an environment in which all living things would be treated kindly.

I maintain that these results that the Buddha discovered, and effectively lived, come to one's life without being forced when intuition is used with excellence—that we can prove the truth of his vision when we each use our ability normally as we are born to do.

## Confucius

Confucius was born around 550 B.C. in China, thirteen years after the Buddha's birth in India. His great success as a caring man was the way in which he molded an entire society into a great civilization. Most will agree that his personal intuition was more elusive than the Buddha's. Today we might call him "uncanny." As with the Buddha in India, the political lawlessness of the Chinese government officials and aristocrats disturbed Confucius. Life for the peasantry was so wretched that people then were asking the same desperate question we're asking today—nearly 2,500 years later: With leadership like this, how do we protect ourselves from self-destruction?

People today do not necessarily agree on the status of Confucianism itself. Is it an ethic or a religion? To answer this from the historical view, we can see plainly that roots of his teachings reached deep into the soul of China and have nourished its people for nearly twenty-five hundred years. How was this accomplished? For two thousand of those years a class of scholars comprised the ruling elite; they studied and passed on Confucius' guidelines for holding a society together, much the way educators teach their classical subjects in universities today. Thus his teaching was transmitted from the old to the young, generation after generation. Today Confucianism stands as a "tradition."

The religion of the China in which he lived added a transcendental—or supernatural—dimension to his perspective. Although Heaven and Earth were not sharply separated as they would be in the later times of Jesus, there was a soft separation of sorts; Heaven was merely a progression from Earth. Each dimension was referred to not as a "place," per se, but as a dwelling for the people who lived there. In Heaven were the forefathers, the ancestors who had gone ahead of the individuals living on Earth, and who would, inevitably, be joined by those still on Earth. Death was a promotion to a more honorable state. These two realms had a communication system working between them. Individuals contacted Heaven by making sacrifices for favors; the controlling forefathers called back through various forms of "augury," or "omens," which fall into the categories of behavior described by some authorities as psi effects. The Chinese believed that these omens were very effective in catching Earth's attention.

The system worked as follows: Being familiar with China's long history, personages in Heaven were thought to be able to share their knowledge and to give warnings—when needed—of things to come; for their part, the earthlings had a long list of occult occurrences they could mark and count as enlightening communiqués from their dear departed ones. The signals from Heaven varied widely—from weather changes, to the cloud shapes, to whisperings in the night. All in all, it was generally agreed: These exchanges worked so smoothly that the Heaven and Earth community held a delightfully cooperative relationship.

Confucius was born in this political and religious climate. Though he lived in poverty, he seems to have always enjoyed his life, mixing well from the start in the company of plain people and, as time went by, learning he could cross class lines unflinchingly when the situation demanded. On the whole, however, his adult years appear to have been a roller-coaster ride of personal and professional failures.

In his work he met nothing but frustrations, at least in his early efforts, when he yearned to win a public office and show how his theories worked. He traveled for thirteen years from state to state, offering unsolicited advice to entirely uninterested political leaders and nobility. Reading about him during that period, one begins to understand he was generally treated like a troublesome gnat by rulers and commoners alike. Almost unbelievably, he had to wait until he was fifty to be appointed to a position in which he finally could demonstrate his dream formula for a successful society.

His tenacity is admirable even today, for, regardless of how much adversity he faced, he would not rest. He simply continued searching for the avenue that would allow him to pass down his principle that fair dispensation of justice would lead to a society in which crime would be eliminated and the people would prosper. It would be a fair exchange. His message never changed: Respect but do not depend on messages from Heaven; stay focused instead on this world dimension. Improve your leadership. Build a democratic society.

Despite the widespread disdain, a small band of faithful disciples stood by him. They asked questions; he solved them in conversation. In all his teachings, he was addressing the biggest problem facing every individual in the history of humanity: how to get out of the position of helplessness and into one of individual strength.

In sum, Confucius was a very practical man. He wasn't interested in the popular supernatural communication between Heaven and Earth; it was not a route to timely solutions. However, he did think a supreme power existed somewhere in the universe and that he was mandated to teach in order to help spread righteousness. The point of interest for us is that his ethic and solution for a society in turmoil had elements of wisdom that most scholars agree were not logically within his reach. Huston Smith attributes Confucius' answer to the social problems to intuitiveness, saying that he could not have found the particular combination by any way other than the "feel" of what was right for his people. The reason? No one in China had introduced the concept before him.

Why did he learn the information he did? What made him so uncannily resourceful? Was it his pragmatism combined with his desperate concern for a downtrodden society that led him, as an alert person, to discover that his intuitiveness could solve the problem? We know that the system was out of control and needed correction. Did intuition produce the solution that needed a human helping hand? Inspiration usually puts that demand on the inspired one.

His formula for a great society indeed had all the earmarks of a classic Teleos psi effect—sometimes called "inspiration"; in this effect the neatest, simplest, and most accurate solution appears spontaneously, as "pure knowledge." His was a practical solution, and definitely a correction mechanism that took a lifetime to initiate. It empowered him as a young man but didn't burst on the scene until he was in his golden years, and it didn't stop there. He passed it on to the next generation. The outcome was that the life of his people improved dramatically, rising to new peaks of success.

A telling factor from history that supports the view of his inspiration as intuition is that Confucius could neither have been fully aware of what he was doing nor understood why it would be as effective as it was. Unquestionably, he had no way to know what he was doing with the plan which involved dynamics of human behavior unfamiliar to anyone at that time. Only passing time proved his methods correct.

What did he discover? His solution seesaws on a two-part principle of respect for old learning and willingness to explore the new. By touting the "old," he was encouraging his people to follow their rich tradition. However, he realized that this practice could entrap people and squelch freedom of movement; therefore, he added the perfect antidote. This second proposition appears to be the inspired element of Confucianism. He taught that they should *not* conform when a traditional system might diminish an individual's integrity and compassion. "Examine with fresh eyes and pay attention when change renders old ways impractical," he advised. We would paraphrase: Stay on top of things, and be prepared *at all times* to make fresh adjustments if habits and customs won't work. Scientists would simply refer us to the regulatory mechanism, ask us to identify which systems are off, and design a way to adjust them when they cannot function optimally. Here is the same basic instruction as we find in the Buddha's "Keep awake, use insight and help yourself." All are the formula for using intuitive sensitivity as an aid to peak performance.

Confucius' fame came only after his death, when the full power of his teachings began to spread. His exacting prescription worked beautifully for centuries.

I propose that we frequently learn the same facts through intuition as we would by using the Buddha's "insight" and Confucius' "inspiration." Look at the similarities. So many common phrases apply here: We "have a feeling" about something, or "have a sense," and "suddenly know" what to do. When clear-cut facts are incomplete, yet the circumstance demands exact solutions, intuition will always come to the rescue. This was exactly the situation in Confucius' crisis. He found an answer that had never been known in his land. Whether he would have described the way he was inspired as by sense, feeling, or purely knowing, I suggest that this *was* intuition pointing the direction to the new order and that it was probably caused by this very caring man's desire to help a stagnant system.

## Jesus

While the Buddha and Confucius shunned the supernatural, Jesus of Nazareth did not. In fact, this man, who was to become the central figure in Christianity, had specific training to learn to influence natural events. He always used his abilities for people's benefit. A carpenter by trade and comfortable as a member of the working class, he faced all the challenges confronting any Jew two thousand years ago. As it had been with the Buddha and Confucius, the politics of Jesus' times were dreadful. For nearly a century, the Jewish people had been virtual slaves to Rome; they had no freedom to travel from place to place and were taxed mercilessly.

Struggling among themselves to rectify these desperate conditions, they split into four ideological groups. Jesus joined the Pharisees, the group that agreed to work within society to revitalize Judaism. Hebrew tradition of those times held that theirs was a two-part universe. Their god, Yahweh, was a transcendental figure, otherworldly, not a personage anyone would meet in an ordinary experience. For instance, one wouldn't see "Him" physically walking along the main street, or sitting in one of the coffeehouses.

Jesus, as a Jew, would have perceived himself as living in this two-part world. One was Yahweh's invisible dwelling place that the Jews referred to as "Spirit." Spirit was thought of as a vigorous *power*, a vitality that influenced the natural course of events, including those on the earth. The other side of Jesus' universe was the elemental earth—this planet Earth with its inhabitants and all their concerns. Jews were taught that they could know this Spirit through mediators who were the established prophets and seers in the Jewish community. Those who wished to have this role as a go-between could earn it by leaving the community for a period of solitude and fasting—in order to be immersed in the vitality of Spirit. The purpose was for the initiate to take it into himself and become empowered, or "Spirit-filled." This allowed the new mediator to do the same work as Spirit, or in other words to influence natural courses of events. Jesus spent forty days in the wilderness and returned Spirit-filled. He used his empowerment to ease human difficulties, heal disease, exorcise demons, calm storms, and resurrect the dead. It is written that people called him the "wonder-worker" and thronged to him for help.

Three points are made about his mediation: (1) He went about setting the example of doing good by teaching and healing where he could, ministering his miracles quietly—to help the needy. (2) As a man, he lived as he preached, giving of himself so completely that people said they "felt" his love and compassion. (3) By these works and lessons, he knew that he was showing the people wondrous natural changes that they had never known were possible. He also knew that their behavior would be altered as a result of this new learning. The lessons were about equal rights in life for every individual, the power of love, and being compassionate.

The works, of course, were his miracles. You will discover that these are examples of intuition. As with the Buddha and Confucius, Jesus Christ's life and abilities became a model of behavior available to all human beings.

In discussing Jesus and intuition, we ask first: Who was this caring man? Among the Twelve Apostles, his disciples, Jesus was a human being. He was born to earth. He struggled. He suffered. He knew times of happiness. He died and was buried. He worked and taught from the mind and body of a man. Putting the information all together, Jesus' selfless love, which people felt, and his extraordinary powers to visibly influence nature might have set him apart as unique for all these centuries, but first of all, he was a man made of flesh.

Next we ask: Were the so-called wonderworks of Jesus a product of his intuition? Turning to examples in the world today, I would say yes. Why? Because thousands of individuals have demonstrated mystifying "talents" that fall into the categories of psi effects—including changing the future and influencing the courses of events—many of which are similar to those that we are taught the Spirit-filled Christ was empowered to effect. Further, whether we like it or not, at least some of the psi effects we experience duplicate his works—the healing and the power of his "love" to communicate. We hear examples of people healing spontaneously. Surely our Telepathy is a mystifying—but real—form of interpersonal communication, as is the Teleos effect of interacting with the future.

Finally, the consistency continues: Everyone I have met who has used intuition naturally paints a picture of wondrous experiences that sometimes challenge the way that we think we experience our physical world. They point out that psi effects introduce movements, abilities, and mental experiences that definitely contradict what we have been taught to expect, yet the accounts in these pages confirm that more than visual and auditory effects issue from our senses and rational minds. Many would agree that when they follow through the psi effects, the results often do seem like miracles!

Here we have come full circle. I described earlier the reactions of people to the information I intuited when doing "readings." "Extraordinary," they said. And I heard the word "miracle" on more than one occasion. My reply is the same now as it was then. This behavior is not a miracle.

Have we come to a historical crossroads? Is our worldview about to change? Are these words and works of the greatest teachers ever known examples of simple human rather than supernatural abilities? Were these men, as teachers, introducing humankind to its nascent intuition? I am convinced that the answer to all these questions is yes. Jesus Christ and others who taught similar lessons and demonstrated like abilities appear to have been early intuitionists among us who could discuss and demonstrate their discoveries just as their historical contemporaries, the Hellenistic rationalists, were bringing the power of reason to light.

The issue of miracles presents us with many contradictions, beginning with the definition itself. One dictionary defines it as an extraordinary event revealing divine intervention in human affairs; another, as "an extremely unusual event, thing, or accomplishment." This second description is more along the lines of scientific officialdom in that it acknowledges unusual events.

It is widely recognized that nature is unpredictable. Pioneers in physics have learned this by probing the cosmic microprocesses—the subatomic and supergalactic dimensions of the universe. To access them requires exquisite sophisticated instruments and the finest scientific thinkers our social systems have produced. This is the province of physicists.

Science is an exclusive club. For decades the party line has been that we do not have the power to zoom across the impassable borders and into that dimension-of-the-infinitesimal without the credentials and supplies just mentioned. Conventional wisdom holds that no one can witness its dynamic *without* those fancy, extremely expensive devices and gadgets; our human sensory limitations deny us access.

In short, there is a line in the natural order beyond which no mere mortal could venture alone. As such, the world of miracles was inaccessible; for centuries it has been cordoned off from our concept of "normal" behavior. Note that the biologist is as determined as the physicist about the cellular world—that is, it is likewise impenetrable by anything but technology. It is worth mentioning that these scientific views have been shifting gradually since the late sixties.

This rule of impossible is not limited to the ivory towers and church sanctuaries. In our contemporary society, regardless of our scientific or religious persuasion, the psi effects are generally relegated to territory outside our human potential. To gain entrance to the secret universe, the rule states, requires extraordinary powers by almost anyone's standard. Ordinary people simply cannot get there from here.

Upon asking authorities in the various camps just which individuals might be the exceptions, we hear several answers. "The great teachers, of course. They can perform miracles." "Mystic practitioners of Eastern traditions. They might need years of practice, but, yes, they can do wondrous things." But, your average man or woman on the street? Do they think that any of the rest of us might be a wonder-worker? Here the authorities blanch, because this possibility simply is too much to countenance.

If we pursue this final decree, asking why the ability is so limited, the answer is that we have much to learn. This is the province of those who have great wisdom. If the secrets are handed out wholesale, there is no telling how much havoc would follow. Humankind, then, has a long way to go before the microworld of miracles opens to the huddled masses even if they are yearning to be free.

My reply to this conclusion is: Preposterous! According to the example of Jesus, the man, these wonders represent acts of a caring person who learns to be a mediator. It is said in church lessons that Christ came to teach that he was the son of God, that we all are children of God, and that makes us brothers and sisters.

I would add that it also makes us candidates for being wonder-workers.

## Lessons from the Past Will Lead Us

Here we have the examples of three people who walked the earth. True, they stand tall among the most renowned of human beings in the history of civilization. But, when we see the full picture of their lives against the backdrop of their familial, social, political, and religious worlds, they are very much like us—people living in both town and country who are looking for solutions to human concerns and a way to mend broken systems.

The actual story of their intuition is more complex. They won their exceptional positions as teachers because they were ahead of the pack in recognizing this extraordinary internal sensitivity. If we look at their work as teaching about intuitive sensitivity, we can see evidence that these men became highly effective teachers of a human ability that was so unknown at the time that they had to learn how to use it themselves. They had to figure out how to teach it, how to guide its fate. Looking back from here, we cannot deny that they were impressive!

How much of their achievement can we realistically attribute to their human intuition? I would say that we should examine their work, looking for the practical acts they demonstrated that changed the daily lives of people around them. Look for what empowered them and what the empowerment led them to do. In other words, ask how they learned as they did. There we will find it. We can see intuition in the Buddha's "lamp" that produced his insight; it empowered him. And it is there in Confucius' inspired concept. Christ's ability is very visible. It enabled him to help people, and by so doing, he taught that he was demonstrating what they, too, could do.

How could these very human men be endowed with abilities that we have been taught all our lives are outside the range of normal human senses, intellectual faculties, and skills? Their examples completely contradict this separation. It's well known that all were born as human beings, not transcendent gods or saints, and like the rest of us they used the earth's resources to keep alive as well as to enjoy themselves. They ate food, drank water, sang, and had families and friends.

Were they the front-runners, the embodiment of this developing intuitive sensory system? Were they demonstrating that using intuition is something all humans do spontaneously at first and with training do better later? Or were these three men abnormal because they were exceptional, as some seem to suggest? The intrigue is that their abilities are time-honored visible examples of behavior we seem to be observing in ourselves today. Might they be the pioneers who blazed the trail, the living models for our own intuition?

I've described people in these pages who have demonstrated comparable behavior: predictions ($\psi$-1, 2), discovery ($\psi$-11), telepathy ($\psi$-5), clairsentience ($\psi$-15), with more to come. Should we be astonished that we can find sprawled through the days of our lives the very same kind of mental ability to know and act that we read about in the works of three men who lived two thousand years ago? My answer is that we should be impressed with the correlation. Perhaps if we can understand that we're seeing this same behavior in ourselves, we will be able to look at the great teachers' accomplishments as instructive for us. Not stopping there, if everyone will learn from their examples, we might be awakening just in time to help this world survive.

## The Question of Teaching

Now let's return to 1981, Phase Two commencement day. I had finally arrived at my goal of teaching. The subject would be intuition. I would build a bridge to this ability, legitimize it hopefully, and save others from the confusion of not understanding the very thing that had so confused me.

Recognizing the uniqueness of the task, I knew I needed an ordinary but powerful method, one that I could make available to everyone so that people could encounter and question psi effects in themselves. I wanted them to know what they were experiencing in their heads, that the orderly array of effects is intuition's equivalent to vision's spectrum of colors—red, orange, yellow, green, blue, and violet. It would be important for them to experiment, as I had, and not to be afraid of making mistakes. With training they would understand what I finally figured out— that they were learning facts, and that to have intuition's facts would give them freedom.

By now I had read Dr. Claude Bernard's comments about how freedom to move comes from cellular stability and had learned about the regulatory mechanism. I'd connected the concept of stability with intuition. I hypothesized that by using intuitiveness intelligently, we could fine-tune every personal interaction in ways we never knew possible. I had no doubt that our natural intuitive ability could bring us insight into our talents and play a major role not only in understanding our actions but also in fine-tuning our interactions. Three chief benefits would result:

1. We'd enhance our personal freedom to reach our full potential individually.

2. We would help bring home the same result for the community of humankind.

3. We would become genuine regulatory mechanisms in the bigger picture, helping to keep the entire natural order—nature's interactive life systems—stable and operating optimally.

I wanted to present all of this to the public. But how would I teach? My best clues for teaching methods were in how I operated intuitively myself. People should learn how to use the psi effects as I had—practically, in daily life, with no hocus-pocus, as Officer Jamison had implied. I could also work without concern about anyone's abusing the ability. Students wouldn't have any reason to cheat—which is a common complaint from skeptics of paranormal phenomena. What would be the point in deception? My teaching would be aimed at the individual, introducing a human ability to reach for the heights. There would be no concern about abusing it. Deception defeats intuition's true purpose of self-sufficiency.

In the final analysis, I decided to design everything around the central idea that the psi effects' ability to empower people in making choices would inevitably lead them to their full potential. The greater second and third outcomes would follow naturally.

Thinking through my dream job was one thing, but carrying all this out was another. A few months of searching proved to my satisfaction that no institution of formal education would hear of scheduling such a topic for a regular class. I would have to invent the job for myself. I took my cue from the fine tradition of early educators. Countless individuals, including the Greek Sophists and the philosopher Socrates, spent the greater part of their lives as itinerant teachers. I decided I could do no better than to follow their lead.

CHAPTER 6

# Fact-Finding

*The brakes are going to fail.*

(ψ-19) THE WORDS CAME to me just before I started down the driveway. I turned off the engine immediately and leaned back in the seat.

"The brakes? Going to fail?"

It was 1972, months before that ESP class. I might have been upset if I hadn't had a personal history of spontaneous psi effects. Naturally I disliked the bad news. Who wouldn't? It was profoundly disturbing—about as pleasant as walking in tight shoes. What's more, it didn't help much. I would have preferred a few solid specifics. For example: When would they fail? Where?

But I'd learned not to argue with my intuition. I was certain that its information was meant for me. Even though there was absolutely no physical indication that the brakes were a concern, I could rely on the "impression." It would be accurate. I also had discovered through the years that *I* would have to figure out what to do next—make a plan.

Time wasn't on my side that day. In twenty minutes my son and three of his high-spirited little pals expected me to be at the gate of their nursery school to take them home. With such precious cargo, I could ill afford any sort of automobile miseries, least of all something so serious as brake failure. Sitting at the wheel, with no visible evidence of the predicted problem, I was faced with a difficult dilemma: Should I find an alternate driver right away or test the brakes and set out for the school if they worked?

Although the decision wasn't easy, I chose the latter. One missing detail controlled that choice: I had not intuited *when* the brakes would fail. Today? Next week? Without the time factor as a definite guideline, I would follow my scheduled plan. However, I would drive on red alert just in case the brakes were to fail on this errand.

I re-started the engine and backed out of the garage toward the empty street, deliberately pressing the brakes hard at the end of the driveway. The car stopped without hesitation. Next I pulled up the emergency brake; it was as tight as ever. Two more tests convinced me that the system was fully operational and I could get on my way. The next decision was which route to take.

Normally, I drove the three miles to the school by back streets. This was longer than the freeway, but I usually took the extra minutes simply to enjoy some lovely scenery. On that day, however, I cared only about potential hazards. I began the count: at least five stop signs, a wide railroad crossing, and it was noon. Although I usually timed myself to be at the tracks five minutes after the train departed, sometimes it was off schedule. Then traffic piled up. There was the decisive risk. All things considered, this definitely was no route for an automobile that might lose its brake power at any minute.

The freeway was my alternative. I could travel in the slow lane and have an option of moving onto the repair strip if necessary. The exit was an uphill grade. If the brakes failed for the light at the top, the car would already have decelerated naturally. I then would be on the straight, flat main street, with only three short blocks more to the school. I settled on this as the safest route—under the circumstances. Any friend watching would have thought the whole planning exercise absurd, because we always kept our car in fine condition. However, criticism wouldn't have mattered, because no one could have influenced me that day. I was absolutely sure that this "impression" would prove to be as factual as all the others.

Satisfied that I could take the risk safely, I set my concentration on high and all of my other senses on alert, and drove away. Light traffic allowed me to glide smoothly up the freeway exit ramp. I braked there to a full stop and turned right onto the two-lane main street. Signal lights marking each city block were in sight. Since they were coordinated to favor main-street traffic flow, I knew that if I paced myself, it would be possible to catch all three on green and go without stopping until I arrived at the school.

Plans were working splendidly until a car cut in front of mine without signaling. This forced me to slow down and lose my timing advantage. The driver, on the other hand, was able to pick up just enough speed to slip through the last wink of the green signal, leaving me face-to-face with the unwelcome yellow. I automatically stepped on the brake. Without a hint of resistance, the pedal went straight to the floor—and popped back abruptly. I pushed again. Nothing. The car continued moving slowly toward the intersection and now a blazing red light. Traffic already was entering from the side street. Ah, but there was the emergency brake. I grabbed it and pulled hard. Although it seemed impossible, I felt the lever come back as easily as a knife cuts through soft butter. All the while, the car just kept rolling—a lump of merciless steel on the loose. I remember wincing. This was the failure! It really was happening!

The obvious question grabbed my thoughts: *How* could the whole brake system have shut down completely in one short city block? But of course this was not the moment to reflect on mindless automobiles. I took one more critical instant to check myself. How well was my head working? It didn't surprise me that I was very calm and free to think—probably because I had had the forewarning, put myself on alert, and preplanned every step carefully, except for this—the real and actual failure.

Failure! Full reality struck hard. Self-interest immediately gave way to common sense. I well remember wondering: What will help me here? With two cars crossing directly in front of me, and my runaway car running me, I was in trouble. I scanned the scene for anything that could stop the unstoppable . . . and found it. The center strip to my left was about ten inches tall and made of wonderfully intractable cement. *That* would be a perfect brake! Glad beyond words that I was moving snaillike at less than ten miles an hour, I checked traffic behind me for what seemed like the hundredth time, angled across the open center lane toward the curbing, and rolled straight into it. The front wheels hit. The lump jolted to a halt. I congratulated myself out loud: "What a finish!"

Safe at last, I sat back in the seat, trying to absorb the strange events, and—I soon noticed—creating a sizable traffic jam. I realized later that during those few quiet moments, I was lost in pure fascination that the "impression" had been validated. Those brakes *did* fail, just as it had indicated they would.

And what a good thing the premonition prepared me! So many minute factors were involved that might otherwise have caught me off guard. Had I driven the scenic route, for example, or been going faster, no question that I definitely couldn't have been so calm or, most important of all, so alert. Obviously, I can't say with certainty that I avoided an accident, but, knowing intuition as I do, my judgment is that a mishap was within the realm of possibility; hence the precognition.

## What Is Behind Intuitive Sensitivity?

What happened that day in the car? The Teleos psi effect indicated that I was detecting an interaction already in process. In some way it involved my brakes. An intuitible change in the various components of the brakes caused me to learn about a correctable event that either might, or inevitably was going to, occur at a time in my future—most likely that day. In the event that it did happen, I would have to control the threatening situation by stopping the car safely and avoiding the traffic. I should make plans to control the situation when, and if, it became a true experience. But, everyone asks, how can we possibly know such things?

Although dozens of hypotheses have been advanced to explain the psi effects, I would like to add mine. I'll begin by posing three questions:

1. What natural phenomenon is affecting our bodies when we're intuitive?

2. What does it do to us?

3. What sets off the process?

To answer these three questions requires that we question the nature of a fundamental physical phenomenon in the environment. My calculations reveal that the human intuitive system supplies the world with an extraordinary amount of beneficial information. You can make the logical extension for yourself: If a single psi effect can produce a complete instruction for instantaneous action that prevents one serious automobile accident ($\psi$-10), how many other accidents might be averted? In like manner, food poisoning: How many cases would the intuitive process prevent? How many lost briefcases, or children? Deaths in terrorist attacks? The list of possible interventions is endless. Our intuitive system is specialized to release a factual report about dynamic situations completely concealed in future time, as with the young student intuiting the bomb ($\psi$-2); in time past, as happened in finding the downed plane ($\psi$-11); and in here-and-now conditions like Operation Toothbrush ($\psi$-16).

To find the crucial explanation of the trigger, let's start with the physical energy powering the experiences. As described earlier, our ability to detect psi data in our brains makes this intuition a potential sensory system. This implies that a system of physical receptor neurons exists in our bodies, to convey messages from the environment. The fact that we perceive their information suggests that these psi effects are *not* mere figments of our imagination or early warning signs that we're psychologically imbalanced. Quite the opposite. We are being called on to restore stability to a condition. Since we can do this with the data derived of psi effects, this gives us the right to test what great forces working in the universe control this internal message system. That this information is traveling harmlessly through the body implies that the phenomenon, whatever it is, must be compatible with us. Were it not, we, as organisms, would be designed to reject it, the same as we ward off all foreign materials, poisoned food, and toxic gases.

Therefore, we are looking for an invisible phenomenon that we welcome. What are we accepting? I say we are witnessing interactions between some of nature's fundamental particles moving around in the universe; these are often called "entities" by physicists. These particles, and movements of them, are a source of our communications about interactions in the ethers. Why do I say this? Let's compare these unknown entities with others that we know influence our different senses, and then focus on one in particular.

Scientists have already determined which environmental phenomena influence our senses of vision, audition, smell, taste. Some are physical, others chemical. Vision and audition, for example, are sensitive to electromagnetism, which is a fundamental physical force in nature. We are able to smell, they say, because we are receptive to chemicals, which are traveling as free molecules in the air. Think of the aromatic changes in a room when your friend presents you with a fragrant rose. Without knowing that molecules are exciting the nerves in your nose, you simply enjoy that fragrance. Likewise, we let unpleasant smells stop us from eating tainted food, which we might otherwise enjoy.

Why don't we demand explanations from the halls of science each time an odor appears? Because for most people the scientific basis is irrelevant. Smelling is a familiar experience within us. We know what to do with essences. In childhood we were taught to pay attention to these things, and how to associate this with that. That smell is from the kitchen, the sea, or grandmother's perfume, we were told. Somewhere along the way, we learned that substances and forces have an endless variety of influences over our systems, and we would respond according to whether they are attractive or repulsive. Sensing, feeling, and learning were all part of life.

During those childhood years, we gain control over our lives on planet earth, solving the mystery of being in bodies with all those pure impressions running through them. Now we smile at the thought of being confused by any of the signals, but in infancy, when everything was new, we drank in the life, extracting information like little sponges from the chaos of sensations that bombard an organism's receptors.

Currently nearly the entire world population is confused by signals emanating from the intuitive realm, for, in it, aren't we all the equivalent of youngsters? We don't understand. I predict, however, that before the twenty-first century is over, people worldwide will be responding appropriately to their telepathic, teleosic, and other intuitive experiences.

## Vision, and Why We "See"

My explanation for intuition parallels the process of human vision. The science community has explained why we are visually sensitive to light, which is a fundamental natural phenomenon we know as electromagnetism. This is a physical force that is responsible for the interactions and for the emission and absorption of phenomena called photons. These photons, components of light, penetrate tiny sensory cells, or neurons, called photoreceptors on the retina at the back of our eyes. When a photon and sensor interact, a succession of events is set in motion within the brain that results in our seeing. The internal transmission of light information is completed in the cortex of our brains, as visual effects. Hence we are enabled to detect impressions of shapes, colors, and perspectives of objects in the world.

Now let us put this idea of a fundamental force, like electromagnetism, in the context of intuition. Imagine that intuition's sensors are also tuned to receive their own physical form of energy and that, following nature's pattern, there are receptive cells for several different conditions, such as human passions, earth changes, automobile parts. Further, think of all those sensors being wired to send signals to the brain centers, where their interactions with that natural force are comprehensible to us through the psi effects. In other words, intuition is responding to and absorbing a particular wave of electromagnetism as do our eyes, but we are intuitively sensitive to a different range of its emissions.

When intuition's cells take in their compatible ones, signals are sent to the brain for our detection in psi effects. Having a limited compatibility means the intuitive sensors respond not to *every* electromagnetic wave in space but rather only to the *appropriate* ones. For example, intuition cannot go wild when you are exposed to yellow light; it isn't sensitive to light's photons. Consequently, it won't pick them up, any more than pain receptors in your hand would be affected by your stepping on a tack. (In that case, the pain receptors in the skin on your foot would howl in dismay.) My suggestion is that when we isolate the systems' pathways we can anticipate finding the same kind of specialized reception of a force in each intuitive sensory neuron as we do in vision's sensors.

One of my favorite characters in United States history is the eccentric genius and statesman Benjamin Franklin. His experiment with electricity provides us a metaphor for discovering intuition. He was in search of a way for humankind to protect itself against lightning, the "cosmic scourge," as he called it. His hypothesis was that lightning and thunder are electrical phenomena, that a cloud is an electrified body, and that the lightning is basically an electrical release from the cloud. If it *were* such a discharge, and he could direct that electrical emission by using a metal rod and a wire to take it to the ground, he would know he had the secret for protection from this scourge. Using his now-famous kite of cedar wood and a silk handkerchief, he reached into the thunderclouds charged with electricity. His intention was to prove the value of the Franklin rods, or lightning rods, he had designed. He succeeded by draining the clouds' electric discharge, usually abbreviated to "charge," into a jar partially coated with metal—called a Leyden jar—where an "electric fire" occurred. With this, his evidence was in. The clouds' charge could be controlled and channeled by a metal wire.

We can use this experiment as a helpful analogy to "collecting" the force from intuitible phenomena. While intuition's driving force certainly is not collected in, and discharged from, thunderheads, I am convinced that we are intuitively influenced directly from the atmosphere, where the intuitible force moves uncontrolled until we, the equivalent of kites, conduct the phenomenon to our nervous systems. The body's intuitive system will be found to be the lightning rod, or Leyden jar, drawing the phenomenon, conducting it along our intuition's neural pathways, and finally, organizing it well enough to report its entry with psi effects—the equivalent of Franklin's "electric fire." It is my expectation that intuition will be shown to be associated with electromagnetic emissions.

## What Does Our Intuitive Connection Accomplish?

Knowing that the perception of sensory effects is a normal state of affairs in the nervous system should now help you accommodate the different kinds of information that you will discover you are experiencing intuitively.

As stated earlier, Telepathy effects report *current* human mental states anywhere in space, while Teleos reveals the normal *movements* of objects and interactions that have been set in motion in space. Most people don't have much trouble understanding that we telepathically intuit events in physical space. In fact, the many reports of telepathic encounters that ordinary people relay draw very few oohs and aahs, and almost no rebukes.

Somehow, person-to-person communication via Telepathy goes down like a spoonful of sugar. In contrast we discover a unique dilemma when we introduce the theme of "time," as revealed in the Teleos effects. The difficulty arises when we intuit facts along a continuum of past through present to future time. Then we broil all the circuits of credibility. How many times I've heard: "How can you know what happened in the past?" (Downed Plane—$\psi$-11), and "Who do you think you are, predicting the future?" (No Brakes—$\psi$-19).

To put this into perspective consider more familiar sensory experiences of registering events in motion. Think of watching a car travel along a city street. It comes into view at a distance, approaches, passes in front of you, travels one more block, and disappears around a corner. You could report your perception of the entire sequence as one incident—"A car is traveling along the boulevard"—but couldn't you also describe it in segments? You might open with "I see a car coming" and then estimate its distance from you: "It's about fifty feet away." Possibly you would anticipate: "It will pass us in less than a minute." Once it disappears you might account for what happened "The car stopped at the intersection, proceeded slowly, and was gone."

These statements have described a current event, predicted a future one, and reported the past. Nobody would cry out that it's impossible to know these details because our understanding of "the way things are" allows such experiences. But, while the idea of seeing objects in motion is not subject to controversy, the phenomenon of intuiting movement is—but only because its story has not been written.

As important a specialty as it is, we have to allow that intuition supplies information in present time and both directions of time away from the present. You have read accounts here about interactions that have been set in motion—an automobile driving along a road ($\psi$-10), a plane that traveled ($\psi$-11). Thus, it should seem perfectly reasonable that, since this is a sensory system, we are going to experience the movement of objects in time.

In this vein, predicting incidents with intuition is as much a part of its normal reporting job as identifying colors, size, and shape of objects is the province of the human visual system. What's more, prediction is only one of the frames of our intuitive time-telling; among the three Teleos psi effects, it's the specialized function we call precognition (the other two are retrocognition and direct cognition). Precognition effects report the future, as we know it in our clock and calendar time; retrocognition specializes in reports of time past.

So be it. The future can be accurately described intuitively, and that is a fact we cannot deny. Like it or not, Teleos psi effects demand that we get used to this idea of observing sequences of events.

## How Do We Identify the Force Within Us?

The No Brakes incident was only a tiny step toward my understanding the significant role intuition plays in our everyday problem-solving. My experience that day taught me that we can use our intuitive power intelligently by mixing its facts with clear reasoning to plan the future, just as I did. And, in due time, when I had learned more about the psi effects, I understood that our intuitive power works spontaneously, without abating. While that day was only the prelude to a lifetime of learning, it certainly capped off years of innocence.

The first small cracks in my naïveté developed that morning while I stood dumbly between the mechanic and my husband, who tried every way they could to prove why, in their automotive logic, those brakes couldn't have done what I reported. They were sure of their conclusion, they said, because the entire system performed flawlessly within twenty minutes of the "so-called failure," as they classified it.

More disturbing than the final deduction was their unshakable confidence; it made me wonder whether I had crazily imagined the entire sequence of events. But, as day turned into evening, I came to a firm decision: I was neither wrong nor losing my mind. That whole inexplicable incident *had* happened. And, oh, how I laughed when I realized that, in all the time we stood there discussing our different viewpoints, neither of those men asked why I went to the trouble of crossing a lane and driving directly into the center strip where they found me—just to stop for an ordinary traffic light.

I'm confident now that I understand why I learned about the brake failure that day, but in 1973, when it happened, I couldn't have ventured a guess. I'd never questioned the familiar "rushes of information" in my entire life. Innocent acceptance notwithstanding, experience slowly taught me that these occurrences had three consistent features: they *spontaneously* revealed *facts* that always were *related to the situation*.

## Public Criticism

These three characteristics might be reliable for me, but according to the views of the public at large, I must be dreaming.

On that long-ago morning, intuition's news transmitted through a strong "impression." It was not an Instruction psi effect such as illustrated in the "Move to the left" account in Chapter 2 but, instead, related to future time and presented only one piece of information. These two characteristics signaled that this was what people call precognition.

As was this, *any Teleos report is basically an informational announcement*, which can be likened to a news headline. It typically conveys one relevant item, such as "Interest rate to be raised," or "Winter storms freeze Europe." My particular breaking news— "The brakes are going to fail"—was just as clipped and straight to the point. But, as stated earlier, it didn't give much of a lead.

Two consistently troubling features undermine many people's confidence that intuition is worth developing at all. The first is the appearance of the information. While I describe it as spontaneous, the accusations are that it wanders in from nowhere like a stray dog, and that it's easily mistaken for dozens of other normal mental states, such as thought, memory, hope, and fear. How does anyone know the difference? This is a justifiable concern. The second is the ambiguity of the information. My experience has been that we intuitively learn relevant facts, but critics reject that as well, asking how anyone can be sure that such meager details are meaningful at all. Appearing as they do, without any way to prove them, their information is described as ambiguous at best, if not completely nonsensical. Who is to say they are applicable "facts"?

Again, the serious analysts have their points. If we are going to learn to use this intuitive sensory system effectively, we need to know where to draw the line between intuition and other mental activity. Likewise the information. Who is willing to act on such skimpy details? Let's get the proof first! Look at the account in hand: "The brakes are going to fail." What is anyone supposed to do with such a terrifying snippet? I ask you: What kind of guidance is that?

The critics are thus correct to question this "impression" of the brakes. It is a classic example of both public charges. The effect did drop in unannounced; that certainly would make it seem to have broken loose spontaneously from some unreliable subcontinent in my mental world. To add to the confusion, it contradicted the facts of my life, because our car was always well maintained. Clear logic would have said what that mechanic declared: "Nonsense, nothing could possibly be wrong." Regarding the second criticism of having a fact with no way to prove it: This is true. I had absolutely nothing to support it. This was an unknown, a Factor "U." That information could be known only by intuition; no other sensory system could have confirmed it at the time I intuited it. Pitifully, nothing at all existed to back it up and support my decision when I needed to make it. The actuality is that I had to risk driving that car and learn whether it was true—a trial by fire!

In responding to these criticisms, I am fortunate to have the advantage of consistent previous experiences as my teachers. With respect to the first concern about interference from other mental states: The strength of numerous other encounters with psi effects—many equally frightful—helped prevent me from tossing out the warning as a false notion or meaningless mental noise. And with respect to the charge of lack of validation, although completely unable to prove it at the time, I could never have thought the impression would be wrong. That simply would not have crossed my mind. I cannot emphasize enough that as you sift out the psi effects in your experiences, this confusion about their unique functions will dissolve, as mine did. They are new and unfamiliar only for this time in our history during which intuition is coming into the light of our common experiences. This beginner stage will pass. The boundaries of the various mental states— memory, thinking, anxiety—will eventually draw themselves.

The second complaint of a fact without proof is a serious concern with a simple solution.

The detail in any psi effect is always true, whether or not your evidence supports it. This is because it is information received from a sensor, and sensors never lie. This applies to any healthy sensory system. *Like all the others, intuition reveals only facts about influences on our present and future moves.* We all need to bear in mind that "a rose by any other name is still a rose."

These claims might seem bold now, but as intuition takes on dimension and purpose, you will see that it already is the keystone of a multitude of your daily decisions and moves. You likely have spontaneously experienced intuition many times, probably without realizing it. For instance, how do you make your choices? By your "gut"? From some vague "instinct"? An "urge," or "voices within"? Are your choices ever influenced by a strong "sense" of direction, or distinct "feelings" that "tell" you what to do, or plain "knowledge"? Have you had a "good feeling" about the outcome of a chance you were taking, or perhaps felt "absolutely sure" that something has happened? Have you ever just "known" what to do and done it, regardless of public opinion? Were you right? Was your accuracy disturbing?

If you can answer yes to any of these, then you have been intuitive. You learned facts in every case. These are examples of intuition's Law of Information in progress, as we discussed in Chapter 4. Your brain was issuing genuine information in those incidents, all of which are signs of psi effects.

That leads us to stage two, the Law of Action. Reflect back on those incidents. Did you pay attention and make a decision with the facts? Did you follow through? To confirm that the information was true, can you say now that the effects were appropriate? Were the moves you made ultimately successful? When you can say yes to all of these, you'll have made some progress toward identifying the force of intuition within you.

## The "Spontaneous" Argument: Facts Flow Freely

Now you know the way information comes from "Intuition Central" and that its purpose is to get your attention. As you begin to work with these psi effects, think of them the same way you think of the sensory reports coming in from "Vision Central"—

to release facts about what your eyes are receiving—and from "Audio Central" which delivers real sound effects. The next account highlights how naturally the effects slip into daily life.

The subject of the account, my grandmother, is an astonishing example of a person who coasted with her intuition. She used it constantly and without pretense, and everyone agrees she was always on the mark. During our childhood years, she certainly kept us all in line with it. The incident that follows is one of the most moving examples I have ever heard of human intuitiveness.

($\psi$-20) In the summer of 1923, my mother's eighteen-year-old brother was camping with friends at their favorite swimming hole in an abandoned rock quarry miles from their city homes. The day after they had left for their adventure, Grandmother and my own mother, who was then fifteen years old, were chatting on the sunporch early that morning. My mother says that Grandmother abruptly stopped talking and simply seemed shocked. Her next words to my mother were: "Something has happened to Miles."

She didn't attempt to track down any more details. Whatever Grandmother "knew" was enough to get her moving. She immediately summoned the other children from their activities and telegraphed my grandfather, who was doing business in a town about fifty miles away. Her instruction to each was crystal clear: "Something has happened to Miles. Come home immediately. We must be together."

By afternoon, the four children and Grandfather were gathered when tragic news arrived. His friends came to the house to tell the family that Miles had drowned in the quarry that morning.

Who could deny that Grandmother intuitively "knew the unknowable" that day? Typical of her approach, she didn't struggle with understanding the meaning—and what a blessing it was. It gave her the advantage we all would want in a time of unfathomable grief. Her intuition offered her a better vantage point on the tragedy, and she could turn it to everyone's advantage. By gathering the family around, she managed to soften the pain of loss by providing the richness and strength of a circle, thereby averting the austere isolation that often accompanies a family's learning of a death one member at a time. What a testimony to the value of the ability. One spontaneous insight, only five words, benefited an entire family, probably for a lifetime.

For many people the greatest mental tumult imaginable happens when shocking news stuns us, as theirs did. It's like a cyclone's force whipping through the loving heart and thinking brain. Rather than buttressing our distress with calm, we're generally faced with the immediate demand for organizing a next step, such as gathering the family members and making arrangements for services. This demand almost invariably competes with the desperate need to stop and regroup, for the conflict can be paralyzing, especially in times of grief. While Grandmother's seems to be an ideal example of the intuitive process flowing freely, it also demonstrates that intuition essentially has a heart. When we have to learn about an event that will send our passions off the scale, our intuition sends in an advance team, to give us enough facts to prepare.

## The Bad with the Good

Many times people have told me that they don't want to be intuitive—because, they say, they aren't interested in learning all the "bad" things. But I reply that we do benefit from knowing in advance when matters of the heart are involved. Those moments and hours when passions command are naturally profound, life-shaping milestones. Falling in anguish. Falling in love. Discovering the all-consuming field of interest that will capture the intellect and set it to wondering for life. For good or for ill, these instances are meant for the heart, not the head. They are inspired times, private and personal.

In these moments when life is going to be swept by an overwhelming effect and throw us "out of our mind," shouldn't we be grateful that we are intuitively prepared for the blast? Think about my grandmother's actions that helped the whole family. Her early notice made time for doing the "sensible" things while her thoughts were still fluid. That swift summons she issued could only have forged closer ties among them that day, settling quiet strength in the place of dull nothingness.

Of course, it was long after Miles's death that my sister and I personally encountered Grandmother's intuitive prowess. When we were young, she told us herself about the old wives' meaning of her well-defined widow's peak, which promises the gift of prognostication to those born with the feature. In a short time we were true believers, learning the hard way just how much she could intuit.

($\psi$-21) That lady seemed to turn up everywhere. She would catch us whenever we fibbed and managed to intercept us, without fail, each time we were heading, on tiptoe, toward the kitchen pantry—and the always tempting cookie jar. According to her, those most unwelcome meetings in the hallway were only a "coincidence." We doubted it but had no other explanation. Young though we were, we understood only that when our grandmother was in charge, neither of us could ever get away with a thing; to our constant amazement, she would be in on our secrets the instant we became rascals.

## Intuition Is Natural

You might find it hard to believe that intuition's driving force could be a fundamental natural phenomenon like the other physical senses that we constantly use intentionally, and that we need only learn to recognize its effects when they enter our heads. The difference, of course, is that we learned to use our other primary senses in infancy; now they are old friends and effortless to employ.

Intuiting information is no more difficult in its way, except that we are in a jumble. To learn as well from it as my grandmother did, we need only repeat what we did to learn about those effects associated with our other highest senses. It will always be spontaneous, hence learning will always be a matter of recognizing the psi effects and making the moves.

Therefore, as you begin to refine your own intuitive sense, the secret is to remember that the fine art of developing it demands that you treat it as normal. When its effects occur, remember that they have all the earmarks of a normal sense. We say so in the way we speak about it: "I sensed it was true." "I have a feeling." "Something happened in me, and I knew it was so."

We need to give the effects their proper place, by understanding how to "grasp" them. We must teach ourselves to base our decisions on them—then we can use them properly to accomplish anything we'd like. Don't complicate it. Just keep the spontaneous learning process simple. Follow the three steps.

▲ Identify the effect.

▲ Make the decision.

▲ Follow through.

## Constant Orientation

So far, this chapter has given you an overview of how the intuitive system interacts with forces of nature that deliver information that we use to guide our behavior. The remainder focuses on what our intuition is doing.

In general, it is constantly orienting us, or spontaneously moving us to the best position.

Every account so far presented is an example of finding our way intuitively. Think of the young lieutenant, who, without the psi effect, would have learned too late about the erosion, and of the dancing mathematician, whose confusion triggered a chain of corrective events. Typical of this sensory system, these accounts demonstrate that when we need direction, intuition is there to nudge the conditions favorably.

In my years of observing living examples of our intuitive sensitivity, I have been overwhelmed by the role it empowers us to play in cocreating the universe by involving us in this well-established, ceaselessly interacting structure. Every indication is that we universally underestimate the wealth of data that is running through us intuitively. The problem begins with our not knowing that intuition is a viable sensory system, and it ends in our being wholly unaware not only of its operations but also, and much more important, of the immense span of events in which we can, and should, assist.

## People Helping People

We often hear of intuition working telepathically between people, especially those in troubled mental states.

(ψ-22) My minister friend was smiling to himself while he reported a brush with his intuition, which he calls "loving energy." He described the incident itself as an "odd invitation."

He was making a scheduled call at the home of a parishioner one day, but when he arrived, the woman who answered the doorbell was openly astounded. The pastor, too, was taken aback, for upon seeing her, he realized he was at the wrong address. They stared mutely at one another until she broke the frozen silence. Stumbling over her words, she explained as well as she could that she'd been trying unsuccessfully, for several hours, to reach him by telephone, to ask him to come help her critically ill husband.

He says today that he simply did not notice when he turned at the wrong corner. In fact, he was several blocks away from his intended meeting. Every member of that church would call this very strange behavior for a man whom they all know as extremely reliable. And he still smiles for that same reason. To this day, he cannot explain what happened. He had had to wander fairly far afield to land at the couple's house. Had he received her desperate call? How? He will say only that it didn't come by telephone.

In situations like this, one must begin to wonder whether we are alone in the world. This woman had run out of solutions, so she was attempting to reach him. What a connection! We support others' mental wobbles; others do ours. Think of the dancing mathematician.

# Making Decisions

One example of intuition filling in the mental blanks is a story I particularly love to tell. The reason is that intuition was playing Cupid that day. Uncountable numbers of people can tell a comparable story. This account and the next underline those features I have just described of how confusion spurred intuition to action, and turned the intuitor on a course of supreme satisfaction.

(ψ-23) The situation was commonplace. I had to make one small decision—at least I thought it was minor. Boy, was I wrong. It put an extraordinarily wonderful twist in the direction of my life.

In this case, I had received tempting invitations for two casual events on the same evening. The first was a meeting, the other a dinner party. I decided on the meeting because, I thought, I'd rather be the quiet observer than a social butterfly. However, a strong intuitive "urge" immediately overruled:

*Go to the dinner.*

Without the slightest idea what possible difference it could make, I followed intuition, albeit a little reluctantly. The unexpected reason began to unfold that evening when a stranger across the table introduced himself. Neither of us had a hint that this was the beginning of a friendship that would change our lives completely, but two years later we happily married.

A trivial decision? It seemed so, but I couldn't know absolutely, because the future was involved, and I had no logical access to its unpredictable secrets—the Factors "U"—except by intuition. It swiftly set me straight on course to happiness by all but trumpeting the decision-of-choice.

## Striving for Excellence

Intuition's fact-finding frequently boosts performance from good to excellent, as occurred when I was competing in a sailing regatta. ($\psi$-24) Weather that morning was stormy. The wind was strong, the sea rough, and to add to the adventure, it was raining cats and dogs. Although races could be canceled on days like this, the committee decided to start at nine o'clock as planned, because the forecast promised clearing around noon.

Without a doubt, harsh conditions always add to the sailor's challenge, but winning depends as much on strategy as on wind and sea states. The most accomplished racers often are those who make the best tactical decisions. Every choice counts toward success: the course, the turn of the wheel, and the trim of the sails.

Huddled in the cockpit on my way to the line, I was unsure of myself. What would be the best starting position? Because conditions could change drastically, I knew this might be the most important decision of the race. While waiting for the gun, I suddenly "learned," or intuited, what to do:

*Take long tacks.*

"What?" I thought. "In this weather? Nothing could be more unpleasant." To take long tacks, I would have to head offshore. It meant a wild journey. I would have to cross the starting line beating to windward. Bashing through those waves, I'd feel more like the pilot of a submarine than a sailboat!

But, it was one of those familiar experiences of "knowing,"and at age sixteen I already understood that they were a ticket to success. I planned accordingly. As a result, mine was the lone boat heading east across the line. The others set off to the north, zigzagging in a series of short tacks toward the protective shore.

Given the sea conditions, their choice certainly made more logical sense. However, the weather changed sooner than predicted, and they lost most of their wind power within the first hour. In three hours, soaking wet and icy cold as I was, I savored the thrill of crossing the finish line in first place. Intuition and I had won!

Would I have excelled without it? Good question. I can say only that every racer had the same options at the start, but the most celebrated unpredictable of all, the weather, was the decisive factor, and it defies strategy. Intuition took that element into consideration and advised what I should do. In all cases, it is the law of nature that we get additional detail to help in decisions great and small, dark and exhilarating.

## Future Movement

Lost or found—which is our master? Will we become slaves to the idea that we cannot know facts when we need them and fall off our set points, or will we let our need determine where we go from here? Evidence from intuition says that we will be able to manage ourselves if we allow it to work in its own way. We're responsible for learning its rules, not making them. Its method is to produce data the instant we become lost or confused. As most of us spend our lives working to avoid being lost, or overly confused, we have to acknowledge that we are subject to both those states. This, then, is precisely why intuition appears spontaneously. Its solitary task is to guide our movement every single time we face the Factors "U"—unknown and unpredictable, and we certainly do meet them regularly.

Now is the time to shed any doubts about whether it is right or wrong, sufficient or inadequate, and harness the power of this marvelous assistant.

# CHAPTER 7

# If This, Then What?

I STAYED WITH my search to comprehend intuition not because I was looking for ironclad conclusions but because the observations were continually intriguing. So often when I thought that the thick knot of confusion was working loose, three or four more curious experiences would snag it again. No matter, passing time had demonstrated that another thread would soon slacken. So it went for years—like riding a hobbyhorse. I moved back and forth between mystifying observations, asking questions—often outrageous—and tying sundry solid findings onto the ever-strengthening framework of intuition.

The regulatory mechanism fell into place, enlarging intuition's purpose—and my perspective. I realized that this intuitive system has to be evolving in human behavior and would no doubt have an associated cellular structure in our brains. This set me to thinking about the powerful influence it could have on our species' evolutionary process, indeed the entire natural order. More psi effects became distinct—each with real adaptive purpose and value—enabling people to make decisions that would prevent unpredictable illness, accidents, and crime; improve performance; and return the sense of adventure to the halls of schools, churches, and homes, enhancing life in every imaginable way. Only the sleepiest person would experience any one of these effects and not be impressed with their contribution.

Then in 1985, intuition climbed to a new degree of precision. I noticed one day that most psi effects were composed of only one small piece of information or a single instruction, such as "Pick it up," yet the follow-through might require multiple moves, as when the minister traveled to the wrong house ($\psi$-22). This exposed a process I hadn't understood, one that guides us precisely to our goals. I classified it as the Intuitive Positioning System, or IPS. With this identified I realized that the principal snags in this quest were nearly combed out. The facts that remained interlaced so smoothly that my once perplexing blur of inexplicable impressions and actions now looked like a sailor's finest knot-work, forming an intricate design in human behavior that is exquisite in its unity and efficiency.

## Beginning of Mastery

Many people react uncomfortably to even small encounters with psi effects, and in fact vast numbers have resolutely pronounced them impossible. Regardless, after gazing long at human action and our desperate search for solutions to personal and world problems, I decided that, while those holding back can certainly justify their positions in a variety of ways, those of us who remain curious should plod on in our attempt to unveil what controls intuitive behavior and claim its advantages. This stated, I am simply shelving the conflict and speaking to the conspicuous predicament that we will face when all the surrounding philosophic issues are settled. We are going to discover that we are extremely uncertain about it. Let's begin with the most obvious puzzle.

People ask: What is nature's whole strategy here? Why do we intuit the particular things we do? Why this rather than that? Among the gazillion interactions that happen in any given minute to make the universe run smoothly, we have to establish who, or what, decides which phenomenon should trigger the intuitive process in any one person.

Individually the experiences are not very enlightening about this linkup. Looking at the accounts superficially, we see only a peculiar hodgepodge of connections. Start with the people we intuit: On one hand, they might be siblings, which makes some sense—because of familiarity. On the other, they could just as well be complete strangers speaking different languages, like the man in Vancouver; they could even be madmen turned terrorist. Where is the pattern? People?

Moreover, it isn't always about human beings. We earthlings often appear only in the background, making way for objects. Fugitive plastic bottles on floors of cars might generate life-threatening accidents, while half-full ones on counters merely stand the risk of tipping over. How important can two paltry bottles be in the universal scheme of things? Certainly it is impressive that a military platoon and its equipment literally were saved from toppling off a soggy cliff, but what a difference that represents in overall pain and suffering from one small wallet's turning up out of fifteen acres of dust. The only link here is dirt! Those concerned off finding a consistent practical behavior will have thrown up their hands in dismay by now. We definitely need to understand more about the hidden persuaders we're encountering.

The previous chapters were devoted to accounting for intuition's existence. Now it is time to cut into the fabric of intuitiveness and identify the specific connections that trigger the process. Two questions will make it possible for us to understand how to use it reliably.

This chapter and the next explore these two questions:

*First, precisely which phenomena enter through our intuitive sensibility?* In other words: If this is a regulatory mechanism, then what system is varying?

As we've established, once the phenomena are revealed, we're faced with carrying the process to the proper conclusion, which is the whole purpose of the mechanism. Thus, Chapter 8 covers this second question: *How do we get consistently excellent results?* Or, if the intuitive process must conclude with a correction, then what enables us to do so precisely?

## What Systems Vary?

Where does the river of information originate? To answer this first question, we have to sift through the psi effects because they alone reveal intuition's contacts. Therefore, we shall consider them here as messengers carrying information from a natural source that obviously is acting on us. Although the following descriptions might be crude today in comparison with what we will know in the future, they are adequate for our initial step across the threshold into this world of intuition.

After my first insight into the Instruction effect, I cast a wide net for a dozen years in an effort to collect enough accounts to establish the pattern. During the very first observations, everything appeared to be so random that I began to doubt that any order existed. People! Bottles! Dirt! Airplanes! Life and death . . . Too many plots! However, that problem disappeared once I learned to control my own ability and focus sharply on the psi effects. Soon two types of activity emerged from the hopeless jumble.

One is the never-ending mental machinations of feelings and thinking that we generate in our psyches. The other is the constant physical interplay among the myriad substances, materials, and forces distributed through the physical environment. These two—psychical and physical mechanics—turn out to be the framework of our intuitive ability. All of its information flows from these two vital sources.

Why do they penetrate any human's inner sanctum? We are cellular creatures, thus biologically involved in the intricate interchange of events around the universe—the dynamic processes of life, growth, and deterioration that serve and prey upon our systems. As part of them, both vulnerable to and influential on them, we naturally are sensitized to their interactions. Any intuitive awareness implies specific contacts with these phenomena, just as seeing is a known contact with photons from the electromagnetic spectrum.

Among the seven psi effects, as outlined in Chapter 2, Telepathy and Teleos are the only two I have found that reveal the pure mental and physical activity we intuit. Think of them as the primary effects, the two leaders that produce breaking news reports from the microworld about our myriad interactions. Of the remaining, Déjà vu is excluded from this discussion of regulatory interactions because, as the purely aesthetic form of intuition and a window for discovery only, it has no role in the worker groups. Left then are Instruction and Reflex, which are backup to the primary Telepathy and Teleos, along with Clarification and Dreams, which serve as redundant effects for the entire intuitive system, including Déjà vu. The next sections describe many of the variables that we perceive telepathically and teleosically. Then follow analyses of the support roles the last four play in guiding our moves.

## Telepathy

Telepathy is triggered by mental activity coming from people on all points on the earth, including the bottoms of the seas and in the skies. (Although we have evidence from airplanes only, I am sure we communicate telepathically through deep space.) In a nutshell, it links the human race globally. No age, gender, language, racial, social, national, economic, or political borders deny this intuitive sensitivity. Overall I suggest that we can intuit the mentality of any human being in the world and likewise can be intuited by anyone. The rule underlying all contacts is that an individual is in danger of not functioning optimally.

Telepathy is a day-and-night connection for communication; its resource is the human brain with all the variable mental states that drive our individual lives.

Taken from the Greek *tele*, "far off," and *pathos*, "suffering" or "disease," *telepathy* literally means "far off suffering." The conventional dictionary description portrays it as a form of communication "from one mind to another by extrasensory means." Unfortunately, this is far too indefinite and inert for our needs in using intuition intelligently. Therefore, we shall return to its linguistic roots and start again, this time to tie it into the framework of our intuitive experiences. We need to identify the most fundamental features of this effect.

Looking for guidelines in language, we frequently find the prefix *tele-* in our conversation about tele- forms of communication. For instance, transmitting by telephone is reproducing sounds across a distance, and telecommuting is working at home by electronic linkup with a central office that might be in the next town or hundreds of miles away.

So, we ask what happens when we are being telepathic. What did the word wizards have in mind when they cobbled together *tele-* and *-pathos*? Grievings? Arguments? Physical discomforts? Doubts? Snoopings? All of these? Or none? What information really passes human beings over the intuitive waves?

## Telepathic Reception

This psi effect untangled in stages. Initially I unwittingly limited my thinking to the concept suggested by the word *suffering*. I took it in the purest sense as meaning our passions of the heart— joys, loves, sorrows, and so forth. Oh, how wrong I was. That careless assumption created a massive snarl for several months. Then a few loose strands of evidence appeared. Relentless probing led back to my asking what I had met in telepathic communication. The answer came quickly: We perceive others' mental tensions when they are suffering stress anywhere in their nervous system. Technically this tension occurs when our nerves are stimulated. We identify stress as "nervous tension." Aha. There it was. *Whatever strain nerves are enduring influences us.*

For example, how many times had I received signals of panic? That signal is not difficult to separate from other forms of Telepathy; it is the loudest cry in the wilderness. Fury also ranks high on the Telepathy index. Likewise, a bad mood will hit me between the ears as hard as a rock. Rational thinking is there as well, especially when any individual is concentrating heavily. And love: Think of the vital sensations you feel around humans who adore one another.

As the list grew longer, I finally developed a model of the repertoire of tensions we suffer mentally. Finding a spectrum answered the central question of Telepathy's trigger: We intuit the human nervous system at work maintaining *all* of our vital functions. Although there are enough nerve-generated phenomena out and about that we would need a Telepathy index the size of the Manhattan phone book, they can be fairly well divided into a few general groups. Among them are self-control, passions, character, mood, reasoning, and break-down, or collapse, of control. These basic mental states combine and build—or destroy—stable psyches.

The general law of nature appears to be that each of us is the operator of our own psyche, responsible for managing all of its departments as they work internally and with life around, for correcting and compensating for all of our errors and weaknesses, for knowing what to teach ourselves, when to move, and in which direction—to name a few tasks. You can see that this mental part of our humanness could be a massive regulatory nightmare!

At first glance, our mental stability looks precarious at best. How do we manage? The answer is that nature has provided us with an immense variety of ways to help ourselves. Among them is our ability to reach out to others and communicate with them directly through Telepathy.

We all make intuitible noise when we suffer internal tensions during this ceaseless mental balancing act called living. You have read about that panicked, frustrated man missing his attaché case: Telepathy assured him that he was not alone. Think of the accounts of my sister, the prom queen, the couple in our church: fear, joy, grief. This Telepathy psi effect was responsible for my learning in all those situations. Reflect on your own life: Do you sense people by your Telepathy? Their excitement? Restlessness? Fear?

Fortunately for us all, this effect's role is tightly regulated. First and most important: We intuit mental states by Telepathy—*only* these and nothing more. Further to this, *we learn through Telepathy only those states that have fallen off, or are about to fall off, set point.* This charming delicacy seems to be nature's insurance that our heads won't be swimming perpetually with the general hubbub that most certainly would exist if everyone's mental activities were untuitible. Think of the cacophony that would result. Who wouldn't agree that this inherent restriction is very humane? The general pattern seems to be that if an individual's mental world is relatively stable, the rest of us are free. If not, we are on line through Telepathy.

One final word on telepathic reception. We are tuned in to anyone who is struggling psychically, but it is impossible to be telepathic to ourselves. However, the tables turn readily when we are tense and tumultuous; then others in the world will be informed telepathically and have the option to come to our assistance.

## Telepathic Transmission

Shifting psychic stresses are to human Telepathy what a fluctuation in weather is to mariners at sea. We all have to adapt to changes in environmental conditions. For centuries a sensitive barometer on board to measure atmospheric change has helped seafarers making decisions about how to navigate. We use Telepathy similarly. In mental atmospheres, tensions constantly build, then subside, because activity is the norm in the intricate maze of the human psyche. If these everyday strains of living become extreme, they will change the state of the environment—just as the wave of a hand or a butterfly's wings will move the air—and be off into the ethers where they influence the intuitive sensitivity of other individuals. Accordingly, we will expand the definition of Telepathy to read "communication across a distance of a spectrum of mental activities from one individual to another or others."*

Born with the mandate to manage these brain centers of ours, we work lifelong to keep our private worlds hovering safely around set point even while we are driven to high stress points, such as when we marshal the powerful forces of talent within us to reach for the brass ring of success. Looking at this conflicting demand for integrity, we can see how the face-off of opposites introduces the potential for our psyches to become terrifying war zones! Miraculously, they need not.

## Telepathy's Environment

What do we learn through telepathic experiences? So far as I can determine, they arise from the states already introduced: self-control, passions, character, moods, and reasoning—and any failure in these functions.

### Self-Control

At the top of the list is the master mental ability to coordinate our experiences as we make our way through life. I think of this ability as self-control over the entire nervous system.

This human capability to mentally control our nervous system balances is one of the most remarkable evolutionary steps we have seen. An advantage delegated to Homo sapiens only, the self-sufficiency it affords makes available more opportunities than virtually any other capacity endowed to organisms (the thumb and ability to reason notwithstanding). Hence I would say that self-control is probably the greatest advantage the organic world has ever seen. Judging from the number of books, articles, and per-

---

*A note to animal lovers: General consensus says that certain animal species are also telepathic. I have no reason to disagree. However, since my experience is fairly limited, I am not extending discussion to include them.

sonal journals written about it, it is one of the most intensely studied endowments in the social picture. Apparently we want to be masters of our own worldly lives.

This might be our wish, but the authoritarian trend in society—concentrating power in leaders and systems—leaves no place for the small person in running the world. Just to have a fair amount of control over their private lives, thousands daily resort to increasing amounts and kinds of excesses—drug and alcohol abuse, child molestation, rape, self-absorption, power plays. And we see abandonment by the authorities we need to trust: politicians of their constituents, parents of children, and children of basic values that self-control imbues. We are headed toward becoming a species that is chronically out of control and dangerously unable to master our psychic states. Can we turn this around?

What are these states we should be able to control? And how do they figure in the telepathic picture? I have come to see self-regulation as the flexible core of our inner strength, enabling us to be strong and stable but also to slip and become unsteady when we're at a disadvantage. It seems to me that this ability to regulate the moves we make demands that we recognize the difference between those occasions when we are in command and those in which circumstances are confusing, frustrating, or infuriating. When we can single out the differences among these and manage all with aplomb, we are truly whole people.

Throughout life, every one of us goes through all of these states of mentality at some time or another. Watch long enough and you will see that even the most uncertain individual has moments of confidence and that self-assured people become undone occasionally.

We readily intuit degrees of self-control by telepathy. In your own experience, how many times have you "sensed" confidence in a person, "felt" that someone was confused, or "known" an individual's frustration? And with that information to orient you, how did you respond? Did you feel relaxed with the confident man or woman? Could you help the confused person reorient, or lead the frustrated one back to a steadier position? We all have to learn that these three mental states—confidence, frustration, and confusion—work like beacons in the night, revealing to your Telepathy what people can give and what they need.

Examples are everywhere. A parent might talk too quickly as she explains her decision and confuse her child. The child's confusion will inform her telepathically. A teacher who leaves half the class behind when explaining a complex point will discover the mistake telepathically. Or, slightly more earthshaking: Imagine that you are the one in the group who must make a decision, but for some reason, you cannot come to a clean conclusion; you feel confused. Your colleagues should meet that uneasiness head on, again through Telepathy. If one among them has the wisdom to acknowledge your stress and open the discussion, chances are excellent that your crisis will be averted.

Picture the future: A psyche is shouting internally, "How can I alter this condition?" (The attaché case problem.) Someone far away intuits and responds. What marvelous communication! What a difference we will witness when those psyches under duress have hope for help in Telepathy. Right now, most people do receive information telepathically but don't orient their actions by it. This will change, and our fate will be sweeter, when this psi effect directs our interpersonal moves as finely as traffic signals manage the flow of vehicles at a crowded intersection.

### Nerves Under Extreme Stress

Fear frequently invades a psyche caught long in confusion or frustration. A human in fear is an animal trapped. Nothing is showing the way to solution and free movement. Externally we might cry for help, strike out in panic, or cower in dread. Fear signals the absolute end of the system's tolerance. That point when a human being has lost all self-sufficiency is the most terrible form of suffocation. Yet, if that state were not in us, we might not be able to call out in our primitive way, either physically with our voices or mentally with our uncontrollable panic. This acute state of the psyche is virtually an open invitation for help to come immediately. Telepathy receives it.

## Two Rages

On some occasions, rather than panic setting in, there will be passionate rage. This stress signals *near* madness. Often a watershed for the psyche, the tumult can be a turning point that changes the course that person is taking. We express two types of fury. We rage out and in.

Outrage is a very different sensation telepathically from the other, which is internalized by an enraged person. Probably the reason is that it is stirred by deep-seated passion in us and has the effect of giving clear direction for our furies. For generations, outrage has led people worldwide to protest publicly. Students and citizens band together in outrage against leaders who have violated their rights. Revolutions result like the American fight for independence from stifling British law, and the French revolt against a monarchy. These movements truly would have spawned a telepathically perceptible "wave of outrage" that led to the stunning group uprisings.

For psychological reasons, some people internalize rage. They land in a mind-numbing isolation of emotions that allows in no support and call out less and less for interaction. The cemented mentality is one in which the overseeing regulatory mechanism controlling mental health appears to grind to a halt like a car that runs out of fuel or a boat that loses the wind in its sails. Although one can intuit these internalized rages telepathically, of all the mental states described in these pages, only this emotional isolation and the human fiend described later are inflexible states in nervous systems that usually benefit more from trained therapeutic help than our everyday natural interactive caring assistance.

This group of normal mental states—confusion, frustration, fear, and outrage—comprises perhaps the most frequent triggers of

Telepathy, no doubt because we all have these stresses. Examples abound of people intuiting these states in loved ones and total strangers, locally and thousands of miles away. The woman who wanted the minister's assistance was sufficiently fearful that she transmitted her duress, and being telepathic to her, the minister inadvertently responded. When these states appear on the scene, we "know." We can detect mental self-control declining nearly as distinctly as we can see water drain from a tub, and we owe it to ourselves as a species to help the sufferer return to set point. When it comes to intuition and mental health, Telepathy is the direct route to a person's true sentiments; we need to learn to read the map!

From the examples in these pages, it should be clear that when you experience a telepathic psi effect, you might not know exactly what is wrong in a person, but you can be confident that the telepathic data will orient you in the most ordinary affairs. The art is to be awake—as the Buddha suggested.

(ψ-25) The pretty smile on the post office clerk's face definitely did not match the heavy frustration she radiated to me via Telepathy. Since I knew I could return later that day I inquired if she would prefer that I come back later. Her whole visage came to life in a shake of her head. No, she said, but asked if I would be kind enough to help her get my bulky package on the scale, because she had hurt her back earlier when another customer handed her a box far too heavy to hold. She explained, "I was so frustrated that he didn't pay attention to what he was doing." Thanks, intuition.

(ψ-26) Another day while in the market I was lifting items from the cart in an effort to help the clerk. What a surprise to intuit her outrage screaming:

*I wish that lady would just stop.*

I did—immediately—and moved out of her way. Standing back and detecting her sudden mental quietude, I couldn't resist testing this Telepathy. So, I asked the benign-looking woman whose name tag read "Gerry" whether she was bothered by my assistance. "You bet I was," came back in an eyeblink. "This is my job! I have things worked out to be efficient. Everybody is like you. You all think you're helping, but you're not!"

A good lesson. I began to pay more attention to the Barometer everywhere. It has proved repeatedly that we are all more finely tuned social animals than we think, and better at getting the truth straight from the sources about who wants assistance and who absolutely does not!

Children need us to use the Barometer with them, for the very same reason. Some days, they eagerly run their entire world; others are filled with confusion and frustration. Learning from children through Telepathy is invaluable in their development. Their strength and maturation depend heavily on our knowing when to help and when to let them find their own self-controls. In my thinking, every parent and teacher should begin using Telepathy as quickly as possible.

Turning to the remaining states of our nervous system that are perceived telepathically, we discover that we intuit human passions, innate character, transitory moods, and breakdown in any of these functions. What does each communicate?

### Passions

We say, "The air is thick with outrage," "The room is alive with excitement," and "The couple's silent struggle held us all in its icy grip." These could be passions swirling in the atmosphere. Call them matters of the heart. They are constructive driving forces propelling us to peaks of joy and love, plunging us into depths of all-consuming grief from loss, by both death and failure.

Passions are largely ungovernable driving forces, bursting out as love, joy, true fear, sorrow, zeal, and outrage from deep within us. They create enormously strong internal forces that well and truly "speak" for us telepathically.

Note: In the purest sense, passions are *not* emotions. Consequently I separate the two completely, recognizing passion as one form of healthy expression and motivational, and emotions as unhealthy repression, numbing and immobilizing. Since they are as different as night and day—one supportive, the other destructive—I assign them to two separate categories of behavior.* Due to the amount of discussion required, I have chosen not to enlarge here on my reasons, but I do encourage recognizing the contrast when being telepathic.

## Character

Call character our innate qualities. We meet these in that helpful "first impression." Have you ever had an immediate "impression" that a newcomer would be a good friend, an honest business partner, or a dedicated leader? Where did that information originate? Telepathy. Characteristics such as courageous, shy, confident, contentious, trustworthy, reckless, and excessively sensitive break into our awareness sometimes before a person has said a word.

To be able to "read" character is an invaluable advantage for strangers meeting strangers; for public relations professionals of any kind, such as human resources groups who hire and place employees; and for any social worker from law enforcement to educators to elected leaders. It helps, too, in the general public where many low-life characters are out to take advantage.

## Mood

Different from characteristics, which are rooted in our makeup, moods come and go like breezes and tempests. They pierce our psyches and vanish, but they should not be ignored. A mood creates the atmosphere. You are being influenced. Respond if you can. Leave the room if it disturbs you; stand by if you're enticed. Subtle though the contrast might be, you will know the difference between a person who is temporarily "agitated" and one who

---

*By contrast to the expansiveness of passions, emotions carry with them a need for rigid control. Examples are hate, jealousy, nostalgia, and shame.

is bursting with murderous rage. Shades of gray? Yes. And a challenge to differentiate. But with intuition as helper, we now are responsible for evolving, for fine-tuning ourselves—sometimes for our own survival. This is probably why we are telepathic.

As with the other Telepathy triggers, these states often "hang" in a room and "stir" the air. We say we get certain "vibes" from a person. Someone might sweep through who is bright-spirited, another who is gloomy. Can you "feel" the mood lift or drop? Generally speaking, most of these atmospheric changes are harmless. If you don't like the one that pervades the room, just wait until another person enters. The balance of mental power might shift.

## Intellect

Have you ever "felt" that a person was in deep concentration or "known" someone was figuring out an answer? Intellectual states range from profound absorption to intrigue, open-mindedness, and straight on to boredom. Every good teacher knows the difference telepathically. One early lesson for every parent to learn is that under no circumstance should we interrupt a genius at work! Take a Barometric reading first, and then proceed as permitted. A library is also an excellent place to intuit intellectual concentration. In a room filled with thinking people the mental "work" is usually so strong that it hits Telepathy like a wall when you enter.

## Human Freak

Last, but not the least telepathically transmitted states are the very detectable inhumane ones so treacherous to all forms of life. This malevolent strain of our species runs its world remorselessly, corrupting life at will. In a vicious psyche there will be no gray zone. It is black. Often concealed behind a smile, or dressed conventionally, the murderers, abusers, and terrorists in the species will always be perceptible through Telepathy.

Nearly all of us gain control of our defiance early, as part of youthful self-mastery over confusion, frustration, and rage, yet there is no denying that some people become a rare phenomenon in our species—the malevolent fiend. Along with her other elements that elevate to devastating proportions—earthquakes, tornadoes, hurricanes, wildfires, floods—nature has occasionally spawned some human freaks.

The horror notwithstanding, we are well protected from it because, like all the raging monsters in nature's elements, this distorted human impacts us intuitively first, often long before embarking on a real-life dastardly assault. While we learn about the weather freaks of nature through the Teleos effect, Telepathy reports loud and clear when this unhealthy psyche is abroad.

Perhaps we shouldn't be surprised that it has such force in its fury that its psi effect overrides almost all other telepathic exchanges, including passion. Reading chilling news reports about adolescent madness and terrorist attacks, we all shudder and wonder how to gauge our movements and teach children the same. Certainly one of the most reliable reporters we have is in our heads with this Telepathy, which is triggered faster than you can blink an eye when a fiend is in search of prey. Don't stay around when you intuit this violent psyche. Do precisely as the effect reports. It will save life.

## Telepathy's Rules of Conduct

By now it should be evident that Telepathy's triggers permeate the environment; they can be likened to familiar constantly shifting weather patterns of pressure. By and large, most wholesome humans beyond adolescence can weather fairly wide swings and variables within their psyches, even when taking risks. The result is that if we travel among fairly mature people, telepathic transmissions only occasionally penetrate our private worlds and usually are welcome.

Telepathy is straightforward. It reports only current states of mental balance, nothing else. By this I mean that it sends its signals in real time. If you intuit that a person is frustrated, this means that individual is frustrated *right now*. If the distress lasts for three hours, you might be aware of it for three hours. As soon as it stops, you will no longer be learning about it.

I once had occasion to ride the tide of a human fiend's fury for ten hours and, like the student sensing the forecoming disaster in Oklahoma City (ψ-2), I tragically had no recourse to intercept and change the consequences. Paralleling this next account with that student's experience, validates that we can know well in advance that a murderous plan is in motion, that we in fact can follow by Telepathy until the raging fury stops. In future time, when we are universally skillful with Telepathy, I have no doubt that precognition centers* will spring up in various locations.

(ψ-27) It was 1981. Around 4 A.M. I received what I describe as an intuitive early-morning wake-up call:

*The world is going to be
changed today.*

I sat bolt upright. This was a telepathic report. Along with this unusual fact, I knew the "change" was surrounded with a dark mood and a heaving mentality frenzied with frustration, or was it several people in that state? I was unsure. The strain was strong. The raging hovered in my head for several hours, ten to be exact. When the humans' heaving mentalities finally relaxed, only then did their exploding disappear from my head.

In this experience I knew nothing more than that fury was on the wind, so I had no way to help. Therefore, like that student, I had to abandon that possibility and went back to sleep. The mental storm raged during the day. I had learned years before that when the atmosphere is troubled by madness, I should

---

*This would be a central bureau where professional parapsychologists and recording equipment would be available around the clock to collect intuitive predictions from individuals calling in their experiences. A team of professionals would make responsible decisions about how to follow through on the reports. Although this kind of center has existed in the past, none are currently in operation as far as I know.

concentrate on everything I was doing, lest the psychic tumult distract me. This rule should hold for all of us. In a windstorm, we have to brace against the blast to walk through it. Likewise in cyclonic mental forces, when terrorists shivering with nearly ecstatic madness are plotting and executing their twisted missions. Remember the reason for the regulatory mechanism: make correction to the system under strain, yours or any others.

Release came in mid-afternoon when we heard on the radio that Anwar al-Sadat, president of Egypt, had been assassinated by Islamic fundamentalists only a few hours earlier. While listening, I noticed that the tension had disappeared from my head. My mental world was free. Analysis of this incident clearly indicates that I was telepathic to the assassins, intuiting their tempestuous psyches all day long while they were planning and anticipating their unthinkable crime.

Finally, a note to those who, like Mrs. Flint in Chapter 5, fear that Telepathy invades their personal lives. For generations, telepathic people have been suspected of delving into deepest darkest private worlds and secrets. Rest assured—this is virtually impossible. The reason is that intuition follows laws. Remember that it is a regulatory mechanism designed to detect and correct, not snoop. Almost perversely, it appears that nature has made this such a specialized sensitivity that if one person attempts to "break into" another's psyche as though it were open territory for thieves, the intruder would not be able to trust the stolen information. The reason is that mental states of strain have to be strong enough to perturb the environment and stimulate Telepathy. It comes to us; we don't seek it out. More likely a thief collects little more than the passing mood.

## The Teleos Effect

When Teleos sends a report, we are learning about the buildup or breakdown of physical substances, materials, and forces in the natural order. It reports nothing of the dynamics of human mentalities known exclusively by Telepathy. Teleos effects seem to be triggered by events and chains of events that will at some time directly affect the intuitor or, just as easily, any organic or inorganic system.

## Teleos Reception

As Chapter 2 explained, Teleos encompasses precognition, meaning to know beforehand; direct cognition, to know at the time of the event; and retrocognition, to know backward. The Teleos effect opens access to a vast frontier that we technically identify as "time"—the future, present, and past. We think of time as a measure of space we fill, or a period during which a process exists. For our own convenience we divide life into artificial segments—eras, centuries, seasons, lifetimes, and appointments, for example. According to our intuitive sensitivity, this territory called "time" is filled with living events in variable states. Call them events-in-motion.

Teleos reports combine both artificial and natural measures. Sometimes we learn about a fixed day or hour when a phenomenon will happen (which appears in account $\psi$-41). Other times we follow the sequence along *its* time line, as with earthquakes, which begin their life as upheaval in the earth's crust sometimes hours, days, and weeks before we who live on top of the ground actually feel it for a few torturous seconds. I picture our teleosic reception rather like a panorama: the event unrolls before us over a period of time. We, the intuitional spectators, are alerted to its progress.

## Definition

Taken from the Greek, *teleos* means "complete." It is best explained by the word *teleonomy*, the concept that a feature would not exist in an organism unless it had survival value. In other words, if a structure such as a wing, an ability such as intuition, or a function such as breathing exists in an organism or animal, we can assume that it is useful to help the creature survive. The belief behind the concept is that everything is directed toward some final purpose.

I selected *Teleos* to represent the three psi effects under its umbrella because they all are abilities that appear to be evolving within us for survival reasons. I am confident that it is appearing to make us learn in advance about dangers we face or are creating, and advantages we can introduce to nature because of our own reasoning power. The finest current example of its promise relates to our untiring creativity. After several historically bad decisions, we have learned that our biggest problem is an information gap: we need details about crucial unknowns and unpredictables before we make a radical move.

This has been the case at least since man split the atom. We did not calculate the full repercussions of the discovery. Now we face the same uncertainty about the hazards of transplanting animal organs in human bodies. How far we should go remains an alarming open question. This new power to anticipate the so-called unpredictable outcome of an experiment with potential to change the evolution of life for all time, or international decisions to permanently disturb the elements, will doubtless affect future decisions.

For this reason, Teleos seems a noble name, for its survival purpose seems clear. It will forewarn us when we venture too close to the brink of damage with our rational skill and will report when we don't recognize solutions that we have in the palm of our hands. This intuitive power helps us to create the future with life everlasting in mind.

## What Teleos Reports

We learn about the past and future while living in the present. Although millions of confirmed reports support this concept of continual learning while a panorama unfolds, I will stick to four I know personally.

The first is the Sadat account ($\psi$-27) just discussed, which illustrates how our intuitive sensitivity can be affected over an extensive period of time. While that was a sustained human fury available only to Telepathy, think of what it represents: Someone could literally follow the progress of a mission of madness for hours before and up to its completion.

I believe that we are equally as sensitive to the sequences of change that occur in environmental materials and forces. From expanding cracks and fissures deep in the earth to infinitesimal bonds that combine atomic and molecular materials, from living cells invading food to future positions of objects, we are intuitively sensitive both to isolated events such as food poisoning and automobile brakes and to progressive change as it happens; from the first ripples of transformation that throw the system into fluctuation to the instant it bears down in real-time experiences that might push us off our set points, we get the message. Why? Because humans are part of the ecosystem balance too. We are in the network and are wired to be aware *when we can help ourselves and others*. With intuition guiding, you will discover that you can get caught and rescued in the most unexpected and entertaining ways.

Earthquakes are another good illustration of our Teleos contacts, since the actual violent quaking of the ground that we experience on the "day of the quake" is the result of a long-term breakdown of earth's internal checks and balances. Let us turn to the events building up to that ultimate moment. The fact is, we are intuitively sensitive to the entire unfolding sequence of prior tensions while the plates of the earth's crust are building up to the collision that ultimately rocks our household rafters.

The three following accounts illustrate well that we learn from three different psi effects—Teleos, Instruction, and Reflex— as danger mounts.

From events arising from two separate earthquakes, you will see how well intuition adheres to the pattern of continuous forewarning. We will learn from Teleos initially. This is the pure information. It occurs far enough ahead of the development for an intuitor to make sensible and humane efforts to control the phenomenon or, if this is impossible, to adjust to its impact, thereby changing an otherwise inevitable future. Instruction reports when the phenomenon is imminent. It is more austere than Teleos, giving the option to act or not, but removing the element of planning moves. When event and intuitor are at a crucial juxtaposition, the intuitor becomes a "rock" to be bulldozed. In the third account, observe what happens to the intuitor's right to choose when Reflex takes over.

(ψ-28) The weather was lovely that Sunday morning. My study was sunny and warm, a delightful place for a bit of thinking and writing. I was lost in thought:

*Earthquake today.*

This was Teleos, giving a straight prediction, so stark and unembellished that it might as easily have been a live weather broadcaster reporting another "sunny, warm day in the Southland." True to intuition's form, it was coolly objective, as one learns to expect any prediction to be. Alas, for your average Californian the mere mention of an earthquake breeds quite the opposite psychical behavior. To the quake-sensitive California psyche, it will be nothing short of electrifying breaking news. I was no exception.

I knew I should swing into action promptly. Quite naturally, when faced with a developing seismic calamity, one is fairly certain that it cannot be prevented. Though we might wish it away, the fact is that a system of nature is on the rampage, correcting herself, returning her major elemental systems to set point, just as we smaller ones correct our major cellular systems—only this is correction on a grand scale.

The pattern emerges here of intuition's true scope. It demonstrates that we are truly interacting with processes as vast as earth's crust in upheaval, with its plates on a collision course, yet are linked too with the most pacific variances such as a missing wallet ($\psi$-18). As the interaction this time was of mammoth proportions, I decided to prepare the house, to help it withstand the stresses that were about to rip through it.

On that day, I hesitated, wanting more data. It was frustrating that the effect offered no detail on the quake's size, epicenter, or precise time. This might be only the slightest tremor or, just as likely, the dreaded Big One, which has all of us who sit on a fault sitting also on pins and needles. Knowing I was fortunate to have any forewarning, but wanting all that was available, I asked a single question: "What else do I know about this earthquake?" This query frequently gathers useful fine points that help me decide my next move. Typical of intuition, I learned only what I needed to know: It would be "in the area of Los Angeles." That was all. But it was enough. This *was* Los Angeles. I now knew that the earthquake would be happening today, underneath my home and me!

Now was time for action. First, I called a couple of close friends to warn them of the event about to happen. Next, I walked through the house, removing all glass-covered photos from the wall and relocating other objects that might take flight. Once finished, I returned to the study and my thoughts. Three hours later a strong, swift, moderately damaging 5.2 quake shivered through the land. For a few seconds the house swayed to and fro, giving the sensation of a vessel at sea. Although media reports crisscrossing the airwaves were replete with descriptions of damage in our vicinity, nothing was damaged in my little rocking house.

Note that in this account, almost all of the planning and action was my responsibility. There was no specific instruction for moves, neither dos nor don'ts. And, I had plenty of time to prepare before the quake struck.

(ψ-29) Earthquake number two: I left the desk at midnight after a long, heavily scheduled day. On the way to the bedroom, I walked past the tall bookcase in the hallway:

*Push them back.*

This was the Instruction effect. A quick scan of the books already lined up at the back of the shelves indicated that my intuition had to be referring to the dozen bottles of wine that stood on the very top. This was a most curious directive. For some reason they were endangered. I stared at them a moment, thinking they looked perfectly fine exactly where they were. Different bottles had stood there off and on for at least two years; it was a combination wine rack and decorative touch that pleased my eye. While my brain was looking for a worthy reason, end-of-day weariness unexpectedly sent up passionate cries of opposition from another corner of my head. "Oh no, not now!"

I heartily agreed with the resistance. It was late. I was spent. This definitely seemed the wrong time for an interior redecoration project. But practical nature took over. What kind of absurd behavior was this? Intuition's Captain had given an Instruction. It would be accurate. Yet, here I was resisting. What was I thinking?

Clearly, I was meeting a hidden persuader. It would influence the positions of the bottles. Apparently I had an opening to control the outcome. Instruction offered an option, and there should be no doubt that *now, not later*, would be the best point in time for moving the bottles. I reflected on Instruction's elegant simplicity. Characteristic of this particular effect, I was limited to two alternatives for action: I could either do or not do as instructed. Remembering that as long as I followed through, intuition had never failed me. I knew I would be foolish to walk away now!

Thus, as late as it was, I respectfully pushed the bottles, one by one, from an arrangement that suited my artistic eye to the much less attractive sensible new one. Five minutes later a dozen bottles stood about twelve inches back from the edge, flat against the wall, in a long uninteresting row. I grumbled a bit, laughed at myself, and went to bed. It was half past twelve. I had to be back at work on the telephone in four and a half hours.

By eight o'clock the following morning, I'd already been working three hours when the earthquake struck. In a split second, the whole house was swaying. I left the desk immediately and went straight to the front garden to wait out a strong 5.8 temblor. Of course I realized with the usual "Aha" that this was the reason for the midnight Instruction. Fifteen minutes later, I reentered the house and headed straight for the bookcases. It was confirmed. Although every wine bottle stood now at the outer edge of the shelf, not one had escaped and crashed on the unyielding stone tile floor below. I remember smiling, bemused by nature's fine forecasting—and flair.

Intuition's Captain had saved the day—and me. It had prevented two losses: first, and most valuable, my precious time, which would have had to go to the unwelcome task of mopping up the damage; second, and, most assuredly amusing, something so trifling as wine.

(ψ-30) A "textbook" example of the Reflex action on that same morning was described by Winthrop, an architect. He called in the afternoon to ask whether his coincidence was a sign of intuition at work. After hearing his story, I was sure it was. Yet, like most other coincidental incidents, it offers no absolute confirmation.

Before eight o'clock, he was in the bottom-floor office of his three-story mountainside home. He had begun work as usual around six and planned to spend three concentrated hours on a new design. Then he would leave to call on a construction site.

His story begins about twenty-five minutes before the earthquake. For no reason he could explain, he became distracted. Being a normally calm fellow who enjoys his work and has no difficulty staying focused, this bewildered him. By fifteen minutes to eight, he was so restless and frustrated with himself that he decided to clear his mind by taking a short walk in the hills with his dog. As a result, while the quake was rattling his house, he was at least half a mile away. Upon his return, he discovered that the heavy wood bookcase beside his desk had toppled, pitching books and objects helter-skelter. He found dozens of his possessions broken, and the bookcase resting on the chair where he had been sitting. Could he have been injured? Who knows? He says he probably would not have reacted quickly enough to escape a good pounding from a few volumes. He wouldn't speculate about his dog.

Do you recognize his behavior as the Reflex psi effect? We know only by hindsight that massive earth forces and a man were on a collision course. He says he had no perceptible intuitive clue, which would suggest that he was driven out by his distraction. Although his home was damaged, the Reflex effect had moved him out of harm's way. Evidently, he had been in too vulnerable a position proportionate to the time the earthquake would strike—the equivalent predicament of getting too close to a fire. As you can see, he needed that help.

The fact that we have an intuitive Reflex should not be a difficult concept to grasp; we find forewarning in other sensory systems. Think of the comparable situation when an individual doesn't see an oncoming car before stepping off a curb. That combination, too, is a case of being too close to the fire and all but shouts, "Disaster ahead!" Machine and man surely will collide unless the pedestrian's senses take over—either the ears to hear, or eyes to notice—and cause the person to physically recoil in fear. As soon as the pedestrian does see the problem, the nervous system takes over with a physical spring-back reflex.

As stated many times, intuition is the assigned regulatory mechanism for particular phenomena that *we encounter only with its sensors.* As a sensory system, it has claim to a reflex function.

Dozens of personal accounts of coincidental occurrences indicate that we are fully equipped to fall into a strong safety net with help from the Reflex psi effect when time is up and harm is knocking on the door. My architect friend's is one.

Winthrop thinks he was bulldozed out of the way of the hazard. The reason, he says, is that the distraction could not have been his own; he was simply enjoying his work too much.*

The three subsystems of Teleos reveal intuition's physical domain of that frontier we measure in time. We are intuitively sensitive to phenomena in this territory *because we are one with it.* Whether we can prove it at the time or not, the intuitive process informs us with three completely separate effects, each one reducing our freedom of choice a little as the crisis moment approaches. Teleos is showing us where to work and gives us options to share in molding their outcomes.

## Teleos Rules

The interplay of human and natural microprocesses suggests the rule: We're not guests here on earth along for the ride. So, as long as nature is in motion, humans will be informed and have an obvious role to play. This shaping of phenomena—by giving either form or direction—takes on startling new implications when intuition comes on the scene because with it we can know so much more than ever before.

What if we really *can* know the future, track the changes, and interact at various times during the process? What then? This fact of our tracking like any animal following a scent could have profound consequences in various scientific disciplines. Think of

---

*Regarding the dog in this tale, it is well known that many animals behave strangely just before an earthquake; we have to question what they know that we don't. On that score, however, Winthrop is dubious. He would tell you that he had to wake up his dog for that walk.

medicine that is looking for ways to prevent illness and assist the healing process, of earth sciences searching for prediction procedures that will increase public safety, of physical and life sciences experimenting constantly with radical innovations. The day is near when we will be able to know in advance which alterations will support life and which will not.

In subsequent chapters, the evidence will be more persuasive that we *do* "know" and track organic and inorganic change. Since intuition is so beautifully simple to use, why wouldn't we be able to make continuous corrections in systems that prevent damage to all systems hanging together in the universe?

## Instruction and Reflex to the Rescue

### Instruction

The Instruction effect, as exemplified throughout the book, appears at the point when we are down to the wire and must act immediately if we intend to help the situation. The intuitor already is limited in what he or she can accomplish; there is no time for elaborate analyzing and planning because tension is high and tolerances are approaching limits. Hence, the intuitor has to be "told" precisely what to do in order to accomplish the finest result.

### Reflex

As you know from Chapter 2, Reflex is the low man on the totem pole, the last in line helping the other psi effects. It forces action. In the cascading sequence of events, free time is up. Apparently, the process will begin to fail or immediately collapse unless a human is in a particular position. Manipulating us like a child's remote-control toy, it forces us to take part in bringing about change.

In these opening stages of our intuition's evolution, almost everyone experiences the Reflex effect. It might represent our first baby step, but since it appears to foster satisfactory change and fine-tune our interactions, it should never be discouraged. There is every reason to assume that it, like all other reflexes, will continue to provide emergency service as the paramedic of intuitive sensitivity. The benefits in this effect show through in Winthrop's story ($\psi$-30). He was so distracted that he left what he was doing without understanding the reason at all.

## Failure Unacceptable: The Role of Clarification and Dreams

No regulatory system could exist without detectors. Imagine driving a car without headlights on a dark night. At best, you will proceed slowly, because you cannot find your way without seeing where you're going. The psi effects are the equivalent of intuition's headlights. We need them to be aware when we run into an interaction in the territories we're traveling. But, for a variety of good reasons, the primary and backup psi effects sometimes cannot deliver their reports; then the system's headlights go out. It should not be surprising that nature has decreed this failure unacceptable, and long ago evolved a solution to potential breakdown. She installed Clarification and Dreams to serve as redundant systems.

Even the sturdiest devices experience some resistance or collapse once in a while, and when they do, we hope their planner has provided a satisfactory redundant system so that the intended result cannot fail. Manufacturers of machinery frequently design their products with more components than necessary. The extras serve as duplicates to prevent failure of an entire machine when a single component falters. Spacecraft have them. Cars have them. I have numbers of them on our boat. For instance, the cabin water is pumped electrically, but in the event of a power failure (frequently!), the builder installed a hand pump to ensure that lifesaving drinking water is always available. How foolish we would be not to have that insurance.

Intuition has them—one for waking hours, the other when we rest.

## Clarification

Recall from Chapter 2 that Clarification comes in at least three guises: clairvoyance, clairaudience, and clairsentience. This effect will jump right in if Telepathy, Teleos, Instruction, or even Dream fails to report what the intuitive sensors have received. This cluster of three effects seems to me to be nature borrowing on her own tricks to keep her interactions going. Mimicry, a well-established biological function, works as the protective cover-up for vulnerable creatures; phenomena often have look-alikes. Next time you watch a butterfly, notice how its ingenious paper-thin wings provide a perfect camouflage as it flutters among delicate flower petals. Turn now to intuition for a parallel. Nature has used her clever cover-up techniques again, this time to slip intuition past our restraining religious and rational radar and straight into our lives.

Clarification is an imitator of our most common sensory effects, the ones nearly all of us trust implicitly—hearing, sight, and the physical sensations associated with taste, touch, and smell. I have found that when the other psi effects flounder, most individuals will pay attention to any experience of the Clarification group—because *we all believe what we learn from our familiar higher-order sensory systems.* This backup curbs doubts and fears more easily than any logic ever could, and the information, like the Pony Express, does get through.

Look at this set of convincing copycat artists: clairaudience openly plays the part of hearing, which people describe as "hearing" voices and bells, that remote "inner voice," and getting "transmissions" and indistinct "echoes"; clairsentience convincingly mimics real physical sensations, like the "gut feeling" uncountable numbers of people have described, the "feeling" of a presence, or "sensations" of heat and cold; and "clairvoyance" closely imitates vision by producing dim apparitions, vaporous spirits, "pictures" in our minds, or, as with Saint Joan of Arc, religious "visions." (Note that she was later tried for heresy and sorcery and was burned at the stake for her efforts.)

I suspect that the mimicry might have evolved because we have so vehemently opposed the intuitive system, yet so greatly needed intuition's information. Because the other sensory systems have always been perfectly admissible as fact-finders, the effects might somehow have mimicked their perceptible signals over time in an attempt to skip past the critics. For instance, as organized religions became more powerful the church authorities called psi effects dangerous and denounced followers who experienced them. And once the scientific method justifiably gained the stature of "truth," rationalists condemned intuition's information as false and groundless. Over time humankind accredited these institutions, thus casting out intuition and its censured psi effects.

Historically we have seen that conditions will be preserved if they are useful in some way in the struggle for existence. Our intuitiveness is one such condition, because it alone guides us in certain critical interactions with one another and when mortal danger threatens. For this reason isn't it possible that the Clarification effect is simply a natural act of preservation? I believe that the disguise has enabled intuitiveness to endure centuries of mistreatment and neglect and will continue to do so.

Note: I think it possible that the Clarification system will devolve as we gradually adjust to using the primary effects. It would disappear for much the same reason a snake sheds its skin, or our wisdom teeth and appendixes are vanishing. Simply put, we will outgrow them; however, that disappearing act might take a hundred million years.

## Dreaming

Although dreams are not exclusively intuitive—some are thera-peutic—almost any escaping intuited information will also be rerouted through daydreams and night dreams. Once more, these duplicate the primary effects' information. We are fortunate to have this set of headlights as lifesavers! Whether or not my expla-nation of redundant components will prove to be the real reason for the "Mimic" and "Lookout" effects is far less important than the fact that they exist as the rescue unit.

## The Correction Mechanism

Having described the intuitible systems that vary, the discussion now moves on to the second question posed at the beginning of this chapter, regarding the precision of intuition. People ask: If this is a correction we are supposed to make, then what makes us capa-ble of restoring that variable to its prescribed point? The answer begins with a remarkable example of the entire intuitive process.

# CHAPTER 8

# Small Adjustments

(Ψ-31) IT WAS August 1972 in eastern France. We were picnicking by the Moselle River. My older children were in and out of the water with youngsters from a nearby village. I was reading to my three-year-old. He and I were seated in the shade of the farmer's tall wheat thirty feet from the riverbank.

In the middle of a sentence, Telepathy interrupted, breaking my concentration completely. It was detectable first as a mental sense that something was terribly wrong, and was followed immediately by an impression of terror. I looked up quickly, hoping to see the problem, but the pleasant scene before me could easily have been a painting on an artist's canvas depicting an ideal summer's day at the river. A dozen noisy children without a common language were merrily playing together. Although nothing looked out of order, the alarm pressed in my head: Somewhere a person was absolutely frantic.

## The Intuitive Process from Beginning to End

The information that had alerted me was a strong, swift mental sensation, the kind of nonverbal "certainty" that slips into the head uninvited; it could be identified as "knowledge" or a "sense" of knowing. This sensation carried a combination of impressions filled with information: first, a silent scream—only one; next a wild creature's agitation and extreme confusion.

At the same moment I stood up for a better view across the murky, fast-flowing river, intuition's navigational system took over automatically. This is the compass, or orienting, feature of it that I call the Intuitive Positioning System. This was the familiar control that I knew would guide my next moves. I would be led to the source of the signal.

Hence, I started walking, just as I had with the briefcase. I crossed the field to the riverbank, jumped into the water and stroked straight to the middle of the river, turned ninety degrees to face downstream, then submerged and swam underwater, taking full advantage of the rapid current. Fifteen feet ahead, I spied the suggestion of a thrashing form. Through the haze, it looked like the kind of shadowy specter one meets in a ghostly tale. But this was more. Here was the panic! I realized I was behind a child.

Moving quickly, I wrapped my arm around his body and carried him to the surface. Exhausted from a terrifying battle for life, he rode, deadweight, so limp that he might as well have been a waterlogged rag doll. Once on shore, he collapsed in a gasping heap; when his lungs were clear, he fell sound asleep.

### No Language Barrier in This World

The foregoing is another example of Telepathy's bypassing a solid language barrier. The drowning child was French; he knew no English. My French was extremely limited. But our speech barrier had no sway that afternoon. His language that day was universal: "Life endangered." The vocabulary is derived of raw fear, panic, and inaudible cries for assistance. When sent telepathically, these are distinguishable to everyone.

We learn from this example the never-to-be-forgotten fact that on any occasion, in every nook and cranny of life, peril speaks in its own dialect—fluently. I cannot leave out a comparison to the assassins ($\psi$-27): their telepathic message was also distinct, but it was triggered by a completely different mental state. While both were strong and compelling, one that was murderous fury, the other mortal terror.

## The Action Element of the Intuitive Process

Why did I learn that day on the riverbank? What triggered our contact?

Returning to analyze what happened, we see only that one young life was unraveling in the grand design. We have to assume that the child perturbed the natural atmosphere as he would have by shouting for help. I am certain this was an intuitive contact because the sensations were typically telepathic. They could be equated with any designated sensory process. Hearing, for example, produces a mammoth variety of sounds, but they are always noise. Our audio system is designed only for sound; it is not sensitive to chemicals as is our nose. Intuition likewise is a specialized sense. Its sensations and data are consistent.

When wanting to prove that an experience is intuitive, I find it useful to inquire what else would have caught my attention. In this situation, no one saw the boy, and being underwater, he was unable to scream with his voice for help. What's more, I was reading. If he weren't linked in intuitively, how could I otherwise ever have known?

Who initiated the contact? The boy did. Because he was gulping so much water, his oxygen supply was depleting rapidly. He was in danger of suffocating. This means that a living system was collapsing. As surely as we feel the movement of wind on our face, we intuit shifts within systems when a life is endangered. Nature uses more ways than shouting to call for help: Intuition is always available for the job.

I have stated repeatedly that we are intuitive because we can help when a system is falling off set point. So, I now ask, was a human assist essential here, or could the boy have saved himself? He was ten years old and knew how to swim.

Regardless of his abilities, the answer is he could *not* have saved himself. Look at the facts: By the time his alarm perturbed the atmosphere, he was a complete victim headed for death. Trapped by the forces of nature, he was no physical match for a river that would remorselessly swallow him whole. Recalling the limp form riding to shore, I would say that he was helpless to do anything more for himself—except to be mortally terrified. Note that his panic succeeded as the communication of choice; it triggered my intuitive sensors. Without it? In this case, it is plain that he would have drowned that day.

## State-of-the-Art Navigation

The last element that is fundamental to the intuitive regulatory process is navigation, which in purest terms is the way of directing the movement of a craft from one point to another. The big problem in following up on a psi effect *is* the navigation. How will we return the system precisely to set point? That is a tall order. How can we move exactly from one place to another?

Sure, we have information about what to do. But we also need a guidance system telling us where to move, when to start, and when to stop. You saw one example of intuitively driven navigation in the Vancouver chase ($\psi$-7). In France it appeared again. This section describes how I honed in on the person in danger— and how anyone succeeds in so doing with intuition.

In that situation on the Moselle, my intuition took over in a way that is not at all unusual. It started when Telepathy sounded the alarm correctly. I learned that someone was struggling at that very moment, but I was helpless to see who it was. Now, you have read in two previous accounts—one centered in Oklahoma ($\psi$-2) and the other in Egypt ($\psi$-27)—that we cannot always give a hand even with good intuitive information, because that is only half the process. Neither of the intuitors in those cases had the power to assist—more strong evidence that knowledge can be powerless to help. This time at the river was different. I could follow through. But how did I know?

This goes to that second question about what enables us to make precise corrections. Think about the follow-up sequence: I walked, swam, turned, dived under, and swam farther until I found the trouble. Likewise, in Vancouver we had to navigate through a maze of busy streets in a vast, unfamiliar city. Why were both of these attempts successful, and seemingly so easy?

Many people have told of finding a place by using their internal "radar." They describe managing to locate the proverbial needle in a haystack—houses, people, offices. At the base of all these tracking operations lies the fundamental guidance system leading the intuitor to his or her destination, and the essential key to intuition's precision. The intuitive navigation system is ready and available whenever we need.

## The Intuitive Positioning System

The plain explanation of how I found the lost boy is that I was guided, not by any ritual, supernatural force or spiritual being, but by this Intuitive Positioning System, as I call it, or IPS. I can assure you that this is a normal biological means of following through on psi effects. It led me.

We have an internal orienting system in the IPS; it provides intuitive people precise information twenty-four hours a day anywhere in the world. I am confident that we will discover its structures within our nervous system one day. It has parallels in the organic world. We could compare it to following a trail intuitively with a hound dog chasing a scent—another creature in pursuit of a distant invisible object. I alluded to this dog in the Vancouver chase. A more concrete correspondence is the man-made Global Positioning System, or GPS, used for navigating in aircraft, boats, and even some automobiles. However, the most helpful parallel would naturally be another human sensory system.

Untangling this knot of intuitive orientation begins with the following brief history of navigation, which illustrates the intuitive challenge of making blind moves accurately. From there we'll return to our senses and uncover why intuitively driven action can be precise.

## The Navigation Factor

Early mariners navigated their crafts by closely following a coastline (coasting) or by steering toward a recognizable landmark (homing). The reason for this is obvious. At sea, humans prefer to be oriented; we want to know where we are in relation to where we are going.

The first big advance in navigation came when seafarers began to estimate position by calculating the direction and distance they had traveled from their last known position (dead reckoning). This helped them sail in darkness and out of sight of land. A new era of navigation grew out of the Chinese discovery of the compass in the fourth century B.C. Then it was little more than a magnet floating in a bowl of water. Later, however, around 1120, this little device went to sea. The introduction of a magnetic instrument* along with the subsequent appearance of optical equipment such as the spyglass, and shipboard timekeepers including barometers, promoted the expansion of ocean voyaging. Captains have applauded every new improvement. They were empowered by each to determine their position on the planet with ever-increasing accuracy and to voyage confidently over short and long distances out of sight of land. This is exactly what we have a right to ask of intuition. It gives us accurate positioning when we have no other system guiding us and we are at sea.

The mariner's foremost problem has always been long periods of bad weather and poor visibility; one loses visual reference to both landmarks and celestial bodies. At the beginning of the twentieth century, radio communication changed sea travel forever. Building on that radio discovery, since 1990 we have added the dazzling new Global Positioning Systems which draw their information from dozens of orbiting satellites. These provide precise positioning information around the clock worldwide. Navigation today can be as simple as turning on this sensor system and reading the global position. Now we can know within ten meters (thirty-three feet) where we are on planet Earth at any given time. A far cry from our early efforts at orienting ourselves.

## The Sensory Factor

Looking around, we cannot help but notice that all precise movement is guided. If we want to reach any destination exactly, we have be able to propel ourselves there correctly. This means that some kind of measurement is required that shows where we are in relation to where we want to go; in other words, we need a

---

*As few people understood the forces moving the compass, quite naturally, superstitions evolved. For instance, captains forbade their crews to eat onions, which were thought to destroy magnetism!

navigational system. We have this in our intuition. It steers us in the direction of any phenomenon until required moves are complete. In the river rescue, the child was the destination. The Vancouver chase took us through town to another designated phenomenon—the man whose briefcase I carried.

I spent years trying to explain this homing capability. The first big riddle was how we learn the information. Now you have met the psi effects reporting the systems variables. Using the example of the river, we can go on to solve the second enigma: How did I know where to move to find that panic?

In reply I turn the question back to you. Think about this: If you enter a park on one side with the intention of walking to a bridge that is a hundred yards away from you but within sight, how do you know where to move? Your answer probably is that you would look over at that bridge to know where it is. Basically, you use your eyes to orient yourself to plot your course. (It is there. I am here.)

Now, when you start walking, let's say you notice a small garden about ten feet ahead. Your eye tells you that it is in your direct path. Without thinking, you slightly shift your direction of movement. That small compensation will take you around the edge but not too far off your course. Once past the garden, you automatically reorient yourself to the bridge and adjust your steps to line up with it. Now you are headed correctly, making good progress. But you see a child chasing bubbles who is unaware that he is about to run across your path. You take three quick steps to the left and avoid a collision. When the child has passed by, you notice that this new position is out of line again with your destination. Comparing the difference casually with your eye, you take three small steps to the right to make the next necessary adjustment that lines you up accurately with the bridge. You see that you can cut straight across from where you stand to reach your bridge. In a couple of minutes, you are right at the spot where you intended to be.

What actually happened? You knew where you wanted to go, set your sight on the destination, and moved steadily toward it. Basically, you had an orientation. Each time you detoured, you took your bearing—where you were in relation to where you were going. When necessary, you realigned and continued walking. In sum, your vision provided the information to start with and continually sent you reports while you made constant small corrections to move toward the bridge in as straight a line as possible. The answer to the question of how you knew where to move is that you used a sensory system—your eyes—to get exactly where you meant to be. Whenever you saw slight discrepancies in your orientation to your target, you simply made small corrections so that you could land precisely where you wanted.

A question: If you were to actually take that walk, how much attention do you think you would pay to making those small adjustments—a step here, a step there? The probability is that you would be so focused on the corner of that bridge, or perhaps a conversation, that any corrective actions would be nearly automatic— the small detour here for the garden, make a correction, three steps aside for the little boy, correction. Your center of attention would always be the destination; the rest would probably be mechanical.

To all intents and purposes, in such situations you are the person at the helm turning the wheel, but the directional system is up there in your head sending the subtlest navigational instructions when you fall off the compass point. In plain English, you correct your moves each time your course wanders. We can say that your navigation to the bridge was exact because you used a visual positioning system   a target, movement toward it, a corrective mechanism to adjust the course, and feedback of information about the corrective move. Now let's turn again to the riverbank and the Intuitive Positioning System.

Experience has taught me that the IPS works on the same principle as our visual positioning system, but of course the homing is up to the intuitive sensors. It is not dependent on light and a pair of eyes to see the objective. We still have a specific destination (the scene of the panic) and still continually correct our action (moving toward the panic) to arrive precisely on the mark that the detectors are reporting (the panicked boy). As was the case with the man in Vancouver, I had no idea where I was going; because this was intuition, I had to follow through the whole sequence of events without seeing the destination or calculating the distance to it. However, intuition is a state-of-the-art human navigational system. It guided me through the entire procedure, and it will do the same for any intuitor.

Again the IPS as I conceive it is a twin to vision's positioning system. Both set your true reference point. Both allow you to go on automatic pilot. In the same manner that you skirted the garden and moved aside for the child and then automatically readjusted your steps, you will do likewise as you move toward an intuited mark—say, turning a corner and climbing a hill. This target-move-compare-correct procedure is a completely normal feedback process for steering you, and *it will be accurate*. People who describe reaching a location by "following my nose" often are referring to using using this IPS. Like the detector thermostat in a heating unit, it automatically makes the comparison and initiates correction.

While it is certainly easier to use your vision for orienting yourself to a phenomenon that you want to help, if that objective is a small boy who is not to be seen but only intuited, then you will be very glad for this extra Intuitive Positioning System. I predict that in the future when we all can use our intuitiveness brilliantly, it will seem every bit as normal as sight.

## Sensors in Relay

Finally, in the river rescue we have to inquire: How did intuition know when to stop? What did stop it?

The short answer is that as long as the child was the Factor "U," intuition was in charge. My responsibility was to keep moving until the unknown phenomenon—a boy in trouble—was known. Only then would the searching stop. Experience taught me long ago that this is always so. As long as the emergency existed, the panicked child was the sole object in the "sight." He was the same to me as that bridge was to you.

You will notice in this case that *intuition stopped signaling before the crisis was over.* This is because it was only one of two sensory systems used in the rescue operation. They worked in relay. Intuition covered the portion during which only telepathy and the IPS could supply accurate information and drive my movement. It passed the wand, so to speak, to the visual sensors when I could see him with my eyes. They relieved intuition as soon as the unknown was known. I used my visual positioning system to swim to the shore for the last segment in the near miss with death. Similarly the mathematician: Once I spotted him visually, I worked my way through the crowd, using reports from my eyes.

## Intuitive Navigation

What has happened? In your walk toward the bridge, you became the equivalent of a mariner steering toward a landmark by the traditional method of homing in during the day. Every school-child knows that the same process would be nearly impossible on a moonless night. If we come upon a situation at night and have only this visual capability, we are virtually helpless.

Metaphorically speaking, this is precisely the situation we face today. Too many unknowns. Too much is unpredictable. Our ordinary sensory systems are not able to identify these Factors "U." But while vision doesn't work in the dark, remember that intuition does. It is here, in us, to report the Factors "U."

Human beings have always been required to know things that eyes could not see. Once we all were tribes and nomads looking for wildlife that might destroy us before we could kill it. Now, most of us encounter strangers daily and need Telepathy to know their intentions. As we enter this young world of reason with all of its variety of products, we must be able to identify what is safe and what is not—foods, drugs, machines, innovations of chemistry and physics. Fortunately, as it was in the history of navigation, so it is in the story of humankind: We have a new instrument evolving within us that will assist our interactions in the mental darkness. It is a completely different device, an inner guidance system that we have to train.

How difficult is this going to be? Easier than you think. During my lifetime I have sailed many dark and foggy nights at sea and know that confusion clouds my judgment when I lose my visual references—both landmarks and the stars in the heavens— to steer by. However, the world opened up with our new Global Positioning System on board. We could not get lost. Because of its ability to give us information about our position night and day, regardless of weather, we now sail to places that would have been out of the question in earlier days. Granted, it took a while to learn to use such high-tech equipment—and perhaps even longer to trust it. Charts and dead reckoning had served both of us faithfully all our sailing years. But with thousands of sea miles behind us now, I can say without reservation that this newest technology has saved the day many times when fog and clouds set in and stole our visual instruments of navigation, leaving us more vulnerable than anyone would care to be.

The Intuitive Positioning System has that same effect on daily life. It too opens up new territories for all of us. Using it well might take a bit of training, but that can be done. Trusting might take a little longer, but as you have seen in several accounts, when visibility is down and any human beings are at sea, intuition takes over competently and provides information that assures we will find our way and go straight on to flourish. When we can use it competently and fearlessly, humankind will have indeed begun a new era of navigation on the good ship earth.

# CHAPTER 9

# A New Tool for Humankind

ALL THE WHILE I have been suggesting that we have a new tool for digging facts out of the universe, I have been mindful of the skepticism and wrinkled brows of critics. They question how I can be so confident that these intuited snippets of information from the blue are factual. This chapter further supports my claim.

How do I *know* these are facts? It took at least a year to answer this question sensibly.

## What Is a Fact?

This next step in understanding intuition is a giant one, because it challenges us to define how we achieve anything at all—from thinking through the simplest problem to taking action on a major decision. The fundamental question is: What guides us to success when we have it or, the reverse, prevents top performances?

The most common answer is that achievement depends heavily on *acquiring enough accurate information*. The accuracy requirement implies that the information must be cemented in evidence.

Evidence suggests we have visible signs in hand that lead to a definite conclusion, in a word—facts.

Conventional wisdom says: "One must have sound data to make ideal decisions," and "Winning action comes from precise thinking." We can't argue with this. We're taught not to "jump to conclusions" but to "think things through"; that statistics are the best instruments for predicting; that factual evidence of anything from safety in travel to vitamins in food lends stability to an unsettled world and gives each of us reliable tools for choosing how to control our lives. As youngsters, and oldsters, we're told that success depends on facts . . . facts . . . facts! This dictum, of course, has much merit.

Children worldwide learn early in life that being well informed with exact data can mean the difference between personal and professional success or failure. Consider your childhood as an example. When did you start learning things like: "The house is white," "Horses have four legs," "Two plus two equal four"? You probably can't even remember. What skills do primary and secondary schools emphasize more than anything else? Fact-finding. We're taught simple details at first, to build up storehouses of data—knowledge bases—which finally lead to understanding complex systems that become sciences, languages, history, and arts, both fine and vocational. Such accumulated knowledge of facts and figures becomes the sum and substance of well-developed individual skills and ultimately any society's strengths. Industrial nations are shaped by facts, thrive on them, and often succeed because of them. Of course, we assume that these are *proven* facts, the kind accompanied by visible evidence.

According to lexicographers, a "fact" is information that can be verified as real, that has been proven unequivocally. It has actual existence. For instance, look at the book in your hand. Touch it. Pound it with your fist! Your sensors report what you automatically "know for a fact." You know you are holding a real book because you can see it and feel it. In the truest sense of the word, you can *prove* by its material presence that the object exists.

Now, to a quite distracting fine point: We *assume* that a "fact" is something that can be readily proved. To illustrate: If you can't see the book I'm holding, you have the right to question my statement that I have a book in hand. You, and everyone else, can say that there only is a possibility that I am speaking fact, that I must prove it by showing you the book. Our universal agreement seems to be "Seein's believin'."

Alas, when you turn to the intuitive camp, you discover that this word "fact" takes on an important and equally as accurate second identity. *When using our intuitive ability to collect facts, we gather them before circumstances physically occur.* I was surprised when I found, and proved to my satisfaction, that human intuition always transmits factual reports but that, in complete contrast to our standard definition, it is not possible to authenticate these facts until *after* the activity in question is finished. Remember, for example, that brief announcement "The brakes are going to fail." You now know that statement *was* true, but when did the evidence come to light? After I acted on the *fact!* Likewise the French boy's panic. Although the example of the failing brakes would almost suffice as evidence that intuition breeds facts, as we go on to examine its modus operandi we will discover that we must always treat our intuited knowledge as factual *before* solid proof is home. In time the pattern will appear that shows, without exception, the information we learn via psi effects is accurate.

## Deeper into the Process

The following seven accounts, one for each psi effect, give examples from an intuitor's position in the process from beginning to end. From these we can begin to recognize the fine grain of the events leading the intuitor and the intuitively driven moves that ensue. Recall the three-step process: (1) Detect the psi effect. (2) Make the decision. (3) Follow through. *Information/Decision/Move.*

Put yourself in the intuitor's shoes as you read, and use the following guidelines as an aid in understanding intuition as a regulatory mechanism: (1) Ask yourself why that person learned what he or she did. In other words, what mental or physical situation influenced the intuitive sensitivity. Here is the system variable. (2) Find the factual psi effect. This is the detector. (3) Note when the fact was confirmed. The return to set point. (4) Study the intuitor. How did that person follow through—or not? This will be the correction. Was the IPS involved? (5) Ask yourself what you would have done in the same situation or one that is similar.

Please note that these accounts all occurred spontaneously. They are arranged in the same sequence in which the corresponding effects are listed in Chapter 7. The two leaders, Telepathy and Teleos, with their pure environmental information are first. Instruction and Reflex pick up when time runs short and fewer options are available. Clarification and Dream appear as the very important redundant systems that protect the intuitive process. Déjà vu here is an example of the psyche's microworld processes as described by a child.

### Telepathy: Passions Soar

(ψ-32) When my sister passed away unexpectedly, we who were left soldiered on with true Yankee resolve. Life became a matter of putting one slow moving foot in front of the other, of letting each seemingly endless day heal the pain of her suffering and our loss. A year later, we all were much steadier on our feet. Not yet free from our sorrows, at least we were no longer yielding to them each time they erupted.

When families pass any milestone, legal affairs usually change, and a death is no exception. Therefore, when we'd had enough discussions, and were satisfied we'd taken giant steps toward reclaiming our composure, on the appointed day we confidently sat down with the lawyer. Things were going swimmingly. We talked cordially, discussed and agreed to the cheerless rephrasing required for the various documents, and even managed to laugh a little.

In this comfortable atmosphere we finally arrived at the moment for signing the new papers. The lawyer swept them lightly across his desk in the direction of my mother. When they were in front of her, I noted with admiration that her facial expression held firm. Then, without warning, I felt everything change. I was struck suddenly by her despair. While her physical demeanor reflected a tower of reserve, I felt her determined restraints topple, dropping her without any warning into her carefully buried soul-piercing pain, much the way a person who trips over a rock is unceremoniously pitched to the ground.

How powerful is this vital voiceless mental world we humans inherit! And how suddenly its forces break free! Aspiration, passion, frustration, and emotion—all discharge like lightning into the atmosphere, striking human trees everywhere. I recall the instant I was struck that day. Had I used only my eyes, would I have known this determined woman was struggling yet again with the anguish of separation from a beloved daughter? No. Her face continued to show composure, exposing nothing that could concern an observer. But I had been informed that she was at sea. There I sat, looking at her dumbly, knowing as well as I knew my own name that even though she had summoned every ounce of her iron will, and was successfully maintaining the compulsory New England composure, her natural passions had plummeted her once more into the uncharted territory of a grieving mother's loving heart.

To my continued amazement, with the papers in position, she paused only a second to arrange the pen and then leaned forward, apparently ready to sign the whole bundle. But, because of that lightning strike, I was absolutely sure she should be stopped, even though I couldn't understand what in particular had perturbed her. My voice broke the silence.

"Wait . . . please!"

She and the lawyer stared at me mutely.

I looked directly at her and asked, "Something's wrong, isn't it, Mother?"

She lifted the pen from the paper and leaned back in her chair, looking relieved.

I continued, "Are we leaving something out?"

At last the passion surfaced for all to see. The lawyer looked concerned for the first time.

She replied, "Well . . . yes, I don't want to sign this the way it is. . . ."

Her voice drifted off, providing me with the opportunity to press her a little and get to the reason she had foundered. Happily, the solution was simple, the changes were made, and the papers were signed without further adieu. When all was said and done, that sorrow lifted. A light trace of serenity moved over her and set both of us free.

What happened? Someone was suffering but wouldn't, or couldn't, speak for herself. However, to sign the papers without changing them would probably continue the despair and even add to it. She was miserably unhappy.

This true-life tale is marvelous evidence of the interrelatedness of human beings. Just as the trees in forests are tossed and torn in wind and rain, so can we human beings be buffeted by any storm-tossed human being. The distress signals from my mother's quaking passions that day ripped naturally through the atmosphere we shared. The instant the atmosphere changed in that room, Telepathy detected it—as it happened. This was heavy weather setting in. The Barometer's needle was plummeting. Mental lightning was bolting everywhere. We had an emergency. It was clear that the optimal outcome depended on another human's helping to change the conditions. On this particular day, my intuitive sensitivity received the upset and thus enabled me to call time-out.

Why me and not the lawyer? There are many reasons, no doubt. But the greatest of them is love. It keeps us "awake." She wanted to make excellent decisions to honor both of her daughters and had been thrown off unexpectedly by her still overpowering grief. Telepathy helped bring home the result she wanted for us all and left her heart a little lighter.

## Teleos: Zoom Lens Through Impassable Borders

One afternoon a close friend experienced this psi effect. We discussed it immediately afterward, because she was overwhelmed by the accurate forewarning.

(ψ-33) Jan's account is that she was watching her husband when he reached for an apple from the fruit bowl on our kitchen table. At that instant, Jan knew he would choke if he took a bite. However, she didn't call out spontaneously to stop him, as she might have if he were about to step in front of a moving car. A few minutes later, while he was chewing, a piece of apple lodged in his windpipe; he began choking and struggling for air, just as she'd known he would. Then, of course, she ran to his assistance immediately. He recovered quickly with a few sound slaps on his back.

Consider what this account implies. Intuition is constantly on alert as your personal periscope, providing an unobstructed view of the nonstop movement in matter all around the universe—including a trifling sequence of events in which one man is reaching for an apple. At the exact junction when help is required you can detect enough precise information to steer the developing incident away from damaging life and toward supporting it.

Could I say that my friend's periscope was down that day? Absolutely not. Jan intuited exactly what would occur—bite would lead to choke. What happened, then, to prevent her from intervening? She said, rather sheepishly, that she didn't tell her husband what she knew because she didn't want to sound like his overanxious mother, who interrupts people constantly to predict gloom and doom for whatever they might be doing. Of course, they all know by now that her mother-in-law is simply an anxiety-ridden person, but everyone in the family has become weary of her empty warnings. It's no wonder Jan bends over backward to not be a twin to her. However, her kindly effort deals a nasty blow to the effectiveness of her intuition.

I asked her: If she had seen an automobile approaching rapidly, would she have had the same misgiving? She said, "Of course not. Naturally I would have called out a warning." Virtually anyone would have done the same. Why then are we such timid intuitive creatures?

Jan was precognitive. She knew what would happen before her husband physically took the bite. Sadly, her lack of intuitive experience meant that the avoidable danger would proceed on the course it was traveling, even though a forewarned human being was standing in the room.

Fortunately, nature has devised an internal redundant system for our complete intuitive misses. Without her intuition as the best early warning system, his physical body came to the rescue. When he began choking, nature's gag reflex kicked in and would have expelled the offending foreign body even without her helping hand. Again we see the example of extra systems duplicating functions. The psi effect probably should have been enough, but when it failed, his own reflexes could also help, though he suffered much more distress than he would have if intuition had succeeded.

Here is a classic illustration of our worldview's interfering with our newest sensory ability. A woman was intuitively sensitive to a developing sequence of events. It would cause physical discomfort—or worse. Unfortunately the danger was invisible to the naked eye. Nevertheless, Jan was well advised. The problem for her was that the actual choking was in the future. This threw her off. In her world of ideas, she was convinced we can't know the future. On that account she doubted herself and therefore didn't take responsible action. Poor husband. When he took the bite that might not have been, the chain of events continued to unfold on the track to adversity.

Jan's belief that we can't know the future was unshakable—until that day. Her experience is a splendid example of this Teleos effect and also, unfortunately, of our current response to it. It is clear that she could have altered the future in a small but immensely helpful way by using her option to act.

Think how useful this precognitive ability will be to science. We will know in advance when an experiment is headed for disaster, or advantage. In medicine, this will be an extraordinary aptitude for physicians who prescribe drugs. They will "sense" who among that purportedly small percentage of the population might be allergic to a medication, and will foretell which minor conditions will spread and which won't. What of attacks other than illness? Terrorists, automobile accidents, planes, trains, boats, weather—all are predators, and we all are prey. The potential in our Teleos talents is beyond imagining.

What was Jan's learning experience during the psi effect? Did she have any sensation? She describes it as simply being informed. No rattling bones, whistles, inner voices, Fourth of July fireworks, or any other folderol. She simply detected the knowledge when it came into her head "as being something like having an idea." Unlike a daydream or an idle notion that floats around in one's head and seems "kind of interesting," hers had a definiteness about it. In her words, she was "absolutely certain" she was learning information about her husband.

Jan now understands that hers was bedrock information, the solid stuff that should drive a decision and result in action. She had learned a fact. Her argument for not acting immediately was a nonrational one born of both anxiety about a mother-in-law, and a mind-set of unsupported beliefs that this was not possible. It happens to all of us occasionally, when gravelly mental noise causes us to slip and lose our footing of good judgment.

Jan learned that day, as we all must, that intuition is always right. Trouble was afoot, lurking in the shadow of a thoroughly innocent action. She now knows that since choking is hazardous and can be as deadly as being struck by a car, she should have used that information to brake the sequence. It is a satisfaction to know that one calm statement from her could have tipped the scales right.

## The Instruction: Direction, Timing, and Distance Adjustments

(ψ-34) On entering a room, I noticed an unfamiliar woman who smiled at me pleasantly:

*Keep away from her.*

This effect was as strong in my head as any bright idea might be. Even with the warning, I decided immediately that I wouldn't leave the gathering but would be alert to any more impressions from her. I began to socialize.

A familiar intuitive feeling of "unquiet" at the back of my thoughts erupted an hour later when she approached the group in which I stood. I felt what some people describe as "bad vibes." Even knowing that we were interacting caustically in the atmosphere, I suppose I hoped she would rise above herself in company. She popped that bubble when, without so much as introducing herself, she turned to me and, in an agitated voice, launched into a vitriolic attack on my field as unscientific. She didn't stop there. For what she described as "religious reasons," she expressed shock that I would dare lecture publicly on the subject and, worse, teach privately. When she finally stopped, the small group dispersed without a word, leaving us alone. After commenting confidently that other people held the same viewpoint, I also excused myself from her angry airborne grip.

Her display certainly confirmed my earlier spontaneous impression that she was a menace despite her friendly smile. Intuition had distinguished her as incompatible well ahead of my other senses.

Like Telepathy and Teleos effects, this Instruction occurs in countless situations as a nonverbal "sense" or "feeling," alternatively in stronger mental impressions accompanied by words or phrases. The command might be like a gentle interruption in your thinking—a "sense" that "something here is right—or wrong," a strong "hunch," or a purely mental "feeling of knowing," as this was. (These sensations are not to be mistaken for a "gut feeling," which is associated with the Clarification effect.) The important factor for this Instruction effect is that it definitely is a directive in all cases.

However, while it is a command, it is not rigid. Unlike the Reflex effect, in which the actual move is the only evidence of intuitive sensitivity at work, this category points the direction for action—where to go, when to start, when to stop. Since I was forewarned, perhaps it appears that I was foolhardy to stay at the gathering. You will learn shades of gray in these effects' information. For instance, I am sure that the instruction would have been more urgent if the woman had been a serious physical threat. Being more sour lemon than murderess, she did not have much influence on my sensitivity—that mood breeze mentioned earlier. I would say that the optimal result of my being aware of her as threatening was the ability to excuse myself gracefully, without any overdramatic reaction.

Instruction's commands are never ambiguous. The intuitor is learning exactly what to do. Anyone having such a sensation would be able to distinguish it and say with assurance that it is neither personal opinion nor emotion, nor a memory dredged up from experience. It is instead, incontestably and without exception, a *fresh lead* to action. Many times it overrides an intuitor's fixed opinions and usual social conduct, as in Operation Toothbrush (ψ-16).

## Reflex: We're Getting Pushed Around

(ψ-35) We had been sailing for about five hours with a steady fifteen-knot wind on our beam, crossing from Antigua to Guadeloupe in the West Indies. The swells were smooth and regular, making the boat lift and fall as gently as if it were an infant's cradle. I was settled comfortably in a corner of the cockpit, with the wind at my back. From that position I could check the three sails from time to time.

My husband and I were chatting pleasantly when I excused myself abruptly. For no reason I could explain, I stepped down the gangway and into the main cabin, turned the sharp corner and walked along the narrow eight-foot passageway, then entered the captain's cabin and, finally, walked into the bathroom, called a "head" on boats. Once there, I calmly closed the window above the sink and locked it down by twisting four knobs, or "dogs," until it was watertight. It was unusual for me to shut that particular port light; in gentle seas, such as we had that day, it is ordinarily open to assure good air circulation through the cabin. That done, I headed back to the cockpit.

As I walked along the passage, the boat heeled over sharply and quivered from bow to stern in reply to what I knew had to be an unusually large wave slamming against her. Arriving topside, I discovered that the peaceful place I'd left less than five minutes before was now a pool of sloshing water, and Gayne, seated at the wheel, was dripping from head to foot. Obviously amused, he raised his sopping arms and shrugged in mock helplessness. While he drained off a bit, he described a freak wave that was more powerful and about twice as high as the gentle swells we'd been enjoying. It had pounded us broadside, cascading water up over the rail, unceremoniously dousing both him and the cockpit on its way over the hull. Then, patting my comfortable dry clothes as though I were a sideshow curiosity of some kind, he asked me to explain my shrewd disappearing act at that particular moment. Where had I gone?

I described dogging down the port light. However, I couldn't spell out precisely what made me leave so impetuously, for the move had been entirely spontaneous. At that point I made a quick check to find out whether I might have actually seen the wave coming, but it was obvious that even if it had been visible, my position would have impeded me, because the wind and oncoming sea were at my back.

While recounting my side of the brief story, I noticed Gayne staring at my face intently, as if he were trying to see into my head and find his preferred completely rational answer floating inside there, the way one catches sight of fish swimming among the thick plants in glass tanks. When he began speaking, almost to himself, I understood from his comments that my timing had been impeccable. This was definitely the strong wave I'd felt as I walked the passageway. We concluded together that intuition drove me to action. And, what a move it was! A coincidence of the finest order. Had the port light been open, the head, and our cabin too, would have been inundated. I couldn't help laughing when that salty captain of mine repeated again what he has said many times. "There certainly are advantages to being a 'spook' and knowing such unpredictable things." From my intuitively sheltered corner of the world, I couldn't help but agree.

Reflex is efficient. Was that run to close the port light a coincidence, dumb luck, or intentional? I would say I was driven to it.

Perhaps you are asking why I am so sure this was intuition. Well, consider these questions. First: Why did I learn intuitively? Second: How did it empower me? And third: Did it favorably influence the course of natural events? Or, we could ask one general question: Did the psi effect enable me to detect Factor "U" and create the best possible outcome with the information? I suggest that we all ask this question on each occasion in which we discover intuition at work. It is invaluable in confirming an intu-itive connection. Let us apply the questions to this account.

The answer to the first question—Why?—is that a natural phenomenon was about to throw the room off its ideal. As to the second—empowerment: it got me moving. Did I know where I was going, or what I would do once I arrived somewhere? No. There was no known purpose. I was like a mindless rolling stone. Let us ask how I knew. As is always the case with the Reflex, I simply didn't understand my behavior—until *after* the excitement was over. Obviously, neither one of us knew. Even though the rogue wave was approaching, it was completely invisible and inaudible; apparently only the intuitive system was sensitive enough to it to drive anyone to action in time to prevent the potential damage. It certainly did empower me.

And the last point—the purpose of intuition to optimalize: Did the action bring that result? Absolutely. In this case, we humans were in no danger, but the boat is our home, and we are the assigned caretakers. Yes, it definitely was better off for not being deluged.

In summary, this Reflex effect did the only thing it is sup-posed to do: It thwarted the impending flood from the rogue, using me to do the requisite work. Cockpits are designed to drain, and humans dry naturally, but living quarters are not intended to be awash with any water, salt or otherwise.

## Clarification: A Clear Cover-Up

A representative sample of intuition's Clarification effect comes from the public at large. Uncountable numbers of people report having "gut feelings" or the "gut call." They describe "knowing what to do" because of nonrational, nonverbal signals that seem to help them identify in which direction to take a decision or make a move. Such feelings seem "visceral," like a resonance in the "gut," or like a vague intestinal tension. Most agree that these feelings definitely are not imagined. Neither are they authentic physical symptoms of known physical states such as are experienced during illness—a stomachache or cramp, for example. Almost everyone understands these references to experiences and will usually settle the question of their origin by suggesting that they are "instinct" or "intuition, whatever that is." For my part, such intuition helped me to learn a great lesson in life.

($\psi$-36) This was a beautiful day, the kind when the beauty itself settles gently on the mind, so I was surprised when my concentration suddenly broke into a wispy mental picture of a head bent down. The image caught my attention only briefly, but a distressing feeling of misery held me in its grip for ten minutes, after which time, without any fanfare, it dissolved as abruptly as it had entered. I checked the clock. It was two on the dot. Someone was suffering acutely.

During dinner that evening, my young son recounted a rather unpleasant fifteen minutes during recess when a teacher assigned to yard duty accused him of throwing paper on the school grounds. She had scolded him roundly in front of his friends. He felt disgraced, not only because the woman made a public fuss, but, more important, because she wrongly accused him.

Aha! There it was. The times jibed. I had "felt" that distress at precisely the hour he was feeling humiliated. We had been in contact telepathically. But clearly I had missed the signal. According to the laws of intuition if a primary connection fails, then Clarification repeats the information by creating its sensation-like effects. This explains the wispy semblance of a head; it would have been a clairvoyant effect. The strain of wretchedness was clairsentience.

Now, I had no illusions about this son of mine. This was not the first time he had been scolded, nor would it be the last. He was as mischievous as the best of them. But there was an interesting twist here. Experience had taught me that if the teacher had been right in her reprimand, then I would never have learned about it intuitively. I knew my child well. When punishment was fair and just, he didn't become so upset that his mood meshed with my mentality. Feeling his disturbance as strongly as I had, I knew that his teacher was misusing her authority and abusing him. Otherwise I would not have been involved.

I promised him I would contact the administration and censure the woman for misusing her adult privileges with sensitive children who were learning from people like her how they should behave in life. Needless to say, I was on the telephone with the principal first thing the next morning.

A point of social concern arises in this account. Realizing that this intimate contact is possible, think of what we can learn from children, indeed from all humans, who are suffering wrongly. As stated earlier, we detect only those individuals in dire straits; they are the ones falling off the edges of their worlds. Thus, intuition is important to us all.

More and more we rely on polls, statistics, and generalizations to tell us about people on the street. These anonymous crowds have the effect of displacing individuals who need to be taken into account. While polls don't change us personally, they do depersonalize us. Most of us don't feel like a lump of people, but instead one voice—however small—with value enough to speak our own minds and feel our own feelings. In this context, the remarkable and very significant value of intuition is that it knows us as individuals. It separates the world into units, highlighting the true importance of every life, and of each vital cell driving that life. It honors each person on the street who is frightened, every clerk behind a counter who is frustrated, every child under water who is panicked, and those on the land who despair.

## Dreams: The Watch

($\psi$-37) My heart froze the day I received a telephone call from the principal of my thirteen-year-old son's junior high school in California. His message was ominous at best: "Your son is on his

way home now. But I want to warn you: He's mad at everyone."
He went on with the chilling facts. "There has been a fight.
Although your son didn't start it, he was involved . . . but," he
added quickly, "we checked him. He's not hurt."

As the principal's account unfolded, I began to understand
that a group of students had attacked Jeff without provocation.
The fighters had chains and switchblades. The skirmish happened on the school grounds during afternoon recess.

While listening to the principal's string of apologies and his
muddled explanation for the inexcusable violation, I saw my son
turn in to the driveway. Promising the principal that he'd be
hearing from me before five o'clock, I excused myself and hung
up the phone. At the door Jeff assured me he wasn't badly injured,
although he had a strange story to tell.

Speaking solemnly, he repeated the sequence of events that the
principal had relayed, finishing with the description of the actual
confrontation. He reported, "I didn't get hurt, Mom, because
when they were circled around me, I decided to run for it."

He described how he had managed to get the boys fighting
among themselves. Pausing a moment, he set the stage for the conclusion, which seemed to amuse him: "That worked so well that I
looked for my chance to cut in the afterburners and get away clean."

While his amusement surprised and certainly relaxed me, I
was enormously impressed with his quick-witted self-defense. I
asked, "What ever made you think to do that?"

He took some minutes to explain that he'd dreamed one night
of just such a showdown. It had been several weeks since the dream,
but he'd thought about it a couple of times and even wondered
whether it would actually happen to someone. He then explained
why, even though he hadn't figured out exactly what he would do in
advance, he was sure his actions were the direct result of that dream.

The crowd of fifteen had approached his smaller group of
pals. Intending to provoke, the boys began their attack with

words: "Get outa' our way. This is our place here." His chums scattered instantly. He discovered he was alone with the fighters. They circled quickly.

At that point he remembered how they had drawn around in the dream. Then the dream and reality matched. That solved his confusion, making the rest easy, he said. He knew he could figure out what to do. He was terrified, of course, but being so forewarned, he didn't panic. Once inside their ring of fury, he could physically see the arrangement of the boys from a perspective he hadn't in the dream.

It seems that he had to wait for the living moment to literally see the best way to escape. For example, in real life, his attackers were in complete disarray. Preoccupied with avoiding injury from their own flapping chains and waving knives, they didn't notice when he dropped down and left them fighting one another. In that flash of time, he was inconspicuous enough to scramble out unnoticed and run.

I asked what happened at the end of the dream.

"I didn't get hurt much in there either," he said.

For some seconds following his finish, I sat staring at my vulnerable not yet man-child. He had stayed cool, but that definitely was a three-new-gray-hairs day for his horrified mother! Unsure of myself, I asked him what we should do next. He had already figured it out. First, see that every one of his attackers was expelled. Second, I should drive him to the door of the school for the next week. I heartily agreed to both. As I'd promised, I phoned the principal that same afternoon.

Oh, how that principal worked to change our first decision! Frightened of possible repercussions from the children's parents, he instead wanted me to keep my son away from school for a period of time, for his own protection. I couldn't accept that proposal, since in essence it meant they were expelling Jeff rather than the attackers.

I countered: "Why deny him his education?"

When he finally understood that we wouldn't retreat, the very unfortunate and nervous man yielded to our position. In the end, I think nearly everyone learned something of value from the unappetizing affair: Parents of the expelled children were on my phone that next evening, some yelling and calling me names, others thanking me for putting a steel rod in the backbone of a pathetically weak school administrator; my son developed confidence in the power of his dreams to forewarn him; I saw him grow more independent of us as protective parents because he'd found one more reliable defense mechanism.

Where did the dream lead the dreamer? It prepared him to make good decisions when the chain of events took real life, I think. Without claiming that it predicted the actual altercation, or that it solved the problem completely, at least we can say it set a safety net for potential danger, and did so without frightening him unnecessarily. Who could deny that it gave a young boy several advantages?

## Déjà vu: Close Encounters of a Personal Kind

Déjà vu, the last of the seven psi effects, takes us far beyond our known mental boundaries so that we can personally encounter intuition's microworld and microprocesses. Not by traveling in time, as some say, but instead with our own mental abilities, we meet the physical subsystems influencing us intuitively. We who don't have a scientific bent understand little of "interrelatedness," "mind," "matter-waves," or the "relationship between the inner and outer worlds." Yet, these are the ingredients in the recipe; they hold little meaning for most of us simply because when we are learning through Déjà vu, the world of objects and science ceases to exist. This vanishing act leaves us only images, similes, and metaphors. However, if we make this dimension an extension of ourselves, and become observers of what we are learning, then we are simply members of an audience enjoying the work of the artist. Taking this position as spectator, we are able to get nearer to the heart of the astonishing performance that

Déjà vu affords. We are observing that microworld where creation is a living event.

I could turn to metaphysics and say: "In a Déjà vu we meet the All, which is everywhere, and we are within there, learning." But perhaps the most charming description comes from a child, because, as you'll see in the following tale, it characterizes how an innocent tracks the experience of knowing the intuitive domain.

(ψ-38) Four-year-old David was playing on the floor, contentedly building serpentine tunnels and precariously high towers with his colorful blocks. Across the room I was ironing, entertained by watching him. He stopped, looked my way, and inquired, "Mommy, can you see in here?"

I asked, rather absently, "In where?" He was touching things testily—a toy truck, his leg, the floor, our kitten beside him.

He then asked, "Mommy, what do I look like to you?"

"You look like my little boy," I said, "wearing your favorite shirt and different-colored socks and building wobbly towers."

"Oh."

That completed our conversation. He returned to his engineering. I continued pressing.

Days later, while we were in the car, he asked, "Mommy, where am I?" His voice, coming from the backseat, sounded no different from usual.

I replied, "Now, you tell me. Where are you?"

"I'm inside here. I like this. Oop. I'm out again."

"Inside? Where did you go?" Like other tots, he had always delighted in fantasizing mysterious nooks and crannies into his private world. I was about to assume he was at his best game of make-believe—until he answered my next questions. We were parked now, waiting for a school bus.

I prompted, "Are you in our car?"

"Yes, I am now. But then I was watching it. It had our car in it today. You were there too. But it stopped, so I'm here now."

"Where is 'there'?"

"It's a place. Everything here is inside there."

"Is it in your head?"

He explained, "Mommy, *all* of me is in a *place*. Everything in there is just like here, except it isn't here." He took a pronounced breath to steady his growing impatience with me. "I'm in there watching everything."

I, too, hesitated, because I knew he was straining to understand something, to fit it into his four-year-old universe. Then I began to wonder. In our little discussions, he seemed to be describing this so-called place as an integral part of his whole world. He was shifting effortlessly between two detectable existences.

I realized that perhaps it wasn't fantasy this time. He might be describing Déjà vu. Groping for a way to learn, I inquired, "Is it like looking at yourself in your mirror?"

He was adamant. "No. Mommy, I'm not *seeing* myself. I'm *being* myself! I get inside a real *place*. Everything around me is in there too." He became thoughtful. "It's always moving." He pointed toward autumn leaves drifting to the sidewalk. "It moves like those leaves. *Everything* moves. I am watching it."

"How do you go there?"

"Suddenly . . . like this . . . zzzzip." To demonstrate, he clasped his hands, bent his body, and disappeared down behind the front seat. I was grateful his frustration had faded.

I called to him, "Do you know why you go there?"

He had reappeared. "Mmm, no. I just am there sometimes."

"Do you have to make yourself move?"

"No, Mommy, *it's* always changing. I am *inside* the moving."

"This sounds exciting. You can be in two places?"

He smiled brightly, happy, I think, that I finally was getting smarter. Now he began explaining as though he were my teacher.

"I get in that place, and am out here. I just change back and forth." He turned his head from side to side. "Here, there, here, there. . . ." He paused, then added, "I never get to stay very long."

"Do you know why?

"Mmm . . . no."

Cautious now, I stopped my questions.

I was fascinated. He could identify with two places, yet felt no conflict in their marked dissimilarity. In the Déjà vu, he perceived himself as life going on with endless local interactions—which he called "everything." He spoke as though he were learning clairvoyantly.

For the next several months, he talked fairly frequently about the places. He obviously enjoyed visits to the inside. As he described them, it became clear that he did not have divided worlds but rather separate experiences of life in one world—his world. For an adult, this might have been like the struggle with an optical illusion, but his perception shifted freely.

I learned some things that he knew about himself in each place. For example, on the "inside," he did not have bodily sensations such as hotness, or moods such as happiness. Apparently these were not part of existence "inside." It was a mental impression of life in moving shapes and tempos. When "inside," he detected himself as changing, seemingly as himself but not like a little boy. He was in free flow and felt buoyant, fully aware of himself developing with the surroundings, merged with the whole, and part of the events. In family-on-earth life, on the other hand, he perceived himself as an individual, at liberty to stop and go by choice, moved by his own feelings, as he called them, and liking them.

His encounters in the two worlds covered the full true scope of human life, which definitely does comprise one dimension of concrete objects—such as blocks, planes, and birds—that our visual sensors report, and one of cellular and elemental subsystems—the building blocks of nature. Perceiving both, he was master of the ultimate existential cognitive experience.

He knew himself just as easily in one dimension as in the other. The dominant place clearly was the familiar circle of family and home. The other, the phenomenon of creation in process, or synthesis, was just as detectable. He learned to describe both. He talked about the experiences and compared them more and more, almost casually.

As years went by and he took responsibility for his own development, he stopped reporting his two-world adventures. Growing up consumed his attention. Existence was dominated by the rigors of real-world physical and mental maturation. In his late teens, he commented one day that he missed the frequent visits inside. We reminisced, laughing together about conversations we recalled. He confided his surprise that, although more of a silent partner in his life, the effect still occasionally happened spontaneously, shifting him mentally from concentration on how to manage his life and worldly concerns, to perception of himself as part of creation.

## Look Where We Are Going

I repeat: Intuition is exposing us to the minute structure of matter, as in a mineral and a biological cell. We have a pure view of these very small structures in Déjà vu, whose solitary task is to present them as though they were pictures at an exhibition. In actual life, we intuit the interactive microenvironment in the other six psi effects. The common denominator in all seven is that we are joining in league with the universe. If we doubt this, we need only open our eyes. In a world abundant with examples of intuitive encounters, this sensory system is continually trumpeting: "Don't miss this. Look at what you know, where you have come, and where you could be going."

In Part I, I have proposed that we are evolving a learning capability that rivals no other. It empowers us to meet and interact with the building blocks of nature, to create and change society and ourselves in entirely new ways, and to flourish as we go, to feel the unity of all things, to "know" that we are co-creative with all that exists. With intuition to guide us, we will become wiser to the ways of the universe, a finer species in it, and more enjoyable company for one another. Again, I suggest that it helps us transcend our little selves and follow the paths of our true dreams, talents, and ambitions.

Some say that living so sensitively—that being so "awake"— is to be following a spiritual path. This implies existing at a level of perception that transcends the boundaries of the individual self, or ego, and to be constantly aware of one's existence in a universe governed by a divine or natural order. The purpose in taking such a path is to become so conscious of unfolding events as to never miss a beat in the cosmic dynamic, thus to feel oneself to be a part of the whole. For example, on this enlightened path one might mentally experience multiple dimensions of life, especially the interrelatedness of all things. By living in such a state of unity, this person learns that every move within the grand design is coordinated precisely. He therefore strives to personally participate in harmony, and to consequently live on earth as one with the divine spirit.

Alas, some individuals lack the time and energy to either retreat to the rigors associated with this spiritual life or to regularly follow religious rituals, which make similar promises of salvation for an afterlife. It may even be that they just aren't interested in becoming a member of either discipline, yet they too are certainly alive and want to find their ideal directions. What will guide these people and restore them to steady states free from distresses and harm?

Whether we are disciple of a religious sect, initiate to the mysteries, or questioner of the existence of any kind of higher order, whether God be called Allah, Brahma, Jehovah, or Jesus, our biological systems are our salvation, linking us to the grand design and the phenomena within that influence, guide, and preserve us. Regardless of any inviolable philosophy you may or may not have, your beautifully regulated physical body will spring to action, providing the precise information you need to restore a set point at any time. It exists for this purpose! Perhaps your vision or your sense of touch will guide you, but it could just as easily be this intuitive sense that helps you learn where, when, and how far to move, thereby assuring you that you need not miss a note in the cosmic symphony.

There have not always been schools of mysticism. Neither have we had religious rituals from the dawn of existence. But we *have* been organisms from the start, subject to cellular demands that are bound to the consistent controls of our life support mechanisms—the very regulators that evolved to help each creature survive and propagate its particular species. Spiritual practices and religions each have their place. But the river running deep beneath these uplifting, life-supportive traditions is this life itself, the whole interlocking system of the universe which inspired our devotion in the first place.

Intuition is the one universally available mechanism of awareness that leads us each to exquisite moments of unity with the hidden dimension of things. I maintain that every man, woman, and child can have this ultimate unification experience—alternately called the oceanic feeling, religious revelation, and peak experience—of the infinite wonders of the universe. It is available to all of us *because* we are intuitive. As it has been the source of strength and wisdom behind numbers of our greatest accomplishments, our intuitive sense must not be denied its freedom—or we run the risk of losing the supreme inspiration behind all of our actions.

On the other hand, what if we take this step toward intuitive freedom? Let us draw a picture for our future: the twenty-first century human. We will be a self-assertive element in creation's aggregate of forces, moving with the curiosity, boldness, and tenacity that generally accompany self-reliance. This awareness of participation in a universe governed by a law-abiding natural order, with no hard-and-fast boundary between it and us, will be an indispensable stabilizing element in our decisions. It will forge our epoch-making change from living as a species shivering under the threat of Factors "U" to one that is co-creator at all times. By adding our intuitiveness to our senses of sight, hearing, touch, smell, temperature, etc., we will know that the universe is not a mere experiment in randomness and that our world within it must not be governed recklessly. It will become axiomatic that the moves we make do, indeed, have a bearing on the greater good of all that exists now and forevermore.

In this light we should begin work immediately on the new era of human action and a future we can expect would succeed through the mingling our very human dreams, talents, and ambitions with the vast intuitible order of all creation. It will work because, whether we have graduated from cults of highest wisdom or schools of hard knocks, we know now as never before that everyone must be concerned for the whole, even as we yearn to reach the top for ourselves.

While never losing the thought that spiritual practices and religious ritual have their distinct and valuable roles in our society, I long ago took the pragmatists' path to solving concerns about social and human stability. It has driven my tenacious search for intuition. You have read a few accounts here of spontaneous incidents demonstrating that this is a vital, readily available tool; it is every bit as influential on the future of humankind as the jagged stone that some prehistoric relative discovered he could use to crush materials that he could not reduce with his hands alone. From the first days of my exploration, my chief interest has been to explain its organization—to provide at least a basic foundation on which learning can build. This is why I stood still and observed for a quarter of a century, waiting for it to show itself and prove its reliability.

Now, these twenty-five years later I can say confidently that this intuitiveness affects our lives at every turn. As you know, I finally decided I would like to show people what might happen at those turns—the forks in our individual paths—because it seems to me that if we can only know which direction is the best, in time to take action, then that move will favorably influence everything that follows.

# Part II

# SELECTIVE INTUITION

The plain answer to why we learn intuitively brings us back once more to evolution. This new sensibility probably evolved for the same reason that other senses evolved in their time: to be an ever-available information resource as we ventured into complex new territory. It has always worked spontaneously. Now we are in the first stage of controlling the experiences. Is this our evolutionary leap?

We want to harness intuition's power, of course. Isn't this the way we humans progress? We find an advantage, rein it in, and put it to work ourselves by adding its strength to ours. Intuitive sensitivity is no exception. It has opened another window onto the universe. We now have the prospect of peering through, and learning how best to interact with the new microcivilization that we will find there. This is a new avenue for solving problems—everyday personal questions as well as concerns of state.

Part I discussed intuition in its natural form, with only occasional references to using it intentionally. Part II introduces a way of managing our intuitive sensibility. These final four chapters explain a simple process for calling on intuition to make decisions, plan the future, and take risks safely. These abilities represent the true value of regulated intuition. We need to know how to select it and gather its information in the same way we select reason and call on our other senses to learn about the world around us. When we make this breakthrough, for the first time in history of problem-solving—as far as I know—we will be able to add accurate facts about the unknowns and unpredictables that in the past have too often led us astray. And when we learn to call on our intuition and use it intelligently, this capability will become true power.

Chapter 10 introduces what I have named "the Routine." It is key to controlling the process that enables us to rise above the spontaneity associated with intuitiveness and select our intuition on command. Chapter 11 concentrates on the psi effects. Chapter 12 elaborates on this system, answers frequently asked questions, and provides a self-test to accelerate development. Chapter 13 closes the discussion on why we are becoming intuitive at this particular moment in history.

# CHAPTER 10

# Taming the "U" Beasts

CRUCIAL TO USING any new notion is confidence that it does what we expect. This certainly applies to learning from the psi effects. Only one point need be made: Psi effects mean what they report. The key to intuition's new reality is our endorsment of these powerful hidden persuaders as a new database for making decisions.

As demonstration of how we can run our lives by intuition's facts, the first account in this chapter concerns my own folly in ignoring a clear psi effect that just seemed a bit much to believe. While reading, note three details: (1) intuition's steadfastness, (2) how useless the information is without intuitor action, and (3) the physical size of the phenomenon perceived intuitively.

## The Roots of Intuition

Eighteen years ago I had an experience that finally forced me to wonder seriously how many levels in the hierarchy of nature we are physically able to know. I was completely baffled when one insignificant pocket-size bag of sugarcoated candy impacted my intuitive sensitivity.

(ψ-39) First, a confession: I am a bona fide sweets lover. So it was that one sunny afternoon I picked out a package of pastel-colored confections that boasted a hard sugar coating over almonds. Irresistible! When I reached for the small packet on the market shelf, my taste buds were all set for the approval test, then:

*Don't buy those.*

My initial reaction was: "Uh oh. The Captain!"

I wondered why my intended purchase was unacceptable. You already know, of course, that raising this question was the wrong response. The Captain doesn't give an explanation, only an Instruction. Did I pay attention? Not that day. That was blunder number one.

Yes, I bought them. However, when I removed the little package from the grocery bag, I tucked it way back on a cupboard shelf—out of respect for our ever-accurate intuition. Perhaps I hoped I'd forget it. But that was not to be. Alas, when foraging for something in the cupboard a month later, I spied the forbidden fruit. Being vulnerable that day, I took them out, pulled off the ribbon, reached in:

*Don't take it.*

Good advice . . . but, too late. Woefully, the intelligent sections of my brain, which make all of my rational decisions, were one small step behind my blind devotion to all the confections in Candy Land. It is a realm where my noblest intentions often collapse, which is what happened on this day. I overrode faithful intuition, picked out a piece, and put it in my mouth. Delicious!

Luxuriating now, I began conducting a silent conversation with myself.

"One more, perhaps," thought I, dipping into the bag again. I enjoyed another flash of pure sugar pleasure.

"And another?" I asked.

"Oh, all right," replied the hedonist within.

With this fourth morsel, I blundered a second time, absent-mindedly biting down hard on the unyielding sugar surface. The facts of the situation would strike hard. I was about to be reminded yet again of intuition's extraordinary accuracy. Apparently the pressure was simply too much for one unfortunate tooth at the back of the bottom row. Without warning, a sizable chunk broke off as cleanly as a mass of ice fractures from a glacier and falls into the sea.

Here we clearly see intuition's realm. This time it was protecting a weak tooth. If this is any measure, it is evidence that we are privy to molecular and cellular conditions in our own bodies. Go back now to other elemental phenomena people have intuited. Recall the eroding earth a mile away that was in a vulnerable state—The Young Lieutenant ($\psi$-15)—and the change in the atmospheric pressures brewing on the day of the sailing race—Lone Boat ($\psi$-24). With this access to variables in elements and cells, or systems of elements and cells, we discover that each one of us can both prevent and produce interactions at the roots of the natural order. Think of what this could mean for health in people everywhere. We know! We intuit well before the breakdown where an elemental frailty might succumb to undue stress.

Examine this account. Intuition reported in twice on the same subject, with a month in between! This characteristic faithfulness has taught me again and again how well it protects us from damaging ourselves, and enables us to regulate even the tiniest systems of our body that are essential to our freedom. When any of them fall off their set points, we are handicapped in some way, as I was with that broken tooth. (Note: None of my teeth had ever before fractured, nor have they since.)

Can we draw the conclusion, then, that our intuition will always be available for everyday defense, to keep us in the flow of life and out of harm's way? By the rule of regulatory mechanisms, the answer is yes. This being true, as hard as it might be to accept, there can be no arguing: In the natural order even a tooth in one person's head is worth protecting.

The end of the tale is that ultimately the correction became the task of the dentist, and my pocketbook. Lamentably, it was all avoidable. With intuition's aid I could have shaped a far finer future than that.

## Three Places for Intuition—The Short List

Anyone can get confused and fall off course. While we face hundreds of millions of potential occasions for having problems, these travails can be collapsed into a short list of three types of ordinary life situations. They all involve solving the conflict of not knowing the ideal next step to take. We are at that crucial gap of unknowing when we are:

1. making a plain on-the-spot decision;

2. facing the future; and

3. taking risks, or in plain English, wanting to excel.

In other words, we need to know exactly what to do when opportunity knocks.

These are the times we want to communicate with all the forces in nature, to be aware of every molecular and cellular interaction that can feed us information from the mosaic of events around the universe.

### Immediate Choice

First, consider the process of making any decision: You simply need to choose what you think is best. In other words, figure it out and, Kazaam, you've made a decision. However, to make it sound so simple diminishes the risk inherent in decision making.

In fact, when deciding any matter, you are, roughly speaking, working as delicately as a high-wire artist whose sole concentration is on body balance, because a slip could mean serious injury. Similarly, while making decisions using hundreds if not thousands of uncountable invisible and inaccessible bits of information, your goal is always to be in the finest position, because anything less could throw off your results. You need all the facts, proven or not. There is a place here for intuition.

## The Future

Second, consider the prospect of facing the future. Ah, what agony it is to shift in time from the secure evidence of the here and now into the mists surrounding there and then. In the search for ordinary future knowledge, you are forced into the role of Sherlock Holmes, snooping around for all possible leads because you can't possibly "reason it out" exactly. Enter intuition!

## Excellence

Third, consider wanting to excel. The very essence of excellence is stretching. You are asking your psyche to reach for new information much the same way a young child strains every muscle in his little body to see over the top of a table. By definition, *new* implies something unfamiliar. Send out a call for intuition.

Since the most likely way to succeed is to have all the crucial pieces of missing information in your head, on time, you can be confident that specialized intuitive sensitivity will be reporting any helpful contact spontaneously.

"Can everyone really expect that?" you might ask. The answer, of course, is yes. It is important to remember that we sometimes are orienting ourselves to a position that our other senses and reason cannot reach. Despite excellent ready resources, with the infinite number of changes that affect our movements, it simply is not possible to have all the information we need stored neatly inside our celebrated gray matter, ready for retrieval the instant we need it. Certainly nature hasn't left out a regulatory mechanism for this potential crisis. Her solution for a mentality without enough information in storage has been to install a capability for receiving news when the time is right—in other words, the instant need arises. One can find ample evidence to prove that this is the very role intuition plays to perfection. Crisis control.

# Using Intuition Intelligently

## Immediate Decision

Our most ordinary signal of a problem is confusion at a junction, any junction—your basic, what-to-do scenario. So often, the solution is to know which is the correct path at a fork in the road, so to speak. Intuition is ready to serve here. A real-life example follows. On this day my husband had to make an instantaneous decision while searching for a setting that his film company needed.

(ψ-40) Gayne and the director of the film had traveled far afield from their New York base, until they found themselves in a rattletrap station wagon, riding with a Maine guide along a back road through thick forests. They had described their need in detail: a wild rushing river with a waterfall that the stuntmen could go over . . . and survive. When they finished their list, the guide had nodded knowingly. "Yes, yes." He knew the ideal spot.

City people that they were, the two were grateful to have a seasoned pathfinder take over their frustrating weeklong pursuit. After parking at the roadside, they plunged into a veritable forest primeval, willing to follow wherever their guide would take them.

Gayne barely noticed the route they were taking; he was preoccupied with thoughts about how his crew, with their lights and cameras, could trek through a place where the thick undergrowth forced you to walk single-file. His colleague, absorbed in the natural beauty, likewise paid no attention to the course.

About one mile in, their effort was rewarded; the forest opened onto a wide river and swirling white-water rapids. This was it! Gratified with their success, they set to work immediately, pacing out distances, listening to the forest sounds, and taking a series of pictures just before they left.

Almost the minute they dropped into line again, following behind the guide, the two began a detailed discussion about the complications that would arise with filming in such an isolated setting. In ten minutes' time, the guide hesitated at a vaguely defined fork in the path. Obviously confused, he quietly studied the spot for several seconds before moving on to the trail bound right. The director immediately proceeded to follow. In that instant, Gayne wondered himself which was correct. Without his realizing, that questioning set the intuitive system in motion. It sent immediate feedback to guide him. A feeling of "certainty" informed him that the left fork was correct.

He told the director confidently that he was sure they should be heading that way. She gazed in confusion, first at him, then toward the disappearing guide, who was now too far up the trail to call back. She finally turned back to Gayne and followed him along the left fork. In half an hour, the woods opened again, this time onto the road and the parked automobile. They sat on a nearby knoll finalizing details of the shoot. An hour later the frazzled guide appeared at the edge of the forest.

Gayne says that the direction had come so quickly that it had made his head whirl. How had he known? Try as he might, he could think of no rational explanation for having that information, or for the mysterious sensation of "feeling he knew." He says today that it was disconcerting to learn something spontaneously, and he was ill at ease with its coming from nowhere. Even more confounding, he says, was the accompanying certainty, which was so strong that he didn't hesitate to act on it.

An observer of the incident would have given the intuitive system a blue ribbon for efficiency. Life didn't hang in the balance that afternoon, but a work schedule did. From Gayne's single-minded point of view, time was precious. As long as the guide was leading confidently, the two had followed along blindly, but when he faltered Gayne picked up the reins of responsibility at once. He began to look for the right trail, but having not paid attention on their way into the forest, he was somewhat helpless. His frustration with the potential work delay likely triggered the intuitive process. Witnessing another incident when intuitiveness makes the rescue we see how efficiently it informs us and enables us to control our own destiny.

## Adding Selective to Spontaneous Intuiting

Controlling a sensory system is nothing new. It is only a matter of deciding to focus attention. For example, what do you do if you want to know more about the outdoor noise from the position in your living room where you are sitting? When you first become curious, you might ask yourself what you are hearing. From there you might stop reading to concentrate on the sounds, even cock your head and orient your ear enough to fine-tune. Now the sounds are distinct. It's a dog barking. Once the source is detected, you deduce that the barking dog is Fido next door.

Basically you have switched sensory systems by choice, shifting from vision for reading to audio for identifying noise. According to the type of data required, we continuously cross over from one sense to another. From sight to touch, to taste, smell, and listening, we swing effortlessly among them throughout our waking hours. Now we are adding intuition to this collection, to home in on its facts when they alone will serve. This is what happened to Gayne. In his confusion he wondered what to do and, by so doing, switched naturally to the intuitive process. The new sensory system fed back that "feeling" of certainty.

## Selecting Intuition

The program for making your intuition work for you has a colorful parallel. Metaphorically, you are doing what Ben Franklin did. You have to send the kite up into the clouds to collect your bounty. In your need, however, you reach not into thunderheads but into clouds of the unknown. Once directed, your sensory system, like Franklin's wire, is a natural conductor of the information.

Think of touching a physical object to learn how much heat it has absorbed—say the handle of a car door. You have to decide to reach out with your hand and let its heat sensors report their news. The neurons will do the rest by carrying the signal to your brain, where it decodes into a perceptible thermal effect. There you have it—the basic routine for learning from your senses. First you establish the connection between your system and the stimulus. Then you pay close attention to the effect. So it is with intuitive sensitivity. We could say that we are preparing to ground intuition in the same way that Franklin grounded electricity.

Next we address how we can learn intentionally from intuition. Let's build the "kite" in the form of a five-step routine. It involves asking a question, detecting the psi effect, making a decision, and finally taking action. Detecting, deciding, and taking action are already familar to you. Now we are introducing a new step—one that gives us firm control over the intuitive process. We add a question.

Recall the "short list" of life situations presented earlier in the chapter. When you use intuition intentionally, it will always involve a decision about one of these three types of circumstance: (1) the next immediate move to make, (2) a plan for the future, or (3) the risk of making an improvement to excel.

## The Routine

Step 1: Form the question. Identify the information you need. Your question will reflect your intention. Examples would be:

which fork to take in the path you are currently traveling ($\psi$-40);

whether to attend this gathering or that ($\psi$-23);

what to do with an object or condition you encounter ($\psi$-7); and

how to break out of an established situation and reach for new heights, such as changing careers, leaving a relationship, or averting a dangerous situation ($\psi$-15).

Step 2: Ask your question. We always begin by asking ourselves the same question, no matter what the condition: What do I know about . . . (fill in the detail)? Examples would be: What do I know about . . .

turning right here;

this invitation to join the group; and

my future in this profession?

Step 3: Detection. Pay attention to the psi effect's information that follows.

Step 4: Decision. Using only the facts as you received them intuitively, carefully consider how you will follow through. ($\psi$-15 & 19 are excellent examples.)

Step 5: Take action. Make your move based on the psi effect's data.

For many years, I've used this simple search system to trigger my intuition. The question is enough to establish the connection because you introduce a situation that is off set point. As long as you do not take over and interrupt the natural process at work, your intuition will produce a useful psi effect—either information or an instruction. It will reorient you, as intuitive facts always do. And here we are again, back at the stabilizing regulatory mechanism: System variable detection. Decision. Correction. Now *you* are deciding which system variable you want to detect.

Following are two accounts in which I used the Routine. In the first, I was working as a consultant for another person. He was at a fork in his profession and mightily confused. The second is of a defining moment in my life. Both situations had many elements that millions of other people encounter in their problems. Essentially, we were both faced with a desperate need to find a professional direction and were frightened about our futures.

## Searching for Direction

(ψ-41) Six months after completing his Ph.D., a young scientist still had no offers for an academic position. His wife was unhappy and fearful about their future. While he patiently waited for an offer, he continued working as a research assistant for his faculty adviser. After several months, he came to me in frustration. Frightened for his family and desolate in himself, he yearned to know what his options were. This was late October.

I began the Routine with: "What do I know about Flavio's professional future?" In less than a minute, the Teleos report came to me. I related to him precisely what I learned:

> *In two years, on the Ides of March,*
> *you will receive three job offers.*

He became agitated. "Two years? What am I supposed to do until that great day?" He sounded somewhat bitter.

I repeated the question: "What *else* do I know about Flavio's professional future?" Again, I stated what I learned:

> *Do what you do best.*

He thought quietly, thanked me politely, and left my office.

One day much later, the phone rang. He was calling me in California from halfway around the world.

"Hello," he said. "Remember me?"

"Of course."

He commanded, "Look at the date."

It was March 15, the Ides of March, and the second year since our meeting. Amazed, I asked for his news.

His voice was full of pleasure and amusement.

"About ten minutes ago I received the third offer. All three came today, just as you intuited!"

He told his story. After our meeting, he had decided to remain where he was and further develop his graduate research until something changed. He thought logically that might be what he could "do best." After a couple of months, he had the idea to combine his lifelong hobby of photography with his laboratory work. He began keeping a photographic record of the chemical interactions he was investigating. Early results of his photographs encouraged him to refine his techniques. After six months, he combined beautiful photos with new experimental results into a book that he submitted to a publisher. It was accepted and went on to became the first of its kind in his specialty. The offers came as a result of the book, which was introduced at an international professional conference just before the Ides of March. He received the offers while there.

On reflection, he realized that, even though he frequently received compliments on his photographs, it never crossed his mind when he added photography to his laboratory work that this was what he could "do best." In his opinion, it only added interest to his passing time. Never once did he consider his picture-taking hobby to be the expertise designated by intuition.

We have to ask: If Flavio had known how to use his own intuition, would he have learned the same fine-tuned information? In the general model of the intuitive process as a regulatory mechanism the answer is "yes." Probably he would have used other words, but beyond the inevitable difference arising from individual speech patterns, the information would be similar. Flavio's problem was that he knew nothing about using his own intuition to help himself.

## *Directing the Question*

Next I want to underscore the importance of properly planning the Routine question because the inquiry is so crucial to getting the regulatory process started correctly.

Returning to Franklin: His intention was to pull down electricity, so he selected conductive wire, which he knew would do the job best. Ours is to reach through our brain processes to stimulate that particular sensory activity that will feed back intuitive data. The secret to probing your intuition successfully lies in the question, especially the interrogative, by which I mean the *word* you use in asking it. One in particular triggers the correct search engine.

The question must begin with "What." This is the only interrogative that generates intuition. It introduces an open question about the character, nature, occupation, position, or role of a person, place, or thing. It, like any other question, has the effect of opening the conduit of the particular region or tract in the nervous system that generates a specific process. For a contrast, think of the alternative interrogatives—Who, Where, Why, How, When, and Which. If you inquire with any of these six, you will lead to entirely different answers to a question.

▲ *Who?* aims to learn the person or persons involved. (Who do we know?) That channels through memory, which is not an intuitive process.

▲ *Where?* inquires about a place. (Where are we going?) Although extremely important as a direction finder, this interrogative reaches for information through memory and reason, neither of which is a conduit to intuitive sensitivity.

▲ *Why?* nearly catapults us into the reasoning regions of our brain. We are searching for the chief cause, reason, or purpose for any phenomenon. (Why do I know?) While reason and intuition certainly are companion resources of information, one definitely is not the other and should never be treated thus. It will never do to send one kind of investigator into the other process any more than we would ask a child to keep the financial records of a burgeoning industry. This kind of mix-up would be equally as absurd in the intentional search through the circuits of our brains.

▲ *How?* wants to know the manner or reason a condition exists. (How do I know?) Again, the channel is memory or reasoning. Instead, ask: What do I know? This is assigned to the intuitive process. The other never will get you there.

▲ *When?* is looking for a specific time, and *Which?* asks for particular ones out of a group. Both follow the tracts of memory and reason. Consequently, they are about as useful to us intuitively as a string would have been on Franklin's kite.

Inappropriate conductors would not serve in either his or our search for the specific phenomenon being captured. Not string, not rope, but wire was Franklin's choice because as a metal it would conduct the electrical phenomenon to ground. Turning back to intuitive sensitivity, we learn that the interrogative "What" will throw us into the kind of open mental state that feeds back data from the intuitive realm of microprocesses.

### Define the Problem

Franklin also chose his weather. Being concerned about electricity, he waited for thunderclouds. His theory was that the phenomenon would take place in them. A sunny day would not bring it. Neither would a drizzly one. He had to be smart in his planning, hence he defined the precise weather phenomenon in order to bag his quarry. Thus he offers us another lesson. We too have to aim directly at the system that is off its set point. This means that we fashion the question with the idea of learning what we can do to restore or create stability in the particular circumstances confusing us. The feedback might offer only one corrective step, but it will be guidance, and that is our need. Therefore, in forming the question, we point to the problem, as the system variable. What *exactly* has confused us?

In effect, we know only where we are positioned, but we need to know where we are going. Flavio wanted to learn about his professional options. In this next account, I had to take a risk that could make or destroy the future of at least four people. It had to help me make my very next move. No Whys or Hows would ground the answer. Watch how intuition worked.

## Searching for the Best Profession

This was a family affair. To all intents and purposes I was risking everything that I had left of a marriage of twenty years. My children would be depending on my immediate decisions for their ultimate success. Enter intuition.

Risk makes us nervous about our safety in any situation, but when an intuitor is relying on his or her own intuitive ability for direction in *personal* affairs, the quality of the information might be unknowingly compromised because the stakes are higher. Consequently, since I have no firmer claim on personal reliability under tension than the next person does, I always add a factor of patience to protect the integrity of the Routine. As it is in so many circumstances, the key to dependability is to not be hasty. Patience opens up time, creates space between a crisis and its solution, allows us to "free our mind," as we say—to be more objective and receptive to new ideas and plans and psi effects. I hoped all this would happen to me.

(ψ-42) As far as I know, no one who is honest has ever said that divorce is pleasant. Mine certainly was not. Perhaps it was fortunate that on the course of recovery, the highest jump was this first: How would I support and run the family alone?

With a long future ahead and responsibilities mounting by the minute, I was afraid that there would be trouble if I followed a career as an occupational therapist, for which I'd been educated twenty years previously. It might be too confining for a young woman with a brood of children who were growing so fast that they seemed to need new shoes every other week. What should I do? The question pounded in my brain.

I first tried taking a rational approach. Alas, logic failed. The visible options were dangerously limited. When confusion reached fever pitch, I decided that only intuition's Teleos would report the ideal direction. I knew that there *would* be a best choice, because nature is an optimalizer.

Intuition will always deliver news when a system is rocking wildly around set point. So while it was peak distress for me, this was intuition's paradise.

Thus began the search. Armed only with the one fact—that I would have to surpass all of my own expectations if I was to meet everyone's needs—I prepared my kite.

What was my mental state? Not brilliant. This was 1979, the apex of personal chaos. The adults around me feared my fascination in parapsychology. My reputation had continued to deteriorate on the gossipvine, which was spreading like a weed, and now my marriage had collapsed. I was a casualty. Mind-numbing insecurity, combined with doldrums, complicated every thought that wandered through my head. On one hand, I knew I could make a go of just about anything. On the other, I was aware that this needed to be more than mere work. Life seemed too precious for me to simply become an automaton. It should be an opportunity. Somewhere there would be the ideal direction.

Clearly, the shaky situation offered a fair choice of two directions: I could follow a familiar path or remake myself. This is the general condition of the person who applied to intuition for a job that morning! I called up the "Routine."

First step: Pinpoint the system variable causing the confusion. Finances. Exactly what did I need to know? "How should I earn my income?" The Routine question seemed obvious. "*What* do I know about my next profession?"

However, the question needed fine-tuning because I already had a short list of options. I could go back to occupational therapy, which had been my first career. Having also been a teacher, I added the option of educator. By that time I'd been absorbing technical books and paranormal experiences and was profoundly intrigued, so parapsychology joined the flock (although I had no idea what I could do in that field). And, as the last, to cover any stray option, I added an unknown, Job "X," just in case. I wrote down the final question: *What* do I know about my next profession: Is it occupational therapy, education, parapsychology, or "X"?

It was nine o'clock in the morning. Add the patience factor. Give the process time. I made an arbitrary decision to expect the answer before 3:00 P.M. that afternoon. Next, I took some minutes to assess my attitude. Though I was still profoundly self-confident, I was extremely frustrated. In my opinion, I needed to pledge to myself that I would not fight the final decision; whatever intuition produced would be my directive. I would seize it and run. This little covenant guaranteed my follow-through.

This self-control turned out to be a stroke of genius. The question done, and with a promise to see it through, I asked the question to initiate the routine. At 3:00 that afternoon, the Instruction came through:

*Become a parapsychologist.*

There it was. Plain advice from the intuitible dimension, and a discovery for me. It was not the answer I'd expected. The internal mutiny proceeded: "No, no, no! I'm not educated for this field. It is the only one that is impossible. No, no, no!"

The mutineer continued attacking. "This is too complicated—it will require more education, and what would be the use? No one in the field had much direction; I would be entering a never-never land! No, no, no!" Isn't it interesting how our inner world fights the unknown?

Fortunately, that earlier promise of compliance crushed the internal revolution and opened the future. I recall thinking: Balk if you'd like, lady, but do as you promised. By now my experiences had proven that intuition does not lead people astray. It would be accurate and best for all concerned. The six-hour search had settled all the confusion. The next step would be acquiring the tools.

Beyond the worldly chaos and out of the reach of our reason lies a future. On the side of our experiences sits a complete history of where we have been and how we have fared. Our private memory is easily accessed and frequently serves as the ideal tool for forging immediate decisions, making future plans, and taking enormous risks. At times, however, we need to go outside in search of another option that will be finer and sweeter than our past could hope to produce. Then we are wise to take the intuitive pathway with the one exacting question.

Had I known that day what I know now about where the path would lead me, I would surely have shouted for joy.

($\psi$-43) Unfortunately Kirby knew neither that it would benefit him to get intuitive advice from a qualified professional adviser, nor that he could learn to control his own intuition by using the Routine.

He told me about his intuitive history during an interview we had in the bustling electronics shop where he worked as a salesman. I asked him to answer three questions: (1) how did he define intuition, (2) did he think of it as a safe or risky tool for making decisions, and (3) would he describe what it felt like. His answer to the first was: "Intuition is the feeling that you know something which turns out to be true." To my second question he replied that any decision involves risk but that he uses intuition "all the time."

And my third question: "How would you describe the feelings you associate with intuition?"

"It's always the same—a 'sense of certainty' that seems like the go-ahead to taking action."

"Is it ever wrong?"

He seemed guarded for the first time since we had started talking. "It isn't usually, but," he paused, "yes, it has led me in the wrong direction."

With some encouragement he continued, telling a classic story of frustration stemming from intuitiveness. It began when a friend learned of a job opening and decided the position would be perfect for Kirby. The only hook was that Kirby had to resign from his existing position to be in the running for the new one. He had a "feeling" that this would be the right move—a feeling that had panned out for him in other situations—so he left his job and pursued the opportunity.

"But I was wrong that time. The prospect fizzled almost overnight. There I was with a pocketful of hope and nothin' else."

He couldn't explain his plight any better than that. As for his work, it was his personal tragedy. His position as district manager of an electronics company, had been filled soon after he left. Thinking that he couldn't afford to be unemployed indefinitely, he had jumped at the sales job he currently held because it was the first one that came along. He pointed his finger at me. "Can *you* tell me what went wrong?"

"Certainly," I replied, but knowing so little about the actual circumstances, I had to resort to the theory of regulatory mechanisms that emphasizes the requisite element of follow through. I asked whether he had returned to his intuition since the job fell through.

"Why?" This idea surprised him.

"To learn more information."

"You mean to ask it questions? Can you do that?"

I explained that when any psi effect proves to be too confusing, or even wrong, it is perfectly reasonable to revisit the intuitive system in search of more insight. We do it with all of our other senses and thought processes. Intuition should be no exception.

Kirby and Flavio had similar stories with very different endings. I introduce them here because they are fine examples of why we should use the Routine to get reliable direction. Both men had taken professional risks that should have worked out because each was qualified to be chosen over the competition. Yet, they had been denied and consequently took lesser jobs that proved unsatisfactory. How could intuition have helped these men through their crises?

Clearly in the consummate crisis, Flavio knew what step to take. Wanting the finest results for the years he had invested, he decided to expand his data bank. He visited an intuitive consultant for much the same reason he would a doctor if he couldn't manage an ailment. He knew that a specialist could do the fine-tuning he badly needed but could not provide himself. Because Flavio had attended a year-long series of my private classes, he had confidence in my judgment and integrity. Although he thought himself competent enough to use his own intuitiveness, he sought my assistance with this particular concern because so much uncertainty was affecting his current professional decisions.

He came prepared with "what" questions that would stimulate the intuitive process. After intuiting what I knew about his professional future, I told him he would be successful in his pursuit of the ideal position but that time was not on his side. Frustrated, he then asked me what he should do in the meantime.

Using the Routine pattern I led the second search with: What *else* do I know? His familiarity with intuition's ways probably made it easier for him to swallow the bitter pill of perseverance and agree to bide his time at a lower income until an opportunity developed.

Turning to Kirby: Recognizing that intuition had led him into trouble, we might ask why he would go back for damage control. But suppose he had known that he could turn again to his intuition, either by asking more questions on his own ($\psi$-28) or seeking intuitive help. This would have been beneficial, according to the rules of intuition, because he was truly off track and directionless. (I am convinced that this is the only reason any paid intuitive consultant can offer *accurate* information.)

We cannot prove that Kirby would be a more fulfilled man today if he hadn't risked all he did. But we do have his example of being misled to serve as a stepping-stone toward improving the ways we apply intuition. The model of the intuitive process as a regulatory mechanism suggests that he could have used the Routine to keep the intuitive process going until he stabilized his professional life *at his personal set point.*

Finally, did my responses to Flavio's questions seem like flight of fancy or make you suspicious of hocus pocus? It is obvious that one answer—the reference to the ides—was like a dart hitting dead on the bull's-eye, while the other—"Do what you do best" was so vague that one might wonder if I had simply pulled it from a fortune cookie. And you may have wondered who in modern days would make reference to something as dated as the Ides of March unless he or she was reading Julius Caesar.*

The observation is fair, but the angle is wrong. Psi effects, though confusing to us intellectually, are products of a lawful

---

*The ides—found on the ancient Roman calendar and designated as collection days by moneylenders—were the fifteenth day of March, May, July, and October and the thirteenth day of any other month.

process that continues to produce these undeniable facts in our everyday experience. Historical records reveal that although prophesies have often been stated in nebulous messages that left listeners scratching their heads, others occasionally included a reference that was so on the mark as to seem impossible. This precision might be hard to believe, but it is neither rare nor unnatural. I have recounted Flavio's story here, in part to showcase the psi effects' wide range of explicitness. I have intuitively marked time with similar surgical accuracy on other occasions using references to literature, history, holidays, natural seasons of growth, and more. For instance, in a "reading" for Natalya, my daughter, a life-transforming event for her was predicted for Mardi Gras the following year, and in another consultation I heard myself tell a client that a business deal would close "next year when the leaves on trees change to gold." Both were accurate. (My client later reported that in her front garden she had three liquid amber trees bearing leaves that turned to blazing golden every autumn.)

Perhaps the moral of this story about learning to use intuitiveness is that we cannot forget that by being part of this realm we are encountering the interconnections of life in all its infinite cloaks. In so doing we are in step with the poet and mystic, whose inspiration comes, I think, from precisely the same resource that we all meet when reaching out to intuition's domain to find the natural beauty and majesty of the order therein. Occasionally this reflects in a psi effect.

## Expect Spontaneous, Be Selective

Because we are only beginning our development, we have hardly enough records of individual intuitive moments to prove how an entire intuitive society will be. However, we can look back, since the past so often is an indicator of what will come to be. To see how we managed novel mental capabilities, we need only to turn back to the sixth century B.C. and the Greek awakening to the art of reason. Society initiated unimaginable changes on a scale that could only be described as evolutionary.

Will we do the same with our intuition? Our society has certainly taken a dizzying zigzag course to reach this next stage in mental development. For the powerful, finely educated world that we are, with all of our mechanized methods of gathering precise data and finding workable solutions, this has seemed too unreliable a tool to sharpen. Yet we want to get control of our lives, to tame the unknowns and unpredictables wherever we can.

Apparently evolution is working. The more we test and draw exacting data by this new sensory route, the sooner we will prove whether or not intuition is really able to help us help ourselves. If it is, we can make significant advances in research and development for those who will build on it in generations to come.

Captured as we are at a point in our history where confusion causes more consternation than challenge, intuition has come to symbolize a new phenomenon, even possibly a way out of unknowing. Now, along with other thinkers who have nudged the sleeping giant to life, I suggest that we dig deeper, find its roots, and ponder its implications.

One of the joys of the researcher is to present new data for others to improve or prove wrong. The details I have introduced in these pages are open for any who would like to test them. I suggest that if they should prove to make good sense—enough, that is, to lead us forward—then we will want to move swiftly from the spontaneous to the selective system of intuiting, and start the inevitable chain reaction that leads to integrating it into our behavior.

It appears that reason has reached its limits as the mental world power. We have done all we can safely do with it along the particular lines of discovery we've chosen. I suggest that we are at a fine-tuning point, which invites us to initiate a new departure along a new line. It will be a cross-fertilization among all our forms of knowing that have led us. Together they could push us out to a grand, finer-tuned technique of living.

# CHAPTER 11

# Feeling the Effects

WHAT DOES A psi effect feel like? Most people seem to have a way of describing them. We call them feelings of certainty; feelings that things are right, or wrong; good feelings, and bad ones; feelings of danger; gut feelings; feelings in our bones; feelings about the future; feelings about the past; feelings that we call hunches, impulses, and inklings. We feel vibes and connections with one another. We feel sure that we should take some actions and feel just as sure that we should not take others. Feelings. Feelings. Feelings. What are we talking about? Does everyone have them? What does a psi effect feel like to you, your neighbor, your friends?

Unlocking the intuitive process includes distinguishing these feelings, for they are intuition's true reporters, or, stated more precisely, the inner experiences that intuition produces. This chapter asks and answers the question: What do we actually perceive?

Commonplace as they are, many of these experiences are woven so smoothly through other events in a day that they are thoroughly confusing to most of us. Yet, the key to intuition's power and influence over our lives turns with these experiences.

We must learn to recognize the psi effects' signals, so that we will be able to learn from them, whether they occur spontaneously or we initiate them by following the Routine. This is the next challenge we face on our way to understanding intuition.

## The Importance of Perception

"If I tell you to look at the color blue that I am looking at now, how do I know that you will see the same color that I'm seeing?"

Eight-year-old David was talking. He was pointing at the sleeve of his light blue shirt. The deep frown across his brow punctuated his puzzlement.

From his place at the head of the table, his father inquired why he was asking. David replied, "Well, I was thinking about when we talk. We use so many words. How are we going to understand what people are saying if we don't know what they really mean? So I looked at my shirt and wondered, if blue is the same color for all of us and if I said, 'This shirt is blue,' would all of you see the same thing that I am seeing. If you do, I guess we're fine. But, if you don't, what do we do then?"

In that moment, I was reminded of one of my most inspiring science professors. When any student asked a question that hinted that he or she had stumbled on a fundamental phenomenon of nature without being taught it, Professor Wade would smile blissfully and cast his eyes skyward while exclaiming, not quite to himself, "Ah. A discovery."

I think that the delight he felt was not because he fancied that he had managed to teach the bright-eyed student a minor chemistry-related fact, but rather that he realized by the profoundness of the comment that the youth had made a great scientific find; without assistance, the student had come upon a pot of purest gold hidden deep within the order of nature. So it was with David that day. He had struck upon a basic challenge for psychologists, the fundamental problem of recognizing a sensory pattern—in this case, a color in the visual field. It was his moment for deciphering a piece of the world, the kind of instance that every thinker relishes, and many times, never forgets.

What is to be learned from David's insight? He described our colossal current problem of recognizing intuition's inner experiences. I could almost parrot his observation in reference to perceiving psi effects. Are psi effects the same in all of us? When we talk about intuition, we use so many words: How are we going to understand what people are saying about their experiences? We don't know what they really mean. For example, if I tell you that I know telepathically that the lecturer is frustrated, can I be sure that you and everyone around me will understand what I mean? Then if I suggest that you tune in telepathically to confirm my insight, would you have the same effects that I have encountered? As David said: If you do, I guess we're fine. But, if you don't, what do we do then?

## The Psi Effects as We Perceive Them

We return again to examining patterns in the intuitive process and discover that the psi effects are all about patterns. I have described patterns in their function, showing how one aesthetic, two primary, two backup, and two redundant sensory effects consistently cover a vast spectrum of interactions, yet each is limited to a particular job; how the intuitive process matches those of our other recognized sensory systems; and how the intuitive sensory system follows the pattern of the omnipresent regulatory mechanism that is responsible for keeping the order in a universe of natural diversity. I have shown how, although intuitiveness conforms with the systematic processes of other sensory systems, it is different from them all because it loads into our nervous system only information that we receive from its unique sensors.*

Now the problem remains of identifying any pattern to our perception of the psi effects, so that we can learn to sort and recognize them when they occur to us. Should we be surprised when we find yet another pattern?

I have related accounts in which individuals learned spontaneously by one or more psi effects. Now we are looking at evidence that consistent feelings make us aware of the effects. Except for Reflex, I find that when we detect these psi effects, we experience any one of three types of sensations. They are the basic building blocks of learning beneath the impressively large assortment of accounts we hear from people describing how intuition directs their decisions and actions. These effects are the rulers of our intuitive perception. Consequently, we each are responsible for discovering these inner experiences for ourselves the way we each learned to distinguish visual images and various sounds. Our assignment is to become aware of the sensory signals when they occur in our heads and to learn to distinguish them as intuition's reports.

## Basic Psi Sensations

By its very nature, any sensory information source will have to own an associated effect if it is to catch our attention enough to convey meaningful material. We feel heat and cold, the texture of water and leaves. The intuitive process includes subtle sensations generally classified in three groups. The most elusive are what people often allude to as a "sense" of the intuitive experience. Sounding slightly more tangible is the "feeling" associated with it. In contrast, some say they "just plain know" data, suggesting no sensation at all.

---

*The group of seven psi effects presented here comprises those that have so far been identified. This does not mean that we have discovered all of intuition's effects. Tomorrow's science might isolate more.

As a parallel to this "plain knowing," think of a visual effect—say, a traffic signal. When you look up from the sidewalk and view the familiar green circle of light, would you say that the experience of "seeing" is accompanied by a specific sensation? Do you "feel" yourself seeing it? Does it come into your eye like a warm glow or with a strong pulse? Does it have an associated sensation like physical pain or pleasure? For most people the answer to all these is no, not really. Likewise, with the exception of the Mimic Clarification group—with its gut feeling, wafting fragrances, and clanging bells—the psi effects are uniformly not palpable sensory experiences.

Overall, the body's response to visual and intuitive effects is similar. It is less that we actually "feel" them, more that we are "aware" that we are learning information. In both types of experience, it might seem that a vacant place in your head becomes occupied with an awareness of green light, blue sky, moving car, "Five furrows in," "Pick it up," or human panic. This is learning, which by dictionary definition is "the ability to gain knowledge by experience." The psi effect is our experience.

As earlier chapters indicated, we have a full storehouse of words and phrases that speak universally of an intuitive experience. Take a moment to review this collection. Familiar to us all, they are mysteriously charismatic words that operate the same on most of us and indeed are known to carry meaning of their own—they testify that the speaker has experienced a psi effect.

In the vernacular relating to social contact and interactions we might intuit: that all is well; a change in the atmosphere; someone's negative attitude; conflict; a connection with someone or something; a dark force; bad vibes; good vibes; being influenced; interference; lightness; a strong bond; or getting tuned in. We describe: having been in a place previously; being guided; having certainty; being driven; feeling an urge, attraction, repulsion, or foreboding; being right or wrong; sudden understanding; getting a transmission; having a glimpse of the future; having no doubt;

a hunch, an impression, or an impulse; inexplicable information; inner reaction; inner sense; inspiration; having no choice; making the wrong choice; a peak experience; sensing good; knowing that something is working; knowing that someone is right, wrong, or neutral; uncertainty or feeling unwelcome. When clarification duplicates the other effects, we describe: feeling presences; clanging bells; doors opening and closing; guardian angels; ghosts; hearing voices; inner voices; pictures as visions; feelings of pressure; being taken over; being told what to do; and being possessed.

More pages could follow. The point is that although the usual reaction to intuition is that nothing about it is concrete, when the subject turns to the actual psi experiences, we use a common, specific vernacular to describe them, the same as we use a common, specific vocabulary to describe visual effects: red, orange, yellow, green, blue, violet, square, circular, triangular, puffy, flat . . . a bell, a cow, a house, a photo, a portrait, and on through all the functional labels we assign to a seemingly endless array of objects that we see.

The vocabulary of the *messages* that we receive intuitively is another matter. Rather than being figures of speech or psychologically charged, *the words of intuition are literal.* Occasionally they are ambiguous, because language is frequently indistinct, but they are not to be tampered with.

For example, recently I was thrown by information when Teleos spontaneously reported what would happen to the violent hurricane racing toward us. It occurred when we heard the first weather announcements that Hurricane Bonnie was sitting hundreds of miles south of our position. My head filled with "We'll get a dusting." Although this last word could have any of half a dozen meanings, I was confident that it meant literally a dusting. We would be affected very lightly, as though we were a piece of furniture being cleaned with a feather duster, which is precisely what happened.

While not all intuitive reports are ambiguous, there will probably always be some that are. In any event, if an effect leaves you,
the intuitor, confused and directionless, the wise move to make
is no move at all. Wait for more information.

It helps to know what the effects do not feel like. In Flavio's
case, in which job options needed clarification, the psi effect was
a pure knowing. It "felt" like an idea taking form. Basically my
brain was working. It affected me with a definite internal sensation. As is fairly common, the actual sensation associated with
intuitively learning was of a mental process, an awareness of
information flowing into my head. Call it "having an idea." Or
call it "receiving" a group of words. Both are accurate.

Do not call it "being rational." Thinking is a different feeling
from intuiting. It has the effect of an effort, a grinding together
of questions and answers, as when you're balancing your check-
book or planning how to spend a free Saturday. By comparison,
intuition asks only that we be attentive to the psi effect, to *receive
the report.*

Memory, like thinking, also is an effort. To initiate recollec-
tion you pose a question such as "Where was I?," and it is almost
possible to feel the psyche churning to find familiar details that
come into focus. On the contrary, intuitive information is not a
journey into the past, but ever and always a report we receive.
Some would call the reports "revelations."

In conclusion, intuition repeats neither the effort of reasoning nor the flood of recall, but is ever and always merely a report
that we either sense, feel, or know.

## A Sketch of Intuition's Inner Experiences

Among all of the perceptible sensory and thought-driven mental activity that you detect in the course of any given day, you
will discover that you sometimes (1) "sense" factual information,

(2) "feel" information, and (3) plainly "know" information. All of your inner experiences of intuitive signals issue from these three basic sensations.

Words sporadically accompany the sensations. Sometimes an intuitor perceives a single word—"Run," for example. Other times, a series of words, phrases, or even entire sentences may contribute to the report. You have seen this in accounts here. The lieutenant's forewarning (ψ-15) was wordless; he perceived his situation through a simple feeling. Josephine's insight, on the other hand, included a full sentence—"Don't get it now" (ψ-13). While I cannot explain why some psi effects include words and others occur without them, the words appear regularly enough in psi experiences to be considered an integral part of the intuitive process.

In the course of reporting our multitudes of accounts of intuitiveness, we have developed a rich vocabulary to describe these three basic sensations. This means that by listening to ourselves talk about the psi effects we detect, we should be able to learn what experiences we have in common. Begin to describe your intuitive incidents to yourself and others, and notice how you build a unique vocabulary for the effects. Because our language and storytelling are naturally picturesque, your descriptions will probably be more detailed and colorful than the psi effects themselves, but the actual effect and its message will be unchanged as long as you understand what you were perceiving. Whether you are describing an intuitive experience to yourself or a friend, you want to promise yourself that you will report exactly what happened to you, without embellishment born of beliefs or imagination, so that intuition's patterns will begin to show and help you learn.

Despite their history of elusiveness, I am certain that all of us will become aware of the effects fairly quickly now that we are highlighting them. As time goes by and increasing numbers of people develop their ability to use intuition, we will begin to understand what others are saying and be able to relate to the experiences they are describing. With everyone talking about them, we will eventually synthesize a practical system of thought about them so that we can learn together to recognize and separate one from the other.

## Finding the Feelings

Now let's put this inner experience of psi effects to work and begin to pick out the ways nature packs intuitive sensations into your life. What does it actually report to you? Let us begin with the most common intuitive sensations. We have all probably perceived a sense or feeling of *direction*, a sense or feeling of *threat* or *danger*, and a sense or feeling of *well-being*.

### Your Intuitive Sense of Direction

Let us take the first universal psi effect—the sense of direction. You might have had a pure "sense" of direction, meaning that you knew intuitively to which place you should go. Examples abound in our daily lives. For instance, you might be late for an appointment or meeting in an unfamiliar neighborhood, when suddenly you sense that you should turn at the next corner. Possibly you are confused about which of all the strangers in the room you could approach, when suddenly you have the "feeling" that you should talk with one particular person. Perhaps you have a pile of letters on your desk and too little time to open them all, so you decide to put off the task altogether, but just as you are about to begin another project, you plainly know that you should open at least a few; in the third letter, you find a check that you had not expected to receive. The woman's impulse to run from the federal building ($\psi$-1) falls under this category. These are typical samples of our intuitive sense of direction. We sense, feel, and know precisely what move to make.

All three sensations have probably provided you valuable information about the plan for your next action. Although in the examples just cited, no words actually pronounced that you, the intuitor, should "Turn left," "Introduce yourself to that man," or "Open the third letter from the top," you were clearly introduced to your next decision or action.

At this point, we have to address a serious misconception of the meaning conveyed by the word *direction*, because it greatly influences our understanding of intuitive experiences. We tend to think that our "sense of direction" is limited to fixing our physical position in relation to the points of the compass—north, east, south, west—but this assumption is utterly incorrect. Fact: While a compass is a useful direction-finder for pointing the way for our planetary moves, intuition serves as our perpetual internal sensor of direction, reporting the way and distance we should move both mentally and physically.

This means that countless numbers of intuitive experiences involve directing and redirecting your decisions and actions. Remember that we intuit what moves to make according to the need in us to be involved in a particular interaction. Accordingly, whether we need to make or change a decision, to move physically from one position to a different place, or to select one task over another, our need to make the best of all possible connections stipulates a command performance by intuitiveness.

Listening to our slang, it appears that we already recognize this phenomenon. Decades ago, we established an idiom that unmistakably reveals that intuition is at work. Have you heard anyone comment that he or she had a "sense" or "feeling" of connection with a place or person? Have you heard people lament that they "feel out of touch" with an individual or situation? A person who is out of touch is acknowledging the need for direction. Do you know that in such cases, you are a candidate for your own intuitive direction-finder to send orienting signals posthaste?

Also important to seek out in your inner experiences is the "feeling of uneasiness" that people notice the instant they get cut off from their proper courses of action. For instance, have you ever sensed that you were making a bad purchase and later learned that your sense was correct? (This is a skill you want to develop before buying a secondhand car.) Have you ever felt that you were making a wrong move and that you should rethink it? Were you right? (Many divorced people describe having this feeling minutes before they took their wedding vows.) Have you ever plainly known that you should review a decision you just made and discovered with the doing that it *was* wrong? (Numbers of people report this feeling when they are looking for a new job.) These all are examples of intuition's attempting to redirect you instantly so that you will fall off set point as little as possible. You will have that sense or feeling, or simply know by uneasiness, when you are setting off in an unsuitable direction.

In general, this sense of direction will be among the first psi effects you will begin to notice as you learn to discern them. You will know from it which conditions, people, and ideas are attractive to you and which are repulsive, which are safe and which are dangerous, what will bring comfort and what will bring misery, what will bring out your talents and what will distract you.

## Your Intuitive Feeling of Danger

Now let's go to the next situation we all know well. We sometimes pass the point where it is easy to shift directions and get tangled in extreme conditions. This can happen in everything from love to a wilderness adventure. Somehow we have missed intuition's early-warning directional signals, and now we are in hot water. Here is the place where we sense danger, have feelings of alarm and even plainly know that we are in bad company.

This is one of the most important intuitive signals you will ever have. If there is a murderer in the crowd, your sense of danger should alert you. When the salesperson is cheating you, your feelings of alarm should create enough disturbance to awaken you. When forces of nature threaten harm to you and your possessions, you will be warned by intuition that trouble is afoot. Winthrop realized after the earthquake that probably his intuition was signaling danger when he was distracted and finally left the house for a walk ($\psi$-30).

Again we are caught in a misunderstanding about words. Too many people assume that danger means one thing only—that life itself is at risk and nothing less. Thus, when intuition sends its psi effects as couriers to assist them in slightly less end-of-the road matters, these people pay little attention to their information, thinking that they are building up psychological problems rather than facing true risks in many guises. The fact is that danger means exposure to harm, and this occurs in a million places.

Add to this that danger means different things to different people. In the first chapter, you read newspaper headlines. Each article referred to a particular threat facing people, but everyone would not be encountering all of the conditions. Only some people would be using the taxi, a few others might be subjected to the risky medication, and still others would have to contend with the terror of a schoolchild turned cold-blooded murderer. With this intuitive ability to perceive danger, we can assume that we no longer need to walk in fear night and day. It would take learning to recognize this marvelous sense, feeling, or plain knowing to reach this free state of mind, but as this sense of extremes is available to the entire population, we can begin to learn how to get out of harm's way on those occasions when we step too far into its path.

## Your Intuitive Feeling of Well-Being—The Aha!

From time to time, a condition settles precisely on optimum, and we perceive it. It happens when we arrive at a long-sought goal. It happens with discovery. It happens when love walks in. People report "feeling very satisfied." Sometimes the intuitive feeling of hitting the ideal might be so strong that the person all but bursts with elation. We feel exultant joy and gladness so penetrating that we are "floating on air." We might exclaim: "Aha! I've got it! There it is. Perfect!" This sense of the optimum transcends all other intuitive feelings in its intensely ecstatic happiness.

You might feel such strong "certainty" that you have found an answer that it makes you draw in your breath and exclaim involuntarily: "That's *right*! I have it." Very often, people in love discover that they have found their mate when they "feel" themselves soaring in joy. Ask them what they are experiencing, and they might say that their "love feels right," or that they "know" that this person is *it*. Have you ever had an "Aha" moment? What did it feel like intuitively?

One other extreme experience can occur to any of us. It is the most complete sense of connection imaginable. We feel it in what is called a "religious," "peak," or "mystic" experience. This is known to be the sudden, direct intuitive knowledge of ultimate reality, of perceiving the harmonious interactivity of all that exists in the universe. One "feels the flow" of life, "knows" that the ways of the world are "right." Both the form and the intensity of mystical experience vary. For some, it is a sense of orderliness; for others, pure feeling; and for still others, plain knowledge of the universal mechanics. Thousands upon thousands of people have reported simply that they were caught in a moment of exultation or gladness.

## What We Know

We know that we intuit which directions to go and when to stop, and that if we fall into difficulties, then we will be advised of danger by feelings of alarm or knowledge that something is out of order. We also know when life is running ideally, or when suddenly the last piece of a worldly puzzle falls into place.

What we don't know is how it happens. When you say, "I have the feeling that everything is going to be all right," what do you mean? What is that feeling? Can you describe it as something like hotness or coldness, pain or pleasure? Most people can say only that something is happening in them that "feels." They detect that an unknown internal system is feeding them these elusive sensations or that they are in the sway of an invisible direction-finder.

Does this slipperiness of the psi effects diminish intuition's credibility? Some definitely argue that it does. But their argument falls flat for those of us who know that, however elusive or vague, these sensations are consistent within us. There is a most obvious change in the patterns of activity of our sensations, or mentality, and that is beyond doubt.

Sense of direction . . . feeling of imminent danger . . . plain knowing that someone is watching: We live by these patterns of sense, feeling, and plain knowing. To perceive them means that we are being intuitive. They might pop into our mental picture or drift through the far reaches of our mental world. They might fling themselves at us, a meteoric shower of certain knowledge, or command our attention so that no other form of knowledge can prevail. When we suddenly know what we should do next, or that we are correct, no one but no one can tell us we are wrong.

Do you recognize the theme? Intuition follows rules that point us in the direction of security and increasing excellence. How to develop it? Set limits on yourself. Since psi effects are consistent, you have a measure for discovery. Learn what happens in your head. Analyze the experience. Was it a sense? Sense of what? Was there a feeling? What words describe it? Was there a sureness, a certainty? Would you have bet your life on it, or set your next course of action by it? Why?

To show yourself what is happening intuitively, keep a record, put your intuition into words that describe the effects. Do not fill in the gaps when words fail you. Perhaps a sketch would help, one drawn to remind you of the mental experience—a floating cloud; a simple map of the route you traveled, with a starburst on the spot where you intuited what to do next; the classic radiant lightbulb suspended over your head to represent a sudden flash of learning. The record fixes your very fluid intuitive experience, puts it under your rational microscope, and gives you a tangible cross section of intuition to return to and reflect on. It helps you establish that, although intuitiveness might be as elusive as a hummingbird flitting among the leaves, it can be captured in your thoughts and become an experience to build on. This development of awareness, ideas, and words serves well as your home schooling of intuition.

Next, talk about it. Ask others: What happens to you? Do they use the same words? Do they describe similar experiences? Conversation also teaches. A friend exclaims that he, too, has had feelings of direction and confirms the experience you doubted; a neighbor smiles knowingly, describes her similar doubts, and leaves you satisfied that you both are learning how to analyze the psi effects that you also both experience. If we begin this comparative study of inner experiences of silent but certain orientation in an invisible world, in time these intuitive senses, feelings, and plain knowings will become phenomena we all can recognize.

## What Phenomena Do We Intuit?

*Telepathy* first: Any changing condition in another individual's mental state is highly intuitible. Remember that you will be aware of a person's self-control—whether he or she is confused, frustrated, outraged, or enraged. You also will intuit passion, qualities of an individual's character, his or her mood, degrees of concentration, and, finally, the violent person.

*Teleos*: You will perceive changes in matter, forces, isolated events, and courses of events.

*Timing*: Timing for your decisions and moves is very perceptible.

In any of these three categories, you will intuit the direction you should or could move. You will be made aware too of any danger that threatens or opportunity that will enrich you.

## Samples to Examine

### First Impressions

When you enter a situation, intuition frequently sends fleet signals to give you an immediate measure for your own moves. Begin to notice these first impressions. Describe them to yourself. What is your first sensation? For example, when you meet a new person, you might have the "feeling" that he or she is someone you would like to know better. Or you might have the opposite "feeling," that this is a person you don't want to know. Pay attention to your head when the phone rings. You often know how to respond at the first jingle. Intuition might signal you whether or not to answer the phone, or even report accurately who the caller is. Likewise the doorbell. What impulse or knowledge runs through your head at the first clang? When you enter your office and begin to open one by one a pile of manuscripts on your desk, notice what your head signals each time you pick up a new packet. Do you have a feeling that this one will be good, or a dog? Do you sense with the first sentence whether or not you should continue?

For a while, why not make a habit of noticing these first impressions. Write down each one when the effect occurs, but ignore it—unless, of course, you feel mortal danger. The reason for disregarding it is that you want to check whether you are right, so you must take the incident or task to conclusion, which is probably what you normally would do if there were no predictive intuition. Once you have answered the phone, opened the door, read the manuscript or letter, or whatever you were bid, then check your record. Was that first impression correct? In time, you will discover that those mental effects that sweep through your psyche on initial encounters usually are intuitive signals.

## Off Set Point

Remember that when a system falls off set point, it means that a condition is either improving or deteriorating. You want to know which direction to turn at any given moment.

Having read the accounts in this book, you are familiar with numbers of sensations that others experience when phenomena are getting closer to their set point or falling off. To find the effects in your own life, recall the times when you have known that something is right. Have you ever said, "That feels right"? What were you talking about? Do you remember the feeling you were experiencing when you gave that description? Were there words or not? Likewise, we have feelings when things are "wrong" or "unsuitable." Look for those in your daily activities as well.

Do you "sense" people's moods? Once in a while, a person might enter a room and "change" the atmosphere. This means that he or she has thrown the existing ethers off set point. Have you ever perceived such a shift? What intuitive sensation made you aware of it—a sense, a feeling, or did you just plain know that the person was influencing the environment? This, of course, would be your telepathy signaling.

Do you recall picking up a person's "vibes"? How did you intuit that telepathic interaction?

Sometimes we feel "out of sync" or "in sync" with an individual or even with a group. Do you remember any such telepathic experience? What sensation revealed it?

Perhaps someone proposed a plan that you "knew" could work well. You might have exclaimed, "That sounds right." The signal would have come from Telcos giving you a go-ahead. Do you think that the person with you understood what led you to that conclusion? Next time, ask whether he or she had a similar feeling, or any intuitive guidance.

Did you ever shop for a gift and just "know" when you saw an item that it was the perfect present for that person? Take a minute to recall the sensation that reported your right choice. This would be a Teleos effect. Was intuition proved right when you presented the gift?

Can you recall "having a sense" that something simply was not on set point? Has a friend ever asked for your opinion about an important matter, such as the person he or she was dating? The question might have been: What do you think of us as a couple? You might have "known" that this was not a good match. Perhaps you instantly "felt" that the pair was compatible, or not so. In this case, the psi effect guiding you would more than likely have been Teleos, because you were intuiting a developing condition. Remember that Telepathy informs you only of the current state of the person's nervous system.

How many boardroom decisions are made intuitively? When the chair asks if the members think a project is good for the firm, will you base your reply on intuition or rational thought? How many in that room do you think base their answers on intuitiveness rather than analysis? If you have been in such a decision-making position, or one that is similar, think back to what your reply "felt" like.

Have you ever "known" that a situation was endangered? Possibly the general manager proposed a new business scheme that set off all of your internal intuitive alarms. They might have taken the form of a strong "feeling" of rejection for the plan, or a "gut" feeling that this would not be good, or even vague "knowledge" that all was not well. Take some time to recollect any distinct characteristics of those teleosic and clarification sensations.

## Timing

We intuit when to make a move. Our most common general description of this intuitive capability says that we have a good "sense" of timing, and that our timing is "uncanny." This kind of timing can be invaluable, keeping us out of trouble that would surely have happened if we had ignored the sensation.

Have you ever had an inexplicable "feeling of urgency" and hurried through whatever you were doing without understanding why? In contrast, do you recall "knowing" that you had plenty of time, when the facts seemed to say just the opposite? Can you describe those sensations? Were you right?

We use a cliché: "Timing is everything." Can you "sense" or "feel" when the perfect time is to pick up a phone, introduce a subject, or leave for an engagement? Do the psi effects come to you as definitely as a physical alarm? This capability of timing is a good one to experiment with simply because of the built-in potential for a process to fall off set point when you are late.

Have you ever "known" that you should wait for the right moment to ask a particular question of your teacher, coach, parent, or friend? How would you describe the psi effect that reports the perfect moment?

Do you remember ever feeling that you should not make a move even though you wanted to do so? For example, perhaps you "felt" you shouldn't telephone a friend or colleague and learned later that you were right to hold up your call. What was the sensation that accompanied the feeling? Did it override your desire to do what you wanted to do? That would have been either a Telepathy or Teleos psi effect. One challenge of intuition surfaces here: the battle of will versus wisdom. Sometimes it is difficult to honor the intuitive message rather than bow to your own desires.

Since timing is of greatest importance in most matters, you might look for a simple pattern in intuition's guidance. These sensations that work to keep you coordinated with humankind's clockwork and nature's biological clock work for the same purpose as traffic signals at a crossroads. Both the intuitive sensations and electric lights are indicating whether you should "go," "stop," or "wait." You will sense an urge to move "now," or "not now." Begin to notice these psi effects influencing your decisions, so that you can constantly time your moves precisely.

## How Many Psi Effects Do You Recognize?

These questions should begin to introduce you to the underlying pattern of sensations and signals associated with the psi effects. In general, I have been discussing the effects as they occur without words. Once you can connect the three characteristic core sensations to the wordless psi effects, you will have cracked the fundamental code of intuition's communication with you. By learning what is happening to you intuitively, you also discover how others feel when they are being intuitive.

You will be able to respond sensibly to the call of intuition when you have learned to recognize these practical natural communication signals, all of which are historically well known as psi effects. Generations have described having the "sense" of things happening or about to happen. They have reported experiencing "feelings" that give excellent guidance for action, and they have often "plainly known" about whole courses of events that were influencing them. If you take time to look back into your own life, you, too, will be able to pull out at least a few such encounters with the three basic sensations. Remember that in all cases, the reason intuition conveys information through us is that we are required to know when we, or a phenomenon, are getting closer to set point and the optimal performance.

## The Matter of Mix-Ups

Before going on, we need to face the troubling possibility that we will confuse intuitive experiences with other mental activity,

and vice versa. To those who sincerely want to tame intuitive ability, let me say this one last time: Intuitive experiences of psi effects
are pure processes by themselves and not to be mistaken for any
other mental activity. Our interest should lie now with this cluster of three and all of the fascinating permutations that issue from
them. In the tens of thousands of experiences we have of the
world, we all will no doubt occasionally confuse the intuitive psi
effects with the other mental processes that supply their own
unique data. This will become less of a problem as we develop
individually and as a society.

While the biggest obstacle to our confidently using intuition's
data is that we prefer to have our facts proven in advance, the
greatest challenge to learning to recognize the psi effects' information will be this separation of our old friends—memory, imagination, and subtle reasoning, among other mental activities—from
the intuitive effects. We all have a lifetime of using these resources,
and such strong mental habits are difficult, but not impossible, to
control.

Learning is always a filtration process. We do it continually.
Thus, perhaps a simple example of what lies ahead would help.
How would you separate the pure *imagination* that you are in danger from the *intuitive sensation* of real danger? If we examine the
characteristics, we see that the learning processes behind intuiting and imagining are distinctly different. One difference is that
imagination grows wild, wicked, and wonderful stories in the head
like a cumulus cloud building its vaporous masses of fluff, while
an intuitive effect is unwavering truth. You sense danger.

Let's say you are alone in a dark room, when you hear strange
sounds from the front entryway. While your imagination can
build a tall tale instantly about a menacing intruder stealing down
the hall toward you, your intuition produces no signal of danger—because nothing has fallen off set point. In the event that
there is such a threat, you will know about it as fact by any one

of the basic sensations. Thus, in the case of imagination versus intuitiveness, the solution to the confusion will always be that intuition is a sensory system reporting facts of reality, while imagination's best work is accomplished without benefit of one single fact. In the colorful world of fantasy, elephants can be pink, cows can fly, and the moon is made of green cheese, but in the intuitive domain, there can be no such merriment, simply because it is unable to produce anything but facts about life in fluctuation around myriad set points.

You will learn the differences among the mental activities. True, the psyche is a fast-moving operation and dexterous at signaling to you. This is its job. But while we learn, we stand on solid ground. Intuition is a vital sensory function and not to be mistaken with any other. It conveys reliable information. Nature has even included redundant psi effects in Clarification and Dreams, to guarantee that, should a piece of information become distorted or get lost in the shuffle, these two will duplicate the data. To ensure that we can do our part, we have to pay attention to the psi effects so that we can always get the message right. Now let's get to the grit of the task—beginning to train ourselves to use intuition intelligently.

# CHAPTER 12

# One Hand for You

WE HAVE TRAVELED together now for pages. I have spelled out the cogent points of our intuitiveness, at least as far as space allows in this book. The story woven throughout this book to this point has been mine, a recounting of how intuition has worked for people around me on a daily basis. The time has come to mix intuition in with the world's experiences, with the intention of launching it into whatever future it has. In this chapter, we turn first to lore of the sea to establish the place of intuition in life itself, then to guidelines for using the intuitive process effectively.

## A Time-Proven Maxim

Round and round we go on planet Earth, watching the general imbalance among systems spread like an epidemic. Should we assume that these signs of breakdown mean nature is doing an evolutionary housecleaning? Or does the upheaval begin instead with us? Imbalance appears everywhere in the ecosystem—in soil, air, and water. Likewise the human species has serious disorder in the rank and file, with children in peril, and with women and men in unhealthy relationships. Political and business leaders are forgetting why they are in power. Organizations are sliding by on half-truths. Economic structures are slipping and cracking like glaciers.

Pundits ask: Where is the public outrage at the mind games that those leaders and individuals alike play with one another, transgressing privileges, offending human values? Our self-centered systems are spinning crazily off center, like a child's top winding down. And in all this unbalancing activity, people are asking: Are we safe?

One goal of this book has been to show how the living universe imposes regulated constraints to control what can happen to it. No question, we are deregulating the order of nature. Thus, the primary reason for the spreading upheaval has to lie with us. We are self-centered. So many people among us grab the advantage for themselves. They would let the rest of life tumble as it may. And tumble it surely will.

How did we get here? One explanation is that when power, pleasure, and ease are part of the equation, we are not particularly enamored with changing. Our love of comfort has taken an insidious hold on us. We break one natural law after another to be comfortable. Anyone who thinks can see that we are moving on a course that ends in a lose/lose result for us and the ecosystem alike. It's like waiting for the hurricane to make landfall.

On the other hand, while once we all thought that life meant a joyride through the solar system which served us, we now know better. But, we say, we are stuck for solutions. What's needed is a fresh new perspective. It would thus make sense to look at the opportunities that come with life at set point; then we can certainly recognize the benefit of getting the balances right.

A maxim from sea lore shows us a way to arrest this perilous unbalancing act. The sailor's life is one of implicit cooperation, of playing fair with the elements. The maxim establishes the ideal interaction in nine small words: "One hand for you, and one for the ship." This simply means that at no time should the sailor take care of himself only. For instance, during a gale he does not cling to the mast to save his own skin, but hauls his share of the lines to keep the ship from foundering. Likewise, he knows he should never give all hands to those lines or the wheel and not protect his own life. In short, those who go down to the sea in ships know the importance of keeping the balance of priorities between self-protection and supporting the ship that carries them home. After all, what good is any vessel without a hale and hearty crew? What good is a crew without a ship to sail?

## Continual Exchange

Those who follow the sea live the very equation that we all need. It is the same one that we, as a species, seem to think is an impossible formula for society to reckon. Challenging that pessimism and extending the sailors' metaphor of cooperation to the human condition can put our problem of self-centeredness into sharper focus and finally help us get the balance right.

The critical question any mariner faces in a storm is the same for all humanity: *Who* gets the advantage first, and who second? A sailor learns this in the first days out and never forgets the time-proven rule. *It will be a continual exchange.*

## Exchanges and Interactions

For every person, there is a constant interplay among the events of private life and those in the larger society, and the risks we are willing to consider in order to have the best for both. How does this differ from the life of a sailor? Does the greatness of the ship make any difference? It shouldn't. Whether we are sailing a small boat for pleasure in a Saturday race, running a ship of state, or making passage on good ship Earth in its sea of galaxies, we are all crew and have to follow the ancient maxim. There is not a permanent superior position of advantage for any party. No matter what the issue, life is an interaction—systems working together. No one is exempt. For our leaders, who are handling the lines along with the rest of us, the rule applies. The time-tested ideal is universal. It will always be: One hand for you, and one for the ship.

Born with all the necessary abilities to sign on, the human species has voyaged this far on earth. If we begin again to make a fair exchange, lending a hand here, holding our own position there, chances are good that the flexible environment will keep our species on board for the full passage. This is playing fair. We know that the quality of future life is threatened. But what if we adopt this maxim? If we hold her on course, will she carry us through smooth and tempestuous conditions alike?

Remember that *the individual is ever and always intuition's priority.* "One hand for you. . . ." You have read enough now to suspect that when life is a dangerously confusing affair, we spontaneously intuit whatever we need for ourselves. Yet the tension will always exist between us and anyone or anything else in a state of flux. The human being, as a crew member, helping to keep the earth on her galactic course, will always be called to help with the ship by learning in time about events within its micro-processes and making moves accordingly.

Return to the accounts in which you see intuitive people interacting with forces of nature: an eroding road, a smoldering fire, wind that will change, a wave that is under way, bacteria invading food, an apple that will choke, a fragile tooth. Faced with this perpetual demand on helping with overall stability, we can say that among all of our diverse human capabilities for holding the delicate balance, this intuitive capacity to fine-tune is the most valuable to individuals and to life as a whole. Born intuitively sensitive to nature's ways, we know by intuition's information where and when life will benefit from a human helping hand.

## Personal Encounters

If we accept the premise that an organic intuitive system exists that gives us the advantage of top performance, it follows that we would want to master its operations. With this as the final goal here, we begin by inquiring what happens to us as we use our intuitive sensibilities.

The important points have been established: Predators skulk about in our world, seven psi effects report interactions with them, intuition is a regulatory mechanism for managing those encounters, Laws of Information and Action exist to direct the movement, intuitive facts must be employed before proof comes home, and we can use a Routine questioning process for selecting intuition as the route to those pivotal facts. The humanly regulated intuitive process involves posing a question, detecting information, deciding what moves to make using the data, and making the move.

Since it is not possible to address the infinite number of encounters we might anticipate with intuition, this next discussion presents generalizations culled from years of observation to guide your learning about the intuitive process by: (1) tying together the spontaneous and selective experiences of psi effects; (2) describing nine types of "follow-through"; (3) listing pointers that help you gain from intuitive experiences; and finally (4) probing the answers to questions that people frequently ask about intuitive powers.

### Spontaneous Intuitive Learning and Behavior

The first nine chapters introduced the spontaneous feature of any psi effect. This spontaneity incorporates the psi effects so naturally into daily life that we frequently do not separate them out for the pots of gold that they are. As described already, our role in these unsolicited instances is to be the detector and correction elements in the regulatory mechanism's standard process of:

1. Detection of psi effect

2. Decision

3. Corrective Movement

The failing brakes ($\psi$-19) and earthquake proofing ($\psi$-28) accounts offer a fair illustration that considerable rational planning can follow from the intuitive information produced.

## Selective Learning and Behavior

While nothing is wrong with operating on the spontaneity of psi effects, greater advantage overall results from using intuitive data and instructions intentionally when we make decisions. When you decide to search for information intuitively, you then turn to the Routine.

1. Identify what you need to know. (Determine the systems variable.)

2. Ask: What do I know about . . . ? (Fill in the condition, or variable, you want to regulate.)

3. Detection. (Be patient for the psi effect.)

4. Decision. (Determine the move[s] you will make.)

5. Action. (Make your move based on the psi effect's data.)

Think of Benjamin Franklin. You are reaching into the environment and pulling facts from there along the nervous system's circuitry. Asking the question generates the intuitive process, which, being natural, follows its orderly routine for you and feeds back the correctional cue via a psi effect. Detect it, decide what moves to make, and move.

## Mixing Spontaneous with Selective Learning

While in many respects the first two processes might seem more than adequate, we have a third option for learning intuitively. We can use the information we receive spontaneously as the grounds for searching with selective intuition. This is the same process we follow, say, when we have a fresh idea such as: "I have extra time today. Why not run a few errands?" On occasions when a notion like this pops into our heads, we often think more about it rationally in order to streamline our actions. Hence you might ask a question like, "Do I have anything more urgent?" or, "Where could I begin?" Additional insight comes to light with each inquiry until you have enough data to lead you to the final decision for action.

Should you detect intuitive information spontaneously, this same principle of digging for data works. You have the privilege of reaching for more information if more is necessary. You do so by returning with almost the same Routine question: What *else* do I know about . . . ?

Thus it is possible to run an intuitive check for more details rather than pursuing with the other rational interrogation of Who?, What?, Where?, Why? One example of this mixing is the earthquake preparations (ψ-28). Warning: Do not force the process. Be content with only the facts that intuition reports. We make our greatest mistakes when we press the intuitive process. It often leads to simply becoming rational.

## Subjects for Intuiting

The Factors "U"—Our intuitiveness is our contact with any unknown or unpredictable phenomenon that will have an influence on us or that we can influence. We will always spontaneously learn the information we require. When in search for data that would favorably impact our lives—such as safe direction or timing—the selective option is always open.

## Moves to Correct Systems

This corrective step in the process converts intuitive knowledge to power. It puts us in a delicate position because the information that we learn from a psi effect might offer tantalizing possibilities, yet the demands it imposes can be distressing. This can cause us to make some fairly bad decisions. One case in point is Jan's unwise choice to remain silent rather than impose an urgent warning and seem like her nagging mother-in-law ($\psi$-33).

Courage is never more crucial than in the early stages of mastering the process. However, it's a good rule to not push yourself to make a corrective move unless you are comfortable with the responsibility associated with it. I discussed the challenge of professional accountability in the lieutenant's choice to take an alternate route ($\psi$-15). Breaking social codes can also demand grit; few responsible people enjoy making others uneasy, as I did in the restaurant. The choice was difficult that day ($\psi$-12), as it was at the card table ($\psi$-16). My social graces nearly won in both cases. Because of this kind of awkwardness you might find that you resist intuition's assistance. So be it. Following its lead becomes easier with successes because that is confirmation that intuition works to the advantage of all.

When we get to this make-the-move phase of the intuitive regulatory mechanism we suddenly discover that we are on the horns of this dilemma: While it is acceptable to not follow through on intuitive information, it isn't wise to do so. Intuition is useful for two profound reasons: (1) it informs us about conditions in the surroundings so that we can get our bearings, and (2) it enables us to participate in the evolution of events and systems in the natural order. Looking at its role as a regulatory mechanism in the larger order of nature we see that intuition draws us into the action where we help maintain harmony in nature's grand design.

It is odd that there is a curious twist in this scheme: We assume that we must follow through on the psi effects. But this is an assumption and not entirely true. Except for instances when the Reflex effect bulldozes an intuitor, *the intuitive system cannot force us to make the correction*. We can—in fact, we should—make the corrective move, but we will always have the option to refuse.

The irony of intuition vis à vis our life is that with intuition's guidance we can fine-tune our action and play a beneficial role in the microdimensions of the universe if we'd like, but nature does not insist upon this. This implies that while we might be invited to the party, if we cannot come or arbitrarily refuse, the universe will not fade into oblivion. Alternatives abound. In the absence of our human support, nature will seek and find a route for that course of events we avoided—perhaps by calling on a different person but, possibly, by passing over human aid for another resource entirely. In a word, we can be replaced.

Now, give this sobering fact some careful thought: The natural order can bypass us and survive, but we cannot bypass nature—and survive. Scores of situations support this grim reality. Deserts provide examples. Their delicate ecosystems have survived eons of change. Then human beings arrived. Without understanding the complexities of the systems' balances we began irrigating, burning, and overgrazing in adjacent areas. This frenzy of doing things our way finally damaged the fragile environment enough to enable deserts to spread and overtake habitable land—driving out human beings. Now these spreading deserts pose a serious world problem.

Again and again the exercise of learning by painful experience shows that nature's motives are good for us all, whereas ours, too often, are for our own good only. Consequently, we have no choice but to abide by the law and order of nature; for otherwise, when the environment deteriorates it will take us with it.

Intuition seems to have installed us in the microworld's communication system where we can learn what is optimal for this natural order. The knowledge intuition offers is immeasurably valuable, but the inherent power within eludes us unless we use those options to interact according to the psi effects' information. Thus, we learn at the end of the story that the case of options is closed. If we want to survive and flourish, we are required to take them and follow through, thereby doing our part in keeping the system strong. I would wager that many "felt" they were doing something harmful even as they built up around those deserts.

Although it is wonderful to recognize the psi effects' patterns well enough to be able to make our moves confidently, once in a while we all run into obstacles to using it freely. Following is a list of reasons why we might hesitate to follow through on psi effects, coupled with suggestions on what we should do to overcome the problems.

1. *The information doesn't make sense:* If you are uncomfortable acting on seemingly illogical psi effects, begin by following up only on those psi effects that make common sense—such as "move to the left lane"— so that you can use reasonable data to make decisions for action.

2. *The intuitive message gets lost:* With such a wide range of possible intuitible developments, it is perfectly reasonable that not everyone is going to acknowledge the data every time. In the event that you don't gather the facts on the first encounter, you should make no move. Instead, be patient. If the phenomenon truly needs a human assist, the backup and redundant

systems will come to the rescue. You might even be bulldozed. Remember my folly with the candy? (ψ-39)

3. *Impossible obstacles limit following through:* Sometimes the obstacles to following through are overwhelming, as in the case of the student before the Oklahoma City bombing (ψ-2). If so, acknowledge that the situation is a fact of life you cannot correct under the circumstances, and continue with your daily schedule as planned. *Do not get caught feeling guilty for what you could not save.* Guilt is hazardous to your well-being and does not in any way correct fluctuating systems. Realize that sometimes you are as helpless as the two people who intuited the terrorists' activity (ψ-2, ψ-27). The lesson we learn from this helplessness is that our human communications are occasionally imperfect despite the fact that we have more continuous interpersonal contact now than at any other time in history. If you cannot find a way to lend assistance, your best action will be to move out of the way so that others can step in and solve the problem.

4. *The message is too threatening:* If correction is possible but courage is in short supply, then plan a viable alternative to get the second-best result. In the case of the failing brakes, I might have been too frightened to drive the car. Then I would have telephoned another person to provide transportation that day.

5. *To take action would be embarrassing:* Here we have the problem of not wanting to be publicly mortified by our intuitive actions. As a veteran of this particular inner war, let me tell you that it is better to suffer a red face than the consequences of opting out of the intuitive work.

6. *Skeptical:* Some people want to use intuition but simply do not trust it. If you think that human intuition is merely a figment of our collective imagination, or that it does exist but has dubious value, then you need not endorse it. No man-made law dictates that we must use any of our senses, and nature leaves us the choice whether or not to use many of them, including intuition. Remember that intuition exists for our convenience and advantage. Therefore, if you doubt its value and purpose but do experience psi effects from time to time, I suggest you ignore the effects—it is your privilege. Furthermore, if a natural need arises for your assistance the intuitive process always has an entry behind the scenes through its "coincidences" and "miracles."

Further to this last point, I warrant that on that day when human intuitiveness is trained from birth as is our reasoning ability now, the human race will relegate both "guessing" and "gambling the odds" to its history books as impractical means of problem solving. I hasten to add that our adventures in discovery will in no way diminish; they only will be less fraught with error and, most important, will be nipped in the bud if they put us on a path of self-destruction or doing harm to any other form of creation. On the whole I predict that this new intuition will increase our roaming territory by giving us freedom to move safely because we learn more accurate information at all times and thus can be confident that the actions that follow will lead inevitably to top performance—if we use the information intelligently.

## A Checklist for Developing Personal Intuition

Traditionally we humans have encouraged our offspring to experiment with their world by asking them to report what they see and hear. Thus generations have learned about the external environment. Around 450 B.C. Socrates introduced his question-and-answer method of schooling to teach the boys of Athens about their inner mental faculties, especially the human capability called "reasoning." Now we are beginning to master another phenomenon of learning that mysteriously occurs in our heads. In order to isolate this activity called "intuiting" we again become our own teachers by describing and analyzing our experiences with the intuitive process.

The following questions serve as guidelines to discovering your undeveloped intuition at work. I suggest that you run through these questions each time you intuit any information. The long-term goal is that you will be able to recognize the psi effects when they occur to you and to act on them confidently. This is not a test of right or wrong, but is instead a self-check to help you master the intuitive process as quickly as possible. If you keep a record of your own experiences you will begin to see intuition's pattern as the valuable regulatory function it is.

## Psi Effect Self-Check

### *Instructions*

In this following self-check you will begin by portraying the psi effects you experience. Describe the experience aloud or write a brief account of it. Use words that describe the psi effect.

Examples: I had a *definite feeling* that the plan was a good one; there was *no question in my mind* that the woman was wrong; I had a *hunch* we would be right on target; I had that familiar *sinking feeling* that the boss was wrong when he said that the project was a "go"; my *first impression* was that the group was tense; I *cannot explain* what saved me.

Having repeated your account, next analyze it to:

▲ identify the sensation associated with the psi effect (D)

▲ pinpoint the fact or facts you learned (SV)

▲ distinguish how the facts helped you follow through (SP)

▲ understand the actual move, or moves, you made (CM)

▲ observe your psychological reaction to being intuitive

## Part I: The Intuitive Process

1. Write a brief description of a spontaneous inner experience, called the sensation, or of one that occurred as a result of using the Routine.

_____

_____

_____

_____

_____

_____

2. How did you learn the information?
   1. A sense of knowing ❏
   2. A feeling of knowing ❏
   3. Plainly knowing ❏
   4. Involuntary reflex action without knowing ❏
   5. Accompanied by words ❏
   6. Without words ❏

3. Identify which psi effect or psi effects informed you.
   1. Déjà vu ❏
   2. Telepathy ❏
   3. Teleos ❏ (Retrocognition ❏
      Direct cognition ❏ Precognition ❏)
   4. Instruction ❏
   5. Reflex ❏
   6. Clarification ❏ (Clairaudience ❏
      Clairsentience ❏ Clairvoyance ❏)
   7. Dreams ❏ (Day ❏ Night ❏)

4. If the psi effect was a backup Instruction or Reflex, or a redundant Clarification or Dream, what primary psi effect did it reinforce? Déjà vu ❑ Telepathy ❑ Teleos ❑

5. Have you experienced this psi effect previously? If so, compare the earlier effect with this one. (Example: Although both were Teleos, this was a strong hunch while that was a light impression. This was Clarification—a feeling in my bones; the previous effect was a plain mental feeling with no other associated sensation.)

_____

_____

_____

_____

6. Name what pure fact or facts you actually learned from this psi effect. (Examples: Brakes would fail in the future; something "seized.")

_____

_____

_____

_____

7. Did the psi effect's information enable you to set out on a course of action? Yes ❑ No ❑ Unsure ❑

8. Describe the move or moves you made. (Examples: Looked around restaurant for indicators of low standards but couldn't find evidence. Decided it was necessary to embarrass myself and order only tea because of the feeling.)

_____

_____

_____

_____

_____

_____

_____

9. Determine who benefited from intuition's appearance.
   It gave: self-help only ❑ a helping hand ❑ both ❑

10. Could you have learned this same information by any
    other internal *physical* system in time to be as accurate
    and useful as you were?
    Yes ❑ No ❑ Unsure ❑

11. If your answer to number 10 is affirmative, analyze
    which alternative internal system would have offered as
    much or better data in time to make the move.
    1. Rational analysis ❑
    2. Memory ❑
    3. Imagination ❑
    4. Fear ❑
    5. A sensory system ❑
       (Vision ❑ Hearing ❑ Smell ❑ Other ❑)

## Part II: Your Response

1. Describe your response to the psi effect. (Examples: I
   was reluctant to embarrass myself by taking action; I was
   so "sure" of the information that I didn't hesitate to make
   the move; it made no sense, so I decided to ignore it.)

   _____

   _____

   _____

2. What was your first reaction to the effect's information?
   1. Glad to know ❑
   2. Wanted more details ❑
   3. Fear ❑

   4. Called it absurd ❏
   5. Decreed it impossible to know such a thing ❏
   6. Confused about how to proceed ❏
   7. Other ❏

3. If you used the Routine and detected no informative psi effect, what do you think might have happened?
   1. The psi effect was: imperceptible ❏; overshadowed by other mental effects ❏; ambiguous ❏.
   2. I was impatient, so gave up waiting for specific data ❏.
   3. Other ❏

4. Are you confident that this experience is evidence that you were being intuitive? Yes ❏  No ❏

5. If your answer to number four is no, what else might it have been?
   1. Reason ❏
   2. Memory ❏
   3. Imagination ❏
   4. Fear ❏
   5. Another sensory system ❏
   (Vision ❏  Hearing ❏  Touch ❏  Other ❏)

### Short Test to Assess the Intuitive Process

1. What was the system variable?

_____

2. What would be the set point?

_____

3. What was the detector?

_____

4. What was the corrective mechanism?

_____

5. Was the Intuitive Positioning System invoved?

_____

6. Did your action return the system to set point?

_____

7. Did your action result in visible advantage to anything or anyone?

_____

8. What information did you learn?

_____

9. How did you learn the information?

_____

10. What move did you make?

_____

## Ten Common Questions

1. *Q: When developing intuition, how long does it take to separate true psi effects from other mental activities such as memory, reasoning, imagination, personal desire, doubt, and beliefs?*

A: Two factors control you. One is your need for intuition's particular kind of data, and the other is your determination to make a place in your thinking for intuitive input. Once you know that psi effects will orient you, the second step is to use intuition as a regular conduit of knowledge—and practice, practice, practice.

2. *Q: You have spoken of only a limited number of mental effects. Where do you fit in more dramatic paranormal phenomena like bending spoons, objects flying around, UFOs, out-of-body experiences,*

*and supernatural events such as the appearance of spirits, or chan-
neling otherworldly teachers and personalities?*

A: I think that these widely reported experiences that don't
quite fit into our worldview are all examples of our belief systems defining how we communicate with the environment. In my
mind, most of these so-called anomalous experiences are valid and
can be explained within the framework of intuition's psi effects.

Let's look at the first matter mentioned—spoon bending. Technically this is called psychokinesis, or PK. Perhaps this highly publicized ability to bend metal is the most common example of mind
mysteriously moving matter. Although there is no satisfactory explanation for it happening, thousands of men, women, and children
worldwide have spontaneously bent and twisted spoons, forks, keys,
and other small metal items. While there is a sharp physical distinction between a human mentally bending a piece of metal and
bending an elbow, I am confident that in living science both phenomena are evidence of our cohesion with the natural order.

I have described my theory about humans intuitively learning through psi effects about matter moving; now we turn to
moving matter intuitively—the Reflex effect. Observing the ways
we interact with materials and forces in the environment may help
us understand this psychokinetic capability. Take, for example, the
simple act of getting up out of a chair and walking across the
room to open a window. How do you make that happen? It
begins with the specific decision to make the action, which sets
off a flurry of neuronal activity that prompts your standing,
walking, pulling, and so forth. These complex mental and physical processes result in your moving matter—a body and a window. You set in motion both your entire body and the window
frame—rather impressive by any neurobiologist's standard. Was
that psychokinesis*? In a manner of speaking, yes, because we use

---

*The prefix *psych-*, meaning "mental activity" or "processes," is rooted in the Greek
*psukho*, meaning "soul" or "life." *Kinesis*, also from the Greek, is a suffix referring to motion
and to set in motion.

the word to refer to setting matter in motion mentally. How hard did you have to work mentally to accomplish this particular physical and mental feat of mind moving physical matter? Wasn't it as simple as making a decision? Assuming that your body is physically capable, it would have been only a short programmed step from the idea to action; most likely the entire physical exercise was pleasantly mechanical. Of course, we cannot ignore the fact that your hands were in direct contact with the window frame.

Examples like this demonstrate that we are united by forces that hold us together with the inelastic materials of the earth. When you wanted to pull up that window, for example, you used the muscles of your hand and arm to grasp the solid window frame and lift it. Most of us would not be shocked by this familiar act, probably because it is so completely normal and explicable. We understand that we had to make the decision that led to the movements. Also, we have learned about the internal biological processes driving muscle action, so the result of moving the two objects—body and window sash—is no longer the mysterious event it once was, even though the muscles doing the work are invisible to the naked eye. To bring us closer to allowing intuitiveness to initiate movements of matter, I ask this question: Why does anyone get up from a chair and open a window? He or she *needs* it open. Whether to get fresh air or to speak with someone outside, the action would be motivated by need.

Consider more bewildering interactions of mentality setting matter in motion. We have watched astronauts gain control over an environment in which gravitation is removed. How do they manage to open hatches, eat a meal, stay in bed? Their situation is that everything is buoyant; they have to move their floating bodies midst objects drifting around inside their capsule. Their movements with gravitation removed appear to be more like swimming in the sea than our ground-based walking. Being weightless, their concerns about decisive action are quite different than ours. Of course, astronauts learn how to manage this, just as we all would if need demanded. Our expectation of common situations and our ways of interacting with matter would have to change entirely.

After more than thirty years of human space travel we have proof that where need exists, humans can survive in weightless states. One of the first concerns would have been how to take some control over the environmental materials the astronauts needed to sustain life—water, food, and so on. While on earth we have learned as children to grab and move materials—such as pour liquid and get food from plate to mouth, but these simple functions are entirely different in space. For example, a lunch of sandwich, potato chips, and iced tea would not sit quietly on a plate or in a cup while we loll away our lunch hour, but instead would want to roam hither and yon. Since making the sandwich stick to the plate with either Velcro or glue is unacceptable, and pouring liquid straight down into a cup is out of the question, technicians had to develop alternative methods for eating in a gravity-free environment—to keep the life-sustaining liquid and food readily accessible, as need demands.

The general rule in life seems to be that when we encounter materials such as wood, glass, and metal and forces such as gravity, we learn to control the movement of objects and our bodies so that we can obtain the substances needed to survive and live contentedly.

Now we stretch our thinking to include the psychokinetic moves we can make with the help of intuition. How do abilities like metal bending and materializing objects fit into our worldview of possible human behavior, and how do these relate to intuition? I repeat, intuitiveness appears to be associated with a particular subatomic environmental phenomena called electromagnetic interactions. We all receive and use electromagnetic information daily. Although we know neither how we get this information nor how it affects intuitive communication, we cannot question its existence. The accounts in this book are evidence only that we do receive and use intuitively derived information for making decisions. However, we occasionally need to initiate real physical changes to help ourselves. Then, from time to time, we witness people controlling the movement of matter with psychokinesis and cannot explain how they do it.

So why does psychokinesis occur at all? Remember the reason that intuition is activated: It is a regulatory mechanism. Let us find a place of need for employing this remarkable psychokinesis. Out here in the real world, I think masses of people could benefit by it. Think of the field of medicine, especially rehabilitation. I particularly look forward to the day when we can teach disabled and bedridden people, such as those who are paralyzed or severely arthritic, to use this effect to obtain objects they need but cannot reach physically. Perhaps they could teleport a glass of water from the tap to themselves, or when cold, they could close the window psychokinetically.

Right now it might seem like living in a dream world to say that it will serve anyone, but in this vein, I remind you of Roger Bannister, the Englishman who made us change our fixed ideas about the speed at which we could run. We had built a great wall of belief that decreed that humans could not cover a mile in under four minutes. Then Mr. Bannister did just that. He took only 3:59.4 minutes and instantly vaporized our expectations. Human potential soared that day. With his experience we were empowered to reach new heights—and we have, of course. I am confident that when one patient whose physical body is little better than a padlock on his or her freedom realizes that this intuitive capacity is one key to emancipation, and transports his or her own glass of water from the sink, then we will see a revolution in the future of disabled people.

3. *Q: If intuition is such a wonderful spontaneous correction mechanism when we get off track, then why can't it prevent people from becoming ill at all?*

A: The potential for using intuition to keep and restore our own health is exciting beyond imagination. Remember that intuition is a regulatory mechanism with its own IPS to keep us on course. Once we do employ it regularly, we will have a far more harmonious internal communication system, and far less illness.

For instance, if we are able to convey frustration telepathically, and receive assistance when we need it (ψ-24, 25), we already are on our way to inner contentment. Illness will be less necessary as an outlet for solving our problems. But we can think even more boldly than using it for prevention. There is the possibility of healing. In the event that we become injured, as by swallowing a fish bone, stepping on a rusty nail, or breaking a bone, we could rely on our intuitive connection with the microprocesses to quickly restore the cells to their fully interactive states. Perhaps doctors will be among the first to learn how to use psychokinesis to set bones, for example, but the ability will not be their province only. I am confident that by the year 3000, we all will learn to be self-healing as a matter of course, the way we learn to read, write, and think today.

Although no one could decry the information revolution at the end of the millennium, one by-product is that today we are so preoccupied with technology and all its endless marvels that we too often abdicate responsibility for creative thinking and solving problems ourselves. The good news here is that even though we are obsessed at the moment with the abundant forms of instant communication pouring from screens, printers, and pages alike, we will be reenchanted with our own brains in the not-too-distant future because we will realize that for all the informational wonders of the high-tech world, this glorious gray matter inside our heads continues to be the only complete resource for consistently finding the way to good health, wholesome self-expression, top performance, and freedom to venture into the world. I predict that we will use both spontaneous and selective intuition to lead us.

4. *Q: Given that numbers of people describe their intuition as unreliable, should we assume that an intuitive sensory system can be defective just as a visual system might be?*

A: Logically the reply would have to be yes, we might have "bad" or defective intuition. However, having no evidence of the system in the body we can know neither how intuition would be disabled nor how serious such a handicap might be. So, I work on the premise that, like any other sensory system, intuition does have a normal, or perfect, state that we will be able to standardize in the future.

Think of a possible parallel in our established standard of 20/20 vision, our classification for ideal eye function. "20/20" means that an individual can see specific objects clearly at a distance of twenty feet without corrective glasses. If a person cannot meet this basic condition then his or her vision is considered to be "impaired." This classification does not necessarily imply seriously damaged eyesight, but, rather eyesight that is not perfect. Nearly all human babies are born with two eyes that work, and most have perfect vision. This normality is in nature's plan. We have learned to assist the natural sighting process by training children to use vision to their advantage.

We can put the same yardstick of normality to intuition. Since it is a sensory system it will exist in 99.9 percent of human babies, and in nearly all cases the system will function ideally from the start. However, small numbers of infants will undoubtedly have defective intuitive systems, which may account for the reports of intuition's unreliability. The solution is largely a matter of education. As we look forward to a future society of intuitively active human beings, we can expect to teach most adults and youngsters at a very young age to use their nature-endowed intuitiveness reliably for their advantage, just as we train children now to learn to interact intelligently with phenomena they see with their eyes. Comparative examples of such training are the way I used intuitive teleosic forewarnings of earthquakes to protect my belongings ($\psi$-28, 29) and the protective visual forewarnings of an approaching car that we all heed by moving out of that vehicle's way.

4. *Q: How can we teach our children to use their intuition when we don't know how to ourselves?*

A: Awareness is really the key to teaching children. Listen to them. Ask them casually the questions listed in the preceding Psi Effect Self-Check. Use the early teachers of reason as your role models—Socrates, Aristotle, and Plato. It was Socrates who initiated the question-and-answer method of teaching as a means of searching for knowledge. We now are following in his footsteps. He, too, taught the youngsters, as we are so eager to do.

As it stands, few of us adults are skilled enough with our own intuitive abilities to teach children formally. Consequently, we help them learn from their experiences at the same time we are learning by ours. Also keep in mind that for both young people and adults, the emphasis in learning should be on what *does* happen rather than on what did *not* occur, and on what advantage it brought instead of what was wrong. This gives us all the opportunity to observe and construct with experiences rather than make demands of it and destroy the intuitive process in ourselves.

In line with the advice in question 2, let us begin to learn intuition's limits by observing, not create the limits with narrowed expectations. This way we all are on the same track. We want children to learn so that they will have that critical advantage of self-help that intuition brings which we did not have in our youths. The dream described in the Chains and Switchblades account (ψ-37) is an excellent example of that potential.

6. *Q: Why do I know about only "bad" situations?*

A: The quick answer is that pain and suffering are among the extremes of the human experience. Returning to the reason for being intuitive—that we are learning about systems off their set points—it follows that our concern is with people in the greatest distress.

Because this ability is reporting Breaking News around the planet, we will always know of the great human and organic problems and paradoxes. It appears that this has to be if we are indeed included in nature's support team for correcting the most dreadful imbalances. A final point on this matter of knowing the downside is that of who knows what. Not all people will learn about every ache and pain that man and beast are suffering. Terrorism excepted, we generally intuit only those events that we can assist, not everything that happens on the block.

7.  *Q: When does intuition rest?*

A: Never. It is on the alert twenty-four hours a day, three hundred sixty-five days a year, with one extra for leap year. On alert is different, however, from sending reports. When life is merely a pleasantly exuberant affair, intuition has little to do. It sends effects only when the environment is perturbed enough to be off set point.

8.  *Q: Why aren't all "psychics" winning the lottery or raking in thousands of dollars at the racetrack?*

A: This sensory process is not designed to be a gambler with life any more than a clinical psychologist is taught to play mind games. It is reliable on occasions when it can follow its own rules of natural regulatory mechanisms. While gambling games certainly cause tensions of both joy and despair, these upheavals are self-imposed and thus not "real" in the natural order. Consequently, our intuitive sensitivity is unaffected. The result is that the test of finding precise numbers is quite unreliable because it has no orientation to a system in trouble.

9.  *Q: Could intuition create serious mental conflict for us?*

A: One might think that it would be disturbing because, on occasion, intuition spontaneously exposes us to conditions where laws of nature pit us against objects of our affection. In those times most of us simply don't want the bigger picture, because it might make us betray our cherished loved ones or ideals. However, this exposure is more beneficial than disturbing, because in most cases of inner conflict we are waging a battle of interests that we naturally bypass intuitively.

For instance, you may be telepathic to the frustration in a loved one who wants to escape distress by taking an easier course of action, but you also perceive intuitively that the person's discomfort is caused by a situation that must be played out for the greater good. Sending our men and women to war is an excellent example of this. Another is watching a child get bruised mentally while learning laws of life such as telling the truth, or physically while gaining freedom to roam by riding bicycles. Being in the middle of such situations, you would inevitably have two bits of intuitive data. In the case of the soldier going to war, you would certainly intuit the tragedy and fear in your dear departing warrior and would readily fight for the right of that person to not march into battle. Yet simultaneously you would sense the ultimate importance of routing out a tyrannical leader who, as an aggressor, is an enemy of life itself. You face the quintessential dilemma: Should you defend the one or the all?

Although our deepest loyalties do divide us psychologically, we will come to understand that, as the optimizer, intuition always guides us to lend help in the corner where we can serve best. From this intuitively sensitive position we know no psychological conflict, because we do not have to struggle with the inconsistencies we inevitably encounter in our personal passions and abstract philosophical thought.

10. *Q: In question nine you address psychological conflicts we transcend intuitively. Now could you discuss what happens when an intuitor—who you say is always receiving accurate data—encounters opposing rational facts? Please answer this question using the exam-*

*ple of a business setting. Say, one person intuits that a plan will fail in the long term; the other produces numbers projecting success over the same period. They obviously disagree. In fact, they flat-out contradict one another. What does the intuitor do?*

A: My experience with such situations has yielded the following four-stage rule of thumb for the intuitive party.

Stage 1: Explain the benefit of using intuition's ability to cut straight to the chase of the ever-changing unknowns and unpredictables, whereas by the very fact of the numbers being only statistical and static, equivalent precision is unlikely.

If this fails to convince the other party, move straight to stage 2.

Stage 2: Having shown the sharp distinction between intuition, which brings constantly unpredictable facts to light, and reason that operates on fixed observations, you as the intuitor turn to the Routine to learn any alternative favorable routes to the same or similar conclusions that the plan intends. (What else do you know?) Propose them. If that fails, move to the third stage.

Stage 3: Now you face a dilemma. Your intuitive system's factual report that provides solid evidence for planning is confronting the statistician's factual calculations, which he or she offers as viable evidence for planning. Because there can be few calculated facts in evidence that will be as current as intuition's facts, a line of demarcation is drawn here between the two systems' value in gathering data for decision making. Suddenly you have to decide how willing you are to go along with reasoning on this particular plan while watching intuition lose its moment. You also have to determine how much confidence you have in your own intuitive ability and how comfortable you feel promoting the facts it has reported for the business proposition. The differences in the information-gathering systems force you to determine how confident you are that intuitiveness is reliable and, now that you are eyewitness to its benefits in a world so full of traps, how important it is to fight for intuition's basic rights. You may have to determine at this point how much you want to help build a future in a workplace where intuition's flexibility is mixed regularly with reason's rigidity. Taking all of these factors into consideration, you intuit for yourself the consequences of the strategy according to the rationalist's approach. If you can live with it, compromise. If concession is impossible, you must remove yourself either mentally or physically from the situation, *without leaving angrily*. Face the reality that rationalism in the modern world overrules intuition in nearly all open confrontations. This is not anyone's fault, and certainly not worth losing sleep over. You knew; you introduced your input; it failed. A second attempt was no more successful than the first. You make your decision to either agree or get on with life. This is the way to maintain your own mental stability.

Stage 4: If the outcome is as intuition predicted, you take note and review for yourself how you knew what you did. It is wise to let others remember themselves about the decision at the crossroads where intuition and reason clashed.

## Growing Into Our Intuitive Shoes

The suggestions and observations offered in this chapter might seem somewhat futuristic or optimistic—even, possibly, sparked by a bit of lunacy. Regardless, I stand behind every statement, yet never forgetting that the question of intuition's existence is open. So much hangs upon resolving this question—upon finding the physical cells and system in the body that control the behavior of the phenomenon; upon building a program of study that advances understanding of its ways and means of communicating both the world to us and our inner experiences to the world; upon its potential for changing a species at war with itself to one of cooperative enterprise; upon its convincing us by experiencing our intuitiveness that we are intuitively sensitive; upon its carrying us far beyond the crude incisions we have made in our species' well-being with divisive languages, nations, times, intentions, and dogmas and discovering new limits with their own complexities and possibilities.

While the new tide turns, we all will be changing fairly dramatically. An improved model of human behavior awaits in this next stage of our evolution. It is worth the effort of centuries that this transformation may need in order to take place. Most everyone agrees that we cannot keep following in the destructive direction we have taken. Being so self-centered as we are, and using all hands for ourselves, there can be no argument against the obvious: We have forgotten about the ship.

# CHAPTER 13

# And One for the Ship

My GOAL FOR this book has been to introduce the framework I have found that supports human intuition. Initially I sought it out to learn whether intuitive sensibility is actual or imagined behavior. If real, it would be tied firmly to the natural order. I am satisfied that it is real.

Looking at it from an evolutionary angle, I uncovered what I suspect is the crucial link between intuition and humankind. On one hand, it protects us. On the other, it enables us to take risks to excel. We need both advantages if we are going to thrive.

The story of our development on earth teaches that humans— Homo sapiens—are products of evolution. Confirmation comes when we look within our bodies. There we discover the telltale cellular structures that unite us with the grand design. Searching further, we uncover the complex cellular sections in our brain that provide for intelligent behavior, the hallmark of our species. By dint of this capability, we are the creation at the top of the evolutionary ladder.

This most recent discovery of our intellectual brilliance has kept us fascinated for 2,500 years. During this time, we have opened vast territories with this uniquely human ability to think, analyze, anticipate, calculate, and make plans for action. With characteristic exuberance, we have used it to divine ways to explore and develop the world's systems on land and sea, diving beneath the planet's waters and rocketing into the vastness surrounding it.

Most recently we have discovered subsystems in the natural order that we can explore.* This brand-new territory holds secrets of nature's subatomic technology and cellular architecture. We have penetrated some of those secrets and, in usual fashion, tinkered with them, changing the arrangements—always to our advantage.

Being impatient creatures, we began the subsystem alterations without quite understanding the full range of possible adaptive interactions and modifications that these resilient microsystems would be capable of producing. The result is that we now stand on the frontier of a different natural order, changed because we as the new tinkerer in the microuniverse have introduced systems of our own that we uncovered when we arrived. Even without using fine-tuned mechanical instruments to assist, we see now that some results of our contributions look forbidding. Clearly, they are hazardous to present and future life. We are alarmed. Around us a once-abundant environment is turning hostile—polluted air, contaminated water, littered land, and a new generation of human and other animal babies born with gruesome deformities that only we could have created with

---

*Around 1900 came evidence that the atom of known chemical elements had an ability to decay into other elements. This was a new model of the atom. It enabled physicists to think more clearly about the behavior of chemical elements and eventually led the way to synthesizing elements. In 1953 biologists also came closer to the origin of life with the discovery of the structure of DNA and the chemical basis of heredity. Untold numbers of other discoveries hang on their find.

our myriad debilitating substances and anomalous nuclear materials.

What a paradox. How marvelous it is to be empowered by our reason to peer in at the natural processes in the cellular architecture and atomic technology composing the grand design, to understand all the products of the ancient time-honored system of slow, very very slow, change. How odd it is that when they evolved the human ability to think, the forces of nature sculpted a structure into the living universe that has the potential to damage, even destroy in a nanosecond, the millions of years of these labor-intensive processes and products.

In our search for solutions to this contradiction, we have to ask: Is our newest brain section with its reasoning faculty basically a hostile territory? If the answer is yes, we then have to inquire why this particular cellular system was evolved with the potential to introduce the seeds of our own destruction.

That it is dangerous seems to be true. By using this implicit function, which clearly *could* be developed, refined, and strengthened, we can see that we have precipitated two very strange consequences. First, we have realized that our brain's brilliance is in competition with our own leader—nature—and we know that humans are no match against her forces. The second grows out of the first. By pushing this brain toward its full potential, we have inadvertently set ourselves on a path that leads to the eventual extinction of our species. When we survey these dubious achievements, it seems that for all of the advantages and territories we have won with our rational faculties, these two are quite opposite and distinctly dangerous triumphs.

It would appear that once our rational talent was circulating in the evolutionary mechanics, this deadly condition became a possibility. If the new-creation Homo sapiens were to sharpen its unique system of thinking, it would inevitably uncover the key physical systems, with their subsystems of microprocesses that forge life from life unceasingly. With power to reform these, which is truly a form of supreme regulation, this babe in the woods, this innocent human, *would* have the potential for mass destruction.

We know, of course, that we did chance upon the subsystems and figure them out. (This is not to say that we understood them. For the time being, we have settled our problem of insufficient knowledge by classifying the mechanics as "unpredictable." Typically the lack of proofs didn't stop science—which made more predictions and continued to dig.) In our excitement, we then began to connect the systems ourselves, creating new manufactured products. With this the next leap in civilization occurred—a world powered by nuclear energy.

Tales abound of discoveries exposed by Reason. We hear marvelous stories of adventure across this subatomic frontier. These include nuclear power, lifesaving chemicals, and extraordinary means of transportation.

Our pattern of rational growth looks like a natural expansion into new territory, common in the evolutionary process. Do you recall the system pattern? When a new feature in the form of a function or organ is added to a species, it generally opens new terrain for roaming and foraging for food and water. Inevitably, the creature gains an advantage for survival because more resources are amassed with each new territory.

Scrutinizing our new brain system, we recognize this phenomenon of expansion. When our ancestors received this ability to reason, it did forage in its way—through philosophy, mathematics, and the sciences in general—for information that led to finding those very basic needs of food, water, and shelter. In due time, it happened upon the keys to the microsystems that were invisible to the naked eye.

So it follows. We are evidence of this process of expansion into new territory, having moved into this next dimension of nature with our clever new brain faculty. We found it with our superior intelligence! First we learned we could think. Next we refined the ability with the scientific method and began to dig deeper into the secrets of the universe. Like our ancient predecessors, we too have had to discover tools. Ours would be mental calculations, along with physical machines and scopes, to augment our senses and emancipate us to travel to the new reality. We learned to use all these in order to fill out our observations with more thinking.

The story of evolution presents a new possibility here. We know that as our subhuman ancestors' cellular systems evolved into more complex cellular structures, they seemed to acquire new regulatory mechanisms. Now we stand here in time, staring at our runaway rationalism. It has become a more complex system itself and traveled into strange and dangerous territories. It appears that like other systems, our reasoning ability has begun to require its own biological regulatory mechanism—one upon which it can rely to both bring it nutrients in the form of other data and remove the waste products of dangerous data that it produces.

## The Intuitive Regulator

My conclusion is that this intuitive sensory system will be the means by which we humans can better manage our world of prodigious thought, ideas, decisions, planning, and the products we produce. It will be the control over our information exchanges in the natural order and with one another. Its three main characteristics support the conclusion that intuitiveness functions as a regulatory mechanism:

1. It plumbs the very microprocesses that we have broken into with rational thinking but do not understand.

2. It knows the comings and goings of the materials and forces in those microprocesses and thus is able to report the interactions' past, present, and future

well before any of our other man-made calculating
systems, instruments, or technology or other natural
senses are able.

3. It makes corrections to our errors that come from using
our fixed rational systems.

In sum, intuition plumbs the Factors "U" and gives us more
precise control over our movements than reasoning is able. We all
have both abilities. They get us where we want to go in whatever
territory we are traveling. The only rule is that when reason and
intuition disagree, expect the intuitive sensitivity to be correct.
This is because intuition is *a sensory process producing reports about
events as they are occurring within the ever-changing natural order,*
while reason works with fixed, unchanging models whose para-
meters are established by the rationalist. Sometimes the models are
inaccurate. Other times they are just plain wrong. In still others,
they are correct. In this last situation, intuition will not interfere.

As the regulator of our rational faculty, our intuitiveness fills
the gaps of information where reason will have no access to solutions. It anticipates for us, guiding us toward benefits and away
from traps that reason might never calculate into its equations.
When reason is unable to optimize our performance, intuition
stands by to supercede imperfect reason instructions and lead the
way itself.

Bearing all this in mind, I foresee a future where the human
population is healthier both mentally and physically, and all the
spheres will follow suit. This change is as inevitable as it was that
we would get in trouble with our rational capacity.

# Why So Long in Coming?

For a species that has unknowingly been building problems to
such massive proportions, why has intuition taken so long to
appear? I maintain that it has been with us since the birth of rea-

son, serving as its regulator as doggedly as it does today and will continue to do so into the future. The mystery is that we have missed it so completely.

To find the answer let's revisit the Greek culture of around 500 B.C. and mark the events that were happening just prior to the philosophers' turning the tide of social change through fine-tuned rationalism. Only half a century before Socrates and the Athenian boys were sitting around the Parthenon, and Plato, his follower, was opening his Academy, the Buddha was preaching supreme enlightenment in India, and Confucius was wandering China, touching lives with his wise teachings. Jesus Christ, born five centuries later, also would become the people's teacher. Chapter 5 introduced my suspicion that in these three we meet the harbingers of human intuition. Now I bring them back as part of its history and our understanding of what happened to intuitiveness after they appeared.

The Buddha, Confucius, and Jesus taught their messages by word and deed. They talked about being awake to people's characters and sensitive to their conditions, about allowing insight to show change that would bring improvements, about how to heal illness and know others' needs. The juxtaposition in time of their teaching about human sensitivity to microprocesses and the Greeks' awakening to those same phenomena indicates that in the fabric of evolution, the two systems were paired and emerged naturally together. Reasoning, which would expand our territory, was automatically attached to a sensory system that would report tensions in the new systems.

Given this complementary relation, we can see that it probably was not a random biological occurrence that brought reason and intuition to light simultaneously. Perhaps it was an exact matching up of systems. Such a pairing would create the balanced activity of a new sensory system and a capability for reaching new territory. Remember that this is the evolutionary pattern for organisms: When a creature develops a structure that allows territorial expansion, it also acquires a new internal information system. This makes the destiny of reason and intuition even more problematical, as history shows that they were separated by human beings almost immediately—twins, separated at birth.

One became a tool for everyone's learning; the other was declared a gift for the chosen few. The tool went to work for the people who gathered in small groups around teachers who taught them how to think and gave them practical skills. Professions appeared. Men became doctors and lawyers. The tool was successful, every bit as useful and reliable as the stone ax of our most ancient relatives. Eventually universities were erected to celebrate this ability to reason, and schools turned up across the lands to give billions of youth that followed through the years the opportunity to hone the tool to make them self-sufficient and enrich every facet of their lives.

Knowing a little now of reason's pilgrimage, we return to the point of separation to track the journey of intuition, which would become the "gift." It traveled a very different route to reach the public experience. The exact time when reason and intuition were severed is not clear, but it is safe to say that intuition was taken from the people and isolated, to become a possession of supreme beings and enlightened men. In the course of time, it was sanctified and made a dream to be dearly hoped for, but certainly not without a price. Ritual encircled it. Intuition was locked tight in doctrine and dogma, to be dispensed through agents who would help others in times of need and work wonders with the forces of nature. Individuals had to turn to these agencies when they were unknowing and in need of a miracle. In essence, this avowed gift was held from the common touch. Whereas they could not hold it or call it their own, people were encouraged to draw strength and answers from it through church leaders and kings— who were rulers by divine right, consequently deemed to be representatives of God—and hope to reach the same state by living a lifetime of rigidly defined behavior.

Contrary to the revered positions assigned to them, the three teachers in their times insisted that their followers possessed the same intuitive ability as they. The Buddha taught: "Do not go by reasoning, nor by inferring, nor by argument." A true disciple must "know for himself." Confucius taught his people that they should hold to the established traditions but at the same time *keep alert* to developments, lest they prevent the old techniques from working successfully. Jesus Christ also encouraged people to be aware, to be compassionate, to let down barriers that separated them from their own existence.

A striking feature that these men shared is their persistent lesson of sensitivity to elements of life. They helped people get "in touch" and taught that once in charge of their own ability, an individual would know the true meaning of life in all its multiple dimensions. This would ensure each of us universality. In other words, no human being could be cast out of the world, but instead, with this sensitivity as guide, life could be made whole for one and all.

Is this not the promise of our intuition as a sensory system? It promises to show the ways we can dodge slings and arrows coming from the world. By having this intuitive sensitivity, and bringing it to life we do not have to live in faith that the natural order is a good and fair place but, instead, no matter what our intellectual or religious convictions might be, we can make safe passage through—because we are created to survive. Here in our own bodies, with this guidance system, there is no need for human hierarchies and ritual. The ability is within us, to be discovered and developed during our lifetimes.

I have already made the point that although the faithful have always been able to find their intuition with the help of a variety of teachers and rituals, I think human intuitiveness was never meant to be the consequence of spiritual purity. Instead it appears to be a function of the biological sensory ability within us all. This different view should give us a new perspective on our individual and collective human potential. We have to realize that if it is an evolutionary modification for survival, we cannot be so separated from it that we need to reach it through another human or instruction of any ilk. These established rituals are tools, yes, and certainly the church and spiritual leaders know and teach the secrets of intuition, but the limits to access that they have imposed are not as the evolutionary process intended. The very fact that it is tied to the framework of the natural order, and follows laws made not by mortals but instead that govern the orderly mechanisms of the physical systems we live with daily, is enough to make us understand that intuition is a sturdy mechanism, there for us all and only for the asking. I am convinced that our earliest and greatest teachers were showing us what we are just beginning to realize now. Intuition is ours personally, and it is here to stay as part of us, an assistant to maintaining fine quality in life from first breath forward. The twins should never have been separated at birth.

Turning over the pages of centuries and taking a measure now, we can see the need for this "gift" with our near vision. We are a species headed for even more trouble than we have already created. The time has come to remove intuition's disguises. We need to know that we are awake to intuitiveness and to the natural order as the Buddha taught; to mingle new learning with tradition by using this sensitivity to balance the establishment's laws with traditions as Confucius proposed; to realize that we, indeed, can learn to use our intuition and be as fine-tuned as Jesus Christ showed us he could be.

Intuition's journey as part of our spiritual tradition will continue to play an important role for mankind. But it is time now to let each man and woman begin to employ intuition individually. This fresh opportunity to put our intuition into personal service brings up a new model for humankind. We all have life, a brief but precious opportunity to ride the planet through the galaxy. We all *also* have the natural capacity that history's wisest teachers taught would allow us to ride successfully through the uncertainties of living, all the while making the most of our talents. Now we are adding this intuitive factor to our skills. If we use our intuitiveness to keep our exceptional brain activity in control, letting intuition guide the decisions and actions born of our exuberant rational faculty, we would become a species-of-value and an immense asset to steering the future course of the good ship Earth. I am confident that this is our next giant evolutionary step.

Time is passing. Why not take this ability into the laboratories where neuroscientists can probe and find the living cellular sensory system in our bodies? Why not instruct the finest teachers how to use their own intuition so that they can instruct others? All of us are able to fine-tune now to the psi effects and learn to recognize them. We know the importance of taking action and will be grateful that at last we have a guide to precise moves. It is our opportunity now to live life at set point, to know what being "in touch" and "in tune" really means. From here we will discover the whole meaning of life, not only our own but also that of every system and material that is in existence or coming into existence. All this is possible. It is intuition's time to join the rank and file.

With this change in human learning, the twins that were wrongly separated will at last be working together. Reason and intuition will have their chance to open new territory for us to explore.

The scale of their unification's promise boggles the mind. In the dazzling variety of our personal pursuits, and the challenges we face while stretching to reach the heights in any of them; in the various approaches to living, from unshakable religious belief to dizzying independent thought; in the throes of painful tensions that we suffer with deepest loss and greatest hope; and, outside our little selves, in the global village where the pendulum of human concerns swings a wide arc between our physical and mental demands, helping entire populations find precious nourishment—the best shield for frail life against ravages of illness or starvation—and assisting millions of others in using natural creative talents so necessary to checking the epidemic self-torture and human carnage bred by mental instability; where we are being held together by sheer effort of staggering numbers of caring hearts and toiling hands, but, at the same time, torn asunder by reckless exploitation from greed and for convenience—our intuition is awaiting its moment, to do its part in helping us soar to success individually, and restore balance to the tottering community of humankind.

## A Species for the Future

We might be in trouble, but we are also a bright, talented, and, above all, adventurous species. Our history proves that when a bona fide human need arises, we will throw all our assets behind it and push until we reach the highest levels of expertise and excitement about our new potential.

A need *has* arisen. The ecosystem is unstable. Multiple internal systems are toppling off their set points. Our own species has begun to lose its stability. The options are clear; it is time to begin restoration. Unless we want to continue on the present course to self-extinction, we need to give one hand to the good ship Earth with all its life systems and get back on the course to the future.

# Recommended Reading

Bradshaw, John. *Bradshaw On: The Family, A New Way of Creating Solid Self-Esteem.* Deerfield Beach, FL: Health Communications, Inc., 1996.

Broughton, Richard S. *Parapsychology: The Controversial Science.* New York, NY: Ballantine, 1991.

Carlson, N. *Physiology of Behavior.* Boston, MA: Allyn and Bacon, Inc., 1977.

Csikszentmihalyi, Mihaly. *Flow: The Psychology of Optimal Experience.* New York, NY: Harper & Row, 1990.

Darwin, C. *The Origins of Species.* New York, NY: Oxford University Press, 1996.

De Becker, Gavin. *The Gift of Fear: Survival Signals that Protect Us from Violence.* Boston, MA: Little, Brown and Company, 1997.

Graff, Dale E. *Tracks in the Psychic Wilderness.* Boston, MA: Element Books, Inc., 1998.

Healy, Jane M. *Endangered Minds.* New York, NY: Touchstone, 1990.

Hillman, James. *The Soul's Code: In Search of Character and Calling.* New York, NY: Warner Books, 1996.

Judson, H. *Search for Solutions.* New York, NY: Holt, Rinehart and Winston, 1980.

Kane, Beverley, Jane Millay, and Dean Brown. *Silver Threads: 25 Years of Parapsychology Research.* Westport, CT: Praeger Publishers, 1993.

Koestler, A. *The Roots of Coincidence.* New York, NY: Vantage Books, 1973.

_____. *The Act of Creation.* London, England: Arkana, 1989.

Merton, Thomas. *New Seeds of Contemplation.* New York, NY: New Directions Books, 1961.

Moyers, Bill. *Healing and the Mind.* New York, NY: Doubleday, 1993.

Purves, et al. *Neuroscience.* Sunderland, MA: Sinauer Associates, Inc., 1997.

Siegel, Bernie S. *Peace, Love and Healing: Bodymind Communication and the Path to Self-Healing: An Exploration.* New York, NY: HarperPerennial, 1989.

Tattersall, Ian. *Becoming Human: Evolution and Human Uniqueness.* Orlando, FL: Harcourt Brace & Company, 1998.

Trefil, James. *Are We Unique?* New York, NY: John Wiley & Sons, Inc., 1997.

Vaughan, Frances E. *Awakening Intuition.* New York: Anchor Books, 1979.

# Index of Psi Effects

## The Psi Effects Viewed in Their Orderly Operating Pattern

The psi effects that report your intuitive experiences obey natural rules of order. In general, you will always gather the information through primary effects. However, as you know already, you might not learn directly from the primary effect but, instead, from either the backup or redundant effects that amplify intuition's signal. In this six-column directory, each of the forty-three accounts contained in the book is listed by its $\psi$ reference number, descriptive name, page number, classification as a secondary and primary effect, and associated sensation. The last three columns characterize the intuitor's actual intuitive experience as precisely as possible according to the rules of sequence of the psi effects' appearance. First mentioned is the perceived secondary backup, or redundant, psi effect, if any occurred. Second is the perceived, or missed, primary effect. Last is the actual inner experience, or true sensation, that caught the intuitor's attention. The question marks in the column signify that I do not know the intuitor's inner experience.

**The Primary Effects**
Déjà vu
Telepathy
Teleos (retrocognition, direct cognition, precognition)

**The Secondary Effects**
Backup: (1) Instruction, (2) Reflex
Redundant: (1) Clarification (clairaudience, clairsentience,
   clairvoyance), (2) Dreams (day and night)

**Sensations**
Sense
Feel
Purely know, in words or not with words

## Psi Accounts Condensed

| Ψ | Account Name | Pg | Secondary | Primary | Sensation |
|---|---|---|---|---|---|
| 1 | Run! | 5 | Instruction | Telepathy | Felt an impulse |
| 2 | Bomb Alert | 6 | Dream-night | Teleos—precognition | In words |
| 3 | Drowned Boy | 8 | | Teleos—direct cognition | Plainly knew—no words |
| 4 | Piano Duets | 8 | | Telepathy | Feeling of fear |
| 5 | Prom Queen | 8 | | Telepathy | Feeling of joy |
| 6 | Have to Decline | 8 | | Teleos—precognition | Sense of nonsuccess |
| 7 | A Dancing Mathematician | 23 | Instruction | Telepathy | Directed in words; felt urgent |
| 8 | Behind the Smiles | 33 | | Teleos—precognition | Feeling of sorrow |
| 9 | College Acceptance | 33 | Teleos | Teleos—precognition | Plainly knew—no words |
| 10 | Move to the Left Lane | 36 | Instruction | Teleos—precognition | Directed in words |
| 11 | Downed Plane | 37 | | Teleos—retrocognition | Nonsensical words |
| 12 | Food Poisoning | 55 | | Teleos—direct cognition | Feeling—no words |
| 13 | Bottle Chase | 71 | Instruction | Teleos—precognition | Plainly knew—in words |
| 14 | Olive Oil Spill | 77 | Instruction | Teleos—precognition | Directed in words |
| 15 | The Young Lieutenant | 89 | Clarification—Clairsentience | Teleos—direct cognition | Felt a threat in "gut" |
| 16 | Operation Toothbrush | 96 | Instruction | Teleos—direct cognition | Directed in words |
| 17 | No-Show Madman | 106 | Teleos | Teleos—precognition | Plainly knew—in words |
| 18 | Five Furrows In | 109 | | Teleos—direct cognition | Nonsensical words |
| 19 | No Brakes | 131 | | Teleos—direct cognition | Directed in words |
| 20 | Come Home Immediately | 146 | | Telepathy, Teleos—direct cognition | Plainly knew—in words or not |
| 21 | Cookie Monsters | 148 | | Telepathy | ? |
| 22 | An Odd Invitation | 150 | Reflex | Telepathy | Imperceptible |
| 23 | Reluctant Partygoer | 151 | Instruction | Teleos—precognition | Directed in words |
| 24 | Lone Boat Heading East | 152 | Instruction | Teleos—precognition | Directed in words |
| 25 | A Postal Clerk Wants Help | 167 | | Telepathy | Felt impression—no words |
| 26 | Gerry Doesn't Want Help! | 167 | | Telepathy | Felt impression—no words |
| 27 | Bestial Fury | 172 | | Telepathy, Teleos—precognition | Feeling of rage—in words |
| 28 | Earthquake-Proofing | 177 | | Teleos—precognition | Plainly knew—in words |
| 29 | Midnight Shuffle | 179 | Instruction | Teleos—precognition | Directed in words |
| 30 | Flying Books | 180 | Reflex | Teleos—direct cognition | Feeling of distraction |
| 31 | Little Boy Lost | 189 | | Telepathy | Feeling of panic |
| 32 | Distress In the Air | 204 | | Telepathy | Plainly knew—no words |
| 33 | Don't Bite That Apple | 207 | | Teleos—precognition | Plainly knew—no words |
| 34 | Agitation in the Air | 210 | Instruction | Telepathy | Feeling of distress |
| 35 | The Wave | 212 | Reflex | Teleos—precognition | Imperceptible |
| 36 | A Child's Call | 215 | Clarification—clairvoyance | Telepathy | Impression of a vague image—no words |
| 37 | Chains and Switchblades | 217 | Dream—night | Teleos—precognition | Preview of a fight—no words |

## Psi Accounts Condensed (Continued)

| Ψ | Account Name | Pg | Secondary | Primary | Sensation |
|---|---|---|---|---|---|
| 38 | Two-World Tot | 220 | Clarification—clairvoyance | Déjà vu | ? |
| 39 | How Dumb Can One Be? | 232 | Instruction | Teleos—precognition | Directed in words |
| 40 | A Fork in the Path | 236 | Clarification—clairsentience | Teleos—direct cognition | Feeling of direction—no words |
| 41 | Searching for Options | 241 | | Teleos—precognition | Plainly knew—in words |
| 42 | Career Direction | 246 | Instruction | Teleos—precognition | Directed in words |
| 43 | It Didn't Pan Out | 248 | Clarification—clairsentience | Teleos—direct cognition | Feeling of "rightness" |

# Index